YOUNG SOLDIERS, AMAZING WARRIORS

Inside One of the Most Highly Decorated Battalions of Vietnam

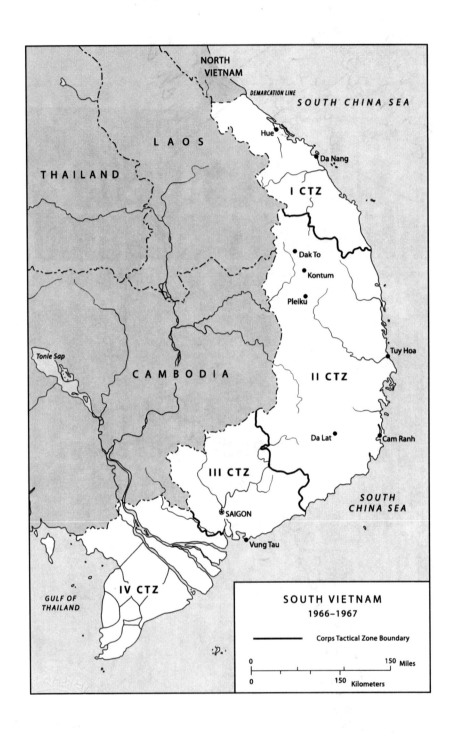

NORTH
VIETNAM

DEMARCATION LINE

SOUTH CHINA SEA

LAOS

THAILAND

Hue

Da Nang

I CTZ

Dak To

Kontum

Pleiku

Tuy Hoa

CAMBODIA

Tonle Sap

II CTZ

Da Lat

Cam Ranh

III CTZ

SAIGON

SOUTH
CHINA SEA

Vung Tau

GULF OF
THAILAND

IV CTZ

SOUTH VIETNAM
1966–1967

——— Corps Tactical Zone Boundary

0   150 Miles

0   150 Kilometers

YOUNG SOLDIERS, AMAZING WARRIORS

Inside One of the Most Highly Decorated Battalions of Vietnam

ROBERT H. SHOLLY
COLONEL, USA (RET.)

Stonywood Publications
Pearland, Texas

Young Soldiers, Amazing Warriors
Inside One of the Most Highly Decorated Battalions in Vietnam
By Robert H. Sholly

Stonywood Publications
Post Office Box 1590
Pearland, TX 77581
Orders@Stonywood.com   http://Stonywood.com

ISBN: 978-0-9796652-3-3   Cover Design: 1106 Design, LLC
LCCN: 2013946434   Maps: S.L. Dowdy

Publisher's Cataloging-in-Publication
(Provided by Quality Books, Inc.)

Sholly, Robert H.
    Young soldiers, amazing warriors: inside one of the most highly
decorated battalions of Vietnam / by Robert H. Sholly, Colonel,
USA (Ret.).
    pages cm
    LCCN 2013946434
    ISBN 978-0-9796652-3-3

    1. United States. Army. Infantry Regiment 8th,
Battalion, 1st—History. 2. United States. Army—
Medals, badges, decorations, etc.3.Vietnam War,
1961–1975. I. Title.

DS558.4.S56 2013   959.704'342
                          QBI13-600130

Printed in the United States

To the men and families of the
1st Battalion, 8th Infantry Regiment,
4th Infantry Division

1966–1967

*"It is foolish and wrong to mourn the men who died.
Rather, we should thank God that such men lived."*
General George S. Patton

Foreword

OVER THE YEARS I have read many memoirs regarding Vietnam combat action; few have come as close as *Young Soldiers, Amazing Warriors* to touching the essential nature of life as a combat infantryman at the cutting edge. The essential characteristics of infantry combat become apparent early in this record, as does the importance of the youthful infantry Soldier—trained, willing and inculcated with an overwhelming loyalty to his fellow Soldiers.

Some aspects of armed combat do not change. The nature of war remains almost primal, and while some of the characteristics might give way to advancements in weapon systems and transportation, the reality is that young, physically fit infantry Soldiers remain one of the most traditional—and capable—combat multipliers. There is little chance of success on the battlefield without small units of capable Soldiers trained in their craft and led by effective and experienced leaders. It is apparent to anyone who reads this account that caring and competent leaders can create effective units.

Preface

THERE ARE MANY ARGUMENTS on many sides as to the rightness or wrongness of the United States' involvement in South Vietnam. Vietnam divided into North and South after France gave up its colony. However, there were powerful Communists in the North who wanted reunification at any expense. This was the middle of the "Cold War" when the Soviet Union and China were trying to expand world Communism. This fact made the North Vietnamese more frightening to the US. The simplistic but famous 'domino theory' speculated that Vietnam, unified under Communism, would force its Southeast Asian neighbors into the Communist bloc, one at a time like falling dominoes. This would deny freedom and democracy to the people of the region. When South Vietnam asked for US help against the North Vietnamese, our senior political leaders decided that Vietnam was important enough to send the US military. U.S. combat divisions deployed.

This book is the story of my men and me, our actions and those of our combat brothers in a combat rifle battalion during its first year in Vietnam.

There have been a few efforts to tell true stories of how it was in Vietnam...the most prominent being the book and movie by Hal Moore and Joe Galloway *"We Were Soldiers Once... and Young..."* That story of the gallant 1st Cavalry Division revolves around the first major US/North Vietnamese battle in the Ia Drang Valley in the western highlands of Vietnam.

A little over a year later, the 1st Battalion, 8th Infantry Regiment (1-8th), along with other battalions of the 4th Infantry Division, thrust into the same Ia Drang Valley and was involved in similar battles as were depicted on the screen. These battles were bloody and horrific with great loss of life on both sides and tested America's young men time and again. This book depicts some of those battles and the courage, determination and valor of those young, yet amazing warriors the United States sent to war.

Tragically, too many did not come back.

Prologue

OLD MEN SEND young men to war.

In the course of history, it has been normal for politicians (old men) to make far-reaching decisions which have resulted in militaries, (comprised of young men) clashing to protect some territory or ideal.

When young men or boys go to war, if they survive, they mature quickly. The phrase "Boys became men..." is an apt description of every war in human history...it is nothing new or original...it is just a sad commentary on the human condition. A great deal of innocence is lost to those who return and they are far more cynical than they might have been otherwise.

At their best, however, those who come back are more mature in their outlook on life than their civilian counterparts who have not witnessed the tragedies and horrors of conflict. How can you compare a returned veteran who perhaps has been wounded, seen his working brothers killed and been involved in a Great Event such as war, with his civilian teen-aged contemporary who has not experienced such life changing traumas?

It is interesting to note that while there are indeed Vietnam veterans who have mental difficulties, who are homeless, and who prefer to stand on street corners for handouts rather than get jobs; the great majority of men and women who served in Vietnam, came home, found jobs, got married, raised families and quietly contributed to society without fanfare. There were no parades with pipes and drums for Korean or Vietnam veterans when they came home from serving their country. The Korean veteran for the most part, was ignored and forgotten. On the other hand, the Vietnam veteran was often reviled and spit upon when he returned...he was called "baby killer" and subjected to all manner of insults, just because he wore his country's uniform. There are still a few Americans who harass those men and women who answer their country's call. Fortunately, they are in the minority. The majority of our today's service members are respected and treated fairly.

I was one of the Vietnam returnees who, upon arrival in San Francisco from my first tour in Vietnam, were subjected to a horrendous outpouring of hate, name-calling and spittle. This treatment hurt and bewildered me. I did not know what to make of it, so I tried to attribute it to ignorant liberalism and went on to join my family from whom I had been separated for a year.

I contrast this reception to that of my return from Desert Storm twenty-four years later. There were different routes for returnees, but my US Air Force C5 aircraft landed at Westover Air Base near Chicopee, Massachusetts for refueling. When we got off the airplane to stretch our legs, we were directed to a large hanger to take our break. There was a band playing and we walked between a corridor made of yellow ribbons with hundreds of townspeople lining both sides slapping us on the shoulder or back and all saying *"Welcome Home!"* The corridor led into the hanger where a free beer wagon was located

Glossary of Terms

1LT – First Lieutenant
1SG – First Sergeant
2LT – Second Lieutenant
4.2 Inch – Mortars found at battalion level
81mm – Mortars found at company level
82mm – Soviet mortar used by the NVA and VC
AIE – Air Force propeller aircraft, excellent close air
    support
AK47 – Soviet assault rifle used by the NVA and VC
Arc Light – Bombing program carried out by B52 bombers
Azimuth – Direction on a compass
B40 – Soviet rocket propelled grenade used by NVA/VC
C&C – Command and Control aircraft
C130 – Air Force cargo aircraft, some served as gunships
C4 –Type of plastic explosive
CG – Commanding General
CIB – Combat Infantry Badge
CIDG – Civilian Irregular Defense Force – Local
    Vietnamese
Click – Used as short hand to designate kilometers
CO – Commanding Officer

COL – Colonel, brigade commanders
CP – Command Post
CPT – Captain, company commanders
CSM – Command Sergeant Major – senior NCO in
    battalion
Dragon Mountain – 4th Division main base camp
FAC – Forward Air Controller, Air Force Officer
FO – Forward Observer for Artillery
FUO – Fever of Unknown Origin
GI – Government Issue, common name for soldiers
KIA – Killed in Action
Kilometer – Unit of measurement, .662 of a mile
LAW – Light Antitank Weapon
LBE – Load Bearing Equipment
LRRP – Long Range Reconnaissance Patrol
LT – Lieutenant
LTC – Lieutenant Colonel, battalion commander
Luddite – Unbeliever in machines or progress
LZ – Landing Zone
M16 – US main battle rifle
M48 – Class of tank
M60 – US machine gun, as used in this narrative
M79 – US grenade launcher
MAJ – Major
Mermite –Type of vacuum container used for food
MG – Major General, or machine gun, dependent on
    context
MIA – Missing in Action
NCO – Non Commissioned Officer
NVA – North Vietnam Army
OCS – Officer Candidate School
Old Man – Term for a commander at company and higher
Perimeter – Oval or circular fighting position

PFC – Private First Class
PVT – Private
R&R – Rest and Relaxation program
REMF – Rear Echelon MF, personnel assigned to rear areas
RPD – Soviet made machine gun
RPG – Rocket Propelled Grenade, generally B40s
RTO – Radio Telephone Operator
Rucksack – Backpack used to carry equipment
RVN – Republic of Vietnam (South Vietnam)
S1 – Battalion or Brigade Personnel Officer
S2 – Battalion or Brigade Intelligence Officer
S3 – Battalion or Brigade Operations Officer
S4 – Battalion or Brigade Supply Officer
S5 – Battalion or Brigade Civil Affairs officer
SFC – Sergeant First Class
SGT – Sergeant
Short Round – Artillery/mortar round that is short of target
Slick – Troop helicopter, unarmed except for M60 MG
SOP – Standard Operating Procedures
Spooky – A C47 aircraft armed with miniguns and flares. It
    was replaced by a C130 version in September 1967.
SSG – Staff Sergeant, squad leader rank
TDY – Temporary Duty
TOC – Tactical Operations Center
VC – Viet Cong, South Vietnamese who fought for north
WIA – Wounded in Action
XO – Executive officer

across my eyes to clear them, I glanced back at Specialists Fourth Class (SP4) Richard Surface and Donald Hunter to make sure they were still following me. At the moment they were our most important guys in the company…they carried our radios, one for the battalion and one for the company… without that capability we were just three guys confined within a hornet's nest of wild bullets and flying shrapnel.

My fourth platoon was pinned down on the left by two NVA machine guns and as the company commander I was trying to see what could be done to clear the problem. I bellied up to a small tree stump for cover and wood chips from the impact of multiple enemy rounds flew into my face, partially blinding me and causing minor scratches. There were several tugs and rips from my rucksack rocking me from side to side. My temporary haven was no longer safe. The stump had disappeared and I was laying on my stomach, unable to see clearly and about to crawl further into a killing zone. Later I found several bullet holes through my pack, poncho and air mattress. It was obvious we were in the sights of a sniper team and to keep going meant being killed. I pointed to where the stump used to be and grinned at the guys to show we had cheated death one more time. I motioned to them to turn around and crawl back the way we had come and received a couple of grateful looks. It appeared they had not been particularly in favor of my idea of moving to the sound of the guns where people were trying to kill us.

And this was all before 9 o'clock when civilians at home were just getting to work. It promised to be a long day, but to us it was just another day at the office! As I kept low and reversed course on my belly, deep in rotting jungle vegetation, dodging bullets, explosions and falling trees, I was reminded of how I found myself in the situation of leading 120 men against a 500-man enemy force located just a few meters away.

CHAPTER TWO

AFTER ATTENDING TEXAS A&M in College Station, Texas for almost two years, as my old New Mexico rancher stepfather, Sam McNatt, used to say, *"I discontinued my matriculation"*.

As many young men do when they find themselves uncertain about their future, I joined the Army. Advancing through the enlisted ranks to Sergeant, I applied for Officer Candidate School and graduated a Second Lieutenant of the US Army Infantry. Attending various skill courses and working through various assignments, I later left active duty to go back to school. In order to maintain a military affiliation and receive a small chunk of change to help with tuition, I joined the 386th Engineer Battalion of the 49th Armored Division of the Texas Army National Guard in Bryan, Texas. To make it official, I had to transfer from the infantry branch and become qualified as an engineer officer, which I accomplished by attending the Basic and Advanced Engineer Courses at Fort Belvoir, Virginia.

Along the way I married a divorcee with five children and my delightful instant family gave me additional responsibilities,

3

which I took on enthusiastically. My original philosophy was that if I could supervise a platoon of 30 guys, surely I could manage five children. I soon discovered there are many skill sets for parenting that have little to do with being a leader in the military. There are some similarities, but they all get forgotten when your sons come to you and tell you they have borrowed a boa constrictor to play with and it was accidentally released into the house and now they can't find it. Or, when they proved another snake was not poisonous because one of them had been bitten and he was still alive. Or, a daughter starts crying because she can't finish her homework for the next day and she is afraid she will lose her A average. Or another daughter falls out of a very tall tree she was climbing, lucky she doesn't break something serious, but knocks the wind out of her lungs and lays gasping for breath and crying because she didn't make it to the high limb she was trying to reach. I learned something every day and am still absorbing those lessons of life.

The night I got married, I was offered the full time job of Staff Administrative Assistant for the 386th Engineer Battalion, which I accepted and continued to take courses as time permitted. In 1965 the years of heavy American involvement in Vietnam began. I was a captain (CPT) at the time. Feeling a calling, I astonished my family and friends by volunteering to return to active duty in Vietnam. Assigned to the Fourth Infantry Division (4th ID) at Fort Lewis, Washington, I joined the unit just a few months before it deployed to the war zone.

The Fourth Infantry Division is one of the core divisions of the US Army. When the US began preparing to send units to Vietnam, it became a "train and retain" organization. This meant the civilian recruits sent to the Division were trained in their various military specialties and then retained in their training units for deployment to Vietnam.

I was one of the late fills before the division deployed, so was assigned to the office of the Division Personnel Rear Detachment office. I was to help coordinate the move of the Division to Vietnam, with the promise that as soon as I got to Vietnam I would receive a permanent posting to a brigade and then, hopefully, to an infantry battalion.

4th Infantry Division Organization

(See Appendix 1 for additional information)

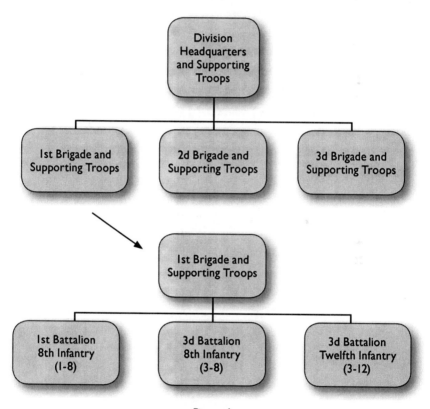

Figure 1
Fourth Infantry Division Organization

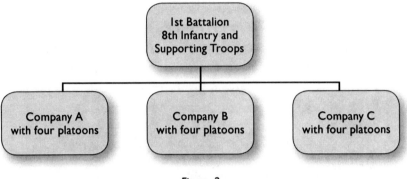

Figure 2
Battalion Organization

The division's move was split into an advance party, a main body and a rear detachment, to which I was posted. Each brigade headquarters and battalion sent a few people by air on the advance party to organize the reception of the main body, which moved by ship. Everything was scheduled for the ships to arrive at the same time as the rear detachment, which traveled by air.

CHAPTER THREE

OUR REAR DETACHMENT AIRCRAFT landed at Pleiku Airbase near the major city of Pleiku in the central highlands of Vietnam on 5 October 1966.

After a couple of days in-processing and several heated discussions about where I was to be sent, I was finally assigned to the 1st Brigade of the Division located on the South China Sea at Tuy Hoa in Phu Yen Province.

The lush coastal plains on the South China Sea were areas of abundant rice harvests. The plains extended from the beaches and sloped upwards into the green coastal mountain ranges that ran north and south along Vietnam's coast. For years the North Vietnamese Army (NVA) and the Viet Cong (VC), had been trying to disrupt the South Vietnamese government by showing that it could not protect its people.

On the coast, the NVA and VC strategy was to infiltrate the villages and towns to gain control over the population. They did this by murder and intimidation. From time to time they gathered in sufficient numbers to ambush the South Vietnamese army units and created a region of instability. As part of their

Getting off the aircraft, I immediately noticed a major difference in the climate. The coolness of the highlands had been exchanged for the hot muggy humidity of the coast. Aircraft were continually taking off and landing and their constant multi-engine roar was the basic background sound. I began to sweat as the heat and coastal humidity caught up with me. I suspected I would start missing the chill of Pleiku before too long.

Another officer had been assigned to the Brigade with me and we flew in on the same aircraft. After claiming our duffle bags, which had been tossed onto the runway, we trudged over to the flight operations tent and inquired where we might find a ride to the 1st Brigade, 4th ID. The operations personnel made a landline telephone call to the brigade to see if they had anything that could pick us up.

After an hour wait, a jeep drove up to the operations tent. The driver asked if we were the officers looking for a ride out to the 4th ID brigade. We said *"yes"* and he drove us the few miles out to the still-new base camp. The route took us on a hard-topped road south of the town of Tuy Hoa with rice paddies and coconut palms on either side. Then we turned off the main road onto a sand trail leading towards a small group of tents. Even though it was getting to be dusk I could see the South China Sea stretching far out to the horizon.

The jeep driver with whom we rode from the airfield didn't know where everything was yet, but he found the brigade headquarters. We were told to report to Lieutenant Colonel (LTC) Tom Lynch, the 1st Brigade Executive Officer (XO).

Colonel Lynch was seated on a gray metal folding chair behind a small wooden field table and the poor light in the tent came from a single dim bulb hanging from the central tent pole. There were two other folding chairs in front of his table and he told us to be seated. Then, without any preliminary chitchat, he proceeded to give us a rousing pitch about pride, professionalism and proficiency. It was a little bombastic and over the top, as if we were young recruits needing a morale adjustment instead of professional officers just wanting to get into the fight. However, he was a lieutenant colonel and we were captains and our assignments were his decision. We nodded enthusiastically with his proclamations. While I was a little uncertain about the reception, it made such an indelible impression I still remember the moment vividly after all these years.

In the coming months I was able to work directly with him and discovered he was an extremely likeable and professional officer.

Meanwhile, the Brigade Personnel Officer (S1), another captain, had been reviewing our files. After our "interview" with the XO, he joined the meeting to recommend our assignments. He wanted me to become an assistant operations officer based upon my previous operations and engineering experience, which he thought, would be useful in planning operations.

I knew I had to overcome the recommendation or be stuck in a staff job for the war. That truly frightened me because I had a very simplistic view of what infantry officers were supposed to do in wartime and that was Fight. Why volunteer for a war if you were just going to sit on the sidelines and watch?

Based upon this view, I pulled out all the stops. I presented a lengthy, and I hoped compelling, argument about my qualifications for a rifle battalion. My ultimate goal was command of a fighting rifle company.

My qualifications included being a graduate of the Infantry Officer Candidate School, my airborne and ranger qualifications, my former assignment as an instructor at the Jungle Warfare Training Center and my certification as a Jungle Expert, as well as my time as an infantry scout platoon leader.

I was a graduate of the basic and the advanced engineer career courses, in addition to the infantry advanced career course. I argued that all of this professional background would make me a better infantry commander.

While trying to remain calm, my intensity must have been apparent. Whether it was the late hour or my impassioned arguments, I was assigned to the 1st Battalion, 8th Infantry.

Whew! Another challenge overcome. It was too late to find the battalion area, so I found an unoccupied piece of sand in the corner of an unfinished tent. I rolled up in my poncho and poncho liner for the night and fell asleep. I was satisfied that whatever tomorrow might bring, my goal of company command was much closer.

CHAPTER FOUR

THE NEXT MORNING I reported to my new battalion commander, Lieutenant Colonel Harold (call sign Pineapple) Lee. After the enthusiastic greeting from the Brigade XO the night before, I was unsure what to expect from my new boss. He was very low key and merely asked about myself and what I wanted to do in his battalion. I repeated my qualifications and told him very directly I had come to Vietnam to be a rifle company commander. *(I thought the most highly prestigious, challenging and rewarding job in the world was to lead a company of United States riflemen against an armed enemy in combat. After 35 years in the Army and several other wars and conflicts, I have not changed my mind!).*

He said he was impressed with my background but he already had company commanders who would retain their commands until their time was up. (In Vietnam, in order to spread combat experience in the officer corps, a command tour was limited to six months.)

I understood this of course, but wanted to ensure he knew I was aggressively seeking a rifle company and would do a good job for him. He acknowledged this and suggested I work on the battalion staff to see what transpired. I became the battalion personnel officer.

After only a few days in country, the battalion companies moved to the field to begin combat operations. This surprised many of the soldiers as they thought they would be permitted some time to finish the base camp. However, as Major General (MG, USA Ret.) Tom Lynch recalls it:

"*Whipcrack* (Colonel (COL) John Austin, 1st Brigade Commander) *wanted to get the troops out into the field as soon as possible. At a big meeting he asked each of his battalion commanders who was ready. The 3-8th CO said, 'We're not ready yet.' The 3-12th CO said, 'Neither are we.' He turned to Hal Lee, the CO of the 1-8th, and Lee, surprising everyone, said, 'We're ready.'*

So the surge was to get the 1-8th equipped to take the field. In order to make room, we had been forced to put our mortars in the lowest hold of the ship, which meant they would be last to unload. We almost had to take over the ship in order to get access to them, but we did.

Then it turned out we couldn't get ammunition yet because of bureaucratic red tape. So we sent some guys over to the 1-101st Airborne ammo depot to steal some ammunition. There was a big fuss about it, but we got it and issued it to the 1-8th so they could deploy.

Lee was a good friend and a very good battalion commander."

The early deployment of the 1-8th permitted a few extra months for the equivalent of a "shakedown cruise" for the battalion and the brigade. It was well worth the time spent in allowing the officers and men to accomplish advanced training and establish routine combat Standard Operating Procedures (SOPs).

The techniques developed at Tuy Hoa established the way the battalions organized themselves for combat.

The base camp provided logistical support directly to the companies in the field. The battalion operations section and the commander operated and guided events from a Tactical Operations Center (TOC) in the Command Post (CP) that was forward in the field, though physically separate from the companies.

We in the rear base camp provided replacements, took care of medical evacuation, made appointments, arranged transportation, provided equipment and generally resupplied the forward companies with whatever they needed. Things moved by truck if they were close to a road, but primarily by helicopter.

The battalion personnel officer was also the morale and welfare officer. It was my responsibility to try and provide certain types of entertainment or distractions for the troops so they could try and forget they were in a combat zone.

Our base camp beach on the South China Sea was not in a bay, but directly open to the high winds, angry surf and strong tides of the ocean. After a few tragic drowning incidents from other units in the brigade, the beach was placed off limits. It was a terrible fact that our first few casualties came from accidents rather than the enemy.

We excavated an almost Olympic-sized swimming pool in the hard packed sand so we could have a protected area to show 8-millimeter movies we ordered from the Post Exchange (PX) in Saigon.

Then the troops in the field commented about their warm beer, authorized 2 per day if practicable, so we figured out how to ice it down in garbage cans and delivered it on resupply days.

I arranged for our mess hall to purchase fresh fish and some shellfish from time to time and even hired boats so the soldiers who were off duty in the rear could go fishing themselves when the weather was good.

All in all, our battalion rear area fast became a comfortable place to recuperate from minor wounds, regular aches and pains and to get away from the slogging for a day or two when authorized by the commanders. What I had not anticipated was that it became so nice that soldiers thought up reasons why they needed to come to the rear and spend a night or two before returning to the field.

On a more serious side, I was also the battalion legal officer. One of the earliest and most unfortunate issues I had to deal with was not a minor matter.

Shortly after the battalion arrived in Vietnam, it became obvious that vehicles could not be used in many operations due to the lack of roads. This required the men of the weapons platoons to carry the very heavy tubes, base plates, sights and other items that were part of the 81mm mortars. Since the companies were on foot most of the time, men throughout each company carried additional mortar rounds in order to have sufficient ammunition for any action. This was in addition to all the other items they carried.

On October 24th, while preparing for one of the early missions, a soldier of Company A refused to carry a mortar round and machine gun spare parts. He was concerned that if his rucksack got shot, the mortar round would explode and kill him. His squad leader insisted and a shouting match ensued. The soldier became enraged, loaded his M16, and shot his squad leader, Specialist Fourth Class Chester Knight, in the chest. The senior medic rushed to treat him, but it was too late and the squad leader died. The assailant ran, but was soon captured and put under guard.

The shot was loud and uncommon enough to be heard in the camp, but I couldn't tell from which direction it had come.

16

Using one of the tactical landline telephones installed in the various companies, we were just contacting Company A's orderly room when I was notified about the incident. I called the brigade headquarters and requested they have Military Police (MP) come and take the soldier into custody since we had no place to keep him safe and under control. After a long wait, the MP's finally arrived and removed him from the battalion area. He was transferred to the stockade in Long Binh near Saigon, charged with murder, found guilty by a courts martial and as I remember, was sentenced to the military prison at Fort Leavenworth, Kansas.

Our first casualty was killed by one of our own.

CHAPTER FIVE

WE ALL HAD A LOT to learn. One night shortly after moving out to the field for example, Company A had one of these experiences. Captain Nick Romaine, the company commander at the time, described what happened:

"... I assigned the first platoon the mission of guarding a hill down near the bottom of the Fort (an old French fort) *to prevent infiltration by the enemy from the South China Sea.*

It wasn't long after everything had settled down and all the platoons were performing their missions, when I heard on the radio a call come in from the First Platoon requesting a "Fire Mission". That could only mean one thing, the enemy has been spotted. Our mortar platoon fired the mission, then quiet, and then came a request for illumination. Quiet. More illumination. Quiet. I got on the horn (radio) *and asked my LT, "What is going on?" He replied "The enemy is on the hill north of us hollering and cussing at us." "Can you see them?" I replied. "Noooo....but we sure can hear them." "Let's try some Arty Lum* (artillery illumination)*," I said. I got my Arty FO* (Forward Observer) *and had him fire the mission...quiet,* *and again, quiet and again quiet…The mortar platoon jumped in and fired up all their 81-mm illumination, then HE* (high explosive), *same with the Arty. This went on all night.*

The next morning at first light I walked down the hill and when I spotted that north hill you will not believe what I saw! That entire hill was covered with white parachutes from the illumination rounds! It looked like a snowstorm had come through during the night. We sent out some search parties and they found nothing. I asked the LT what they were saying and he replied "F…. You!" Later we discovered this is the sound that a lizard makes at night. So it was called the F… You, lizard."

First Lieutenant (1LT) Howard Brooks, a platoon leader in the same company, learned about some of the other wildlife the hard way. In one of his letters home he described his day… *"The company commander* (CPT Romaine) *and I rode down the road a way today to an old deserted village and found a grove of coconut trees. We decided to shoot some down and bring them back to base camp. Well, the first batch I shot at stirred up a damn hornets' nest up in the top of the tree and before I knew it those damn things were all over me. Four got me on my arms where my sleeves were rolled and one found the back of my neck. I mean those damn things really sting. They still hurt."*

Company B, like Company A, was beginning to have men wounded in various incidents, the first of which occurred on October 26. A patrol from Company B was fired upon by a sniper, who was later wounded but escaped capture. However, the patrol called for a fire mission from the company mortars. One of the mortar rounds fired in support of the patrol was a short round into the company's position, wounding three. While these men were classified as having been Wounded In Action (WIA), the enemy had yet to lay a hand on us.

CHAPTER FIVE

A subsequent investigation showed that the propellant charge required to launch the mortar round had become wet and had not burned all the way. This weakened the amount of explosive force applied to the round and caused the shortened trajectory.

A few days later on 3 November, Company B found a large VC force and engaged in an active firefight. When artillery and air strikes were called in, the VC responded with hugging tactics, an approach where they tried to get close to the US unit during barrages or firefights. The VC hoped the US unit would call off the artillery because it was as dangerous to the US unit as to the enemy.

While Company B fell back and formed a perimeter, Colonel Lee ordered Company C, who was not very far away, to move to the location and provide additional support. In the meantime, Company B was still trying to flush out the enemy. When Sergeant Frankie Molnar's squad was sent to check out an area just beyond the perimeter, it was met by VC fire, which they returned even more effectively. Once Molnar determined that the enemy was still present in force, he returned the squad to the main company. When Company C arrived, the enemy retreated, leaving 15. In the action, one Company B soldier was wounded and medevaced to the rear. He was the first man of the company to be wounded by enemy fire.

This action earned Molnar and his men, along with several others of the company, the award of the highly coveted Combat Infantry Badge (CIB). These were the first CIBs awarded to Company B personnel.

Only an infantryman, or an individual who has performed in an infantry position, is authorized to wear the CIB, and then only after being in ground combat with an armed enemy. To the regular rifleman, there is no badge or award as meaningful as the silver flintlock rifle imposed on the infantry's color of light blue, embossed on an enameled bar with a silver border

21

and a silver oak wreath. The CIB is more than a punched ticket, it says the individual has put his life on the line as an infantryman and has done his job. You can have all the medals and decorations in the world, worn from breast pockets to both shoulders, but to a grunt rifleman, if the CIB is not among them, you are just a "wannabe".

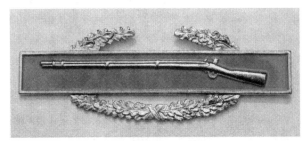

Figure 3
Combat Infantry Badge

Fortunately, the Army recognized that soldiers other than infantrymen also put their lives on the line, so there is a Combat Medical Badge, which all of our medics deserved, and a Combat Action Badge more recently established for those non-infantry MOSs who find themselves in the mouth of the dragon as well.

There were wounded and sick in Company B, but so far none killed. That changed on 16 November when Private First Class (PFC) LeMoine Grow of Company B was drowned while trying to cross a dangerously swollen stream.

Murphy's Law's:

"Weather ain't neutral."

The loss was a result of poor judgment by the company commander who had refused to request a helicopter to move a patrol across a flooded stream. The stream had been safe to cross in the morning when the patrol left. By the time the unit returned however, it had become a raging torrent due

22

to afternoon rains. The patrol leader found a small boat. Not wanting to risk his men, he was able to cross, but the boat broke up as he reached the bank, leaving the rest of the patrol stranded. The patrol leader requested the company commander obtain a helicopter so they could move the remainder of the troops across safely; the commander refused and snarled that they were infantry and to get the f___ across the stream like real soldiers and hurry up about it.

PFC Grow, who was a strong swimmer, tried to swim a rope across the stream so the rest of the platoon could use it to cross, but the current was too swift, he lost his footing and was swept downstream. When this was reported by radio, the company commander somehow managed to obtain a helicopter to search for the soldier, but he could not be found. The helicopter was finally used to move the remainder of the patrol to the other side. Vietnamese found Grow's body a few days later, far downstream, almost where the stream emptied into the South China Sea.

PFC Jim Burch of Company B's fourth platoon, commented on the incident in a letter home:

"...one of my buddies from Indiana drowned Wednesday. We were out on a recon patrol and had left early that morning. It rained all day. We had crossed some streams that were small. When we were returning that afternoon the streams were bank full. Lamoine Grow was his name. He was one of the best swimmers but the river was too much. The third time he went under he didn't come up. They found his body today."

Burch's letters home provide an insight into the normal day of our soldiers. He was not a dramatic writer but described the everyday concerns of a man who is far from home. He was a dedicated letter writer to his family and was hungry for news. His letters describe his anxious desire to keep himself anchored in his family and in the events of the "real" world.

23

(Many soldiers referred to home in the United States as "The World").

He was concerned and interested about his father's crops, his brother's marriage, his sister's well-being and myriads of smaller details: his pay, pictures of friends, care packages and letters from home. Most of all he was looking forward to the future with thoughts of purchasing a new car, getting a room fixed up for himself and saving money. He offered money to his mother if she needed it and assured his sister that she would be able to attend college, intimating as an older brother that he would take care of it in some manner. Like many others from the mid-west who were drafted, he had a full sense of family values and treasured his relationships.

In a later letter home, he reported he was now the point man for his platoon and had been issued a shotgun. A shotgun was considered a better weapon than the M16 for close jungle work.

Burch: *"... they gave me a shotgun. It's a 12 ga. 5 shot pump. Guess I'll like it o.k. We use 00 buck shot shells. Tell Dad to send me a box of Western Xpert deer slugs. We are allowed to use them, but the Army doesn't issue them. Tell him to pay for them out of my money."*

As far as weapons were concerned, most officers carried the M16 instead of the authorized .45 pistol. I figured there would be enough M16s around if I ever got involved in a firefight, but I decided I would carry an M79 grenade launcher as my personal weapon. The M79 was an area type weapon shaped like a sawed off shotgun. It launched a .40mm grenade up to 200 meters. There were several different rounds that fit the M79, one of which was a round that fired 45 fleschette darts, which was later superseded by a buckshot round with 27 double ought buckshot. I felt it would add nicely to any firearms mix.

As the Battalion Personnel Officer, I spent a day or two during the week hiking the boonies with the different companies. I wanted to understand how I could improve my support as well as better prepare myself for company command.

Little combat occurred during any of my walkabout times in the field, but on a routine trip to Company C we found a little excitement. The battalion Reconnaissance Platoon under 1LT Arthur Trujillo, while searching out an area, became pinned down by sniper fire from some rocks on the side of a mountain. Soldiers had been wounded. The unit tried to maneuver against the sniper, but there was a large area at the base of the mountain that was completely exposed to fire from the heights.

There was no need to get someone shot just trying to get into the rocks when artillery fire could cover the area just as well. The Battalion Logistics Officer (S4) and I, with another battalion staff officer were visiting Company C at the same time. When we heard about the situation, we knew it would take a little time for any artillery to respond because other operations that day had much higher priority. A helicopter was sitting on the ground after having just finished unloading. The three of us sprinted for it and told the pilots to take off.

We flew the short distance to where Recon was located and started firing into the rocks to give the platoon time to move away. The door gunner was firing his M60 machine gun into the face of the mountain. The other two officers were firing their M16s and I was the indirect fire support, firing my 40-millimeter grenades into the area. We made a heck of a noise and hit a lot of dirt and rocks. We were successful, as the sniper stopped firing at the platoon (probably out of sheer surprise). No one got hit and things got quiet again. The platoon searched the area but found nothing.

We returned the helicopter (the crew had a great time transforming from grocery bag boys to a real gun ship with shots

25

being fired and everything) and things went back to normal. I thought Pineapple was going to fuss at us for getting involved in stuff that really wasn't our business, but I guess he understood that it all worked out OK; we actually did some good, though it was a little unorthodox. He knew even staff pukes needed to smell brimstone from time to time.

Some VC or NVA were working the region, setting mines and blowing up things after dark. An intelligence report indicated the group was in our area of operations and the battalion was working with the Korean regiment to find them. The company I was walking with at the time (which one escapes me) had flushed a small group of uniformed bad guys. There had been a small firefight in which no one was hurt; the bad guys had disappeared into a tunnel on a destroyed rail line that paralleled the coast. The company had radioed the other side of the mountain and a maneuver force from the Korean unit blocked the other end. Now the question arose of how to get at these guys. No one wanted to go in after them since the attackers would be silhouetted and extremely vulnerable. Again, there was no need for anyone to die trying to dig these folks out and it was hoped an interpreter might be able to talk them into surrendering. If this group could be taken prisoner, then information might be obtained regarding the VC/NVA plans for the region. We fired sporadically into the tunnel to keep their heads down while we waited for an interpreter from battalion.

In the meantime the Koreans moved up with an M48 tank. Our Vietnamese interpreter finally arrived and tried talking to the Vietnamese in the tunnel. We got a burst of rifle fire in response so the company commander decided to wait a while longer. The concern was that when it got dark these guys would be able to break out and get away (individual night vision devices were still in the future). We could use flares to

26

eminded me that soldiers were supposed to be
all times and that it was a pretty sloppy outfit
cure its ammunition properly.

, so the mess hall was next. The 1-8th arguably
finest mess sergeant/chefs in the Division and
won all kinds of awards at Fort Lewis for the
etail, food preparation, presentation and gener-
e troops well. This had not changed just because
ietnam. As in all the brigade units in the rear,
prepared in a small mess tent over field stoves.
ine passed by the front of the tent and food was
aper plates as the troops shuffled by. There was
rator that provided electricity for a freezer and
After observing the mess line and the food dis-
cess, the general wanted to see the refrigeration
ess sergeant explained the ration break down
many rations were received and how they were
efrigerated. The general opened the door to the
and then shut it. As he did so I saw an insect fly
as the door closed and I suspect the general did
didn't say anything, but immediately opened the
and the fly flew out. He then began to accuse the
nt of permitting flies to contaminate food and that
negligence.

rotested that the insect had just flown into the unit
ened it, he just glared at me and informed me that
n was a pigsty and that the rear area supervision
me) was unprofessional and inadequate. In addi-
d me to pass on to the battalion commander that
d the mess sergeant to be given an Article 15 and
r his slovenly standards.

to the XO for some support, but he just looked at
any expression and said he would ensure Colonel

keep the area bright enough to see by but it was not a wise
use of time or manpower.

It all became moot when the tank suddenly lined up its main
gun and fired three rounds at the entrance to the tunnel. The
tunnel opening collapsed, completely blocking the entrance
with large chunks of concrete and dirt. Before we could recover
from the shock of this unexpected action, we heard a distant
boom. The Koreans had blown the other end of the tunnel
with demolitions, removing any worry about what to do with
those inside the tunnel. As far as the Koreans were concerned,
the action was over and we should continue the mission of
searching out other bad guys. This frustrated our force, since
we had hopes of a prisoner, but there really wasn't much that
could be done anymore. It was readily apparent the Koreans
had a different approach to solving problems.

A few weeks later, the battalion was operating north of Tuy
Hoa along Highway 1, which was the primary north-south
highway along the coast. One of the battalion tasks was to
protect the bridges that spanned several streams and rivers that
emptied into the South China Sea to our east. Another task
was to protect the highway from snipers and ambushes so military and civilian traffic could use it safely. Convoys invariably
encountered sniper fire or a roadside explosive when moving.
As soon as counter fire was initiated, the snipers faded away
into the hills or nearby villages until the next convoy arrived.

There was a small hard-packed sand hill on a peninsula
just to the east of the highway. It overlooked several coastal
villages; the highway itself, and several hundred acres of rice
fields. While only about fifty feet above sea level with knee-
high brush, it permitted good observation and fields of fire
in all directions. Because of its elevation, it was selected as
a company-size firebase from which patrols were supported
by 4.2-inch mortars. The companies of the brigade took

moved to
the childr
on the hil
VC, dres
came up
the wire.
grenades
the defen
lesson, bu

The en
if need be

training by allegedly throwing things at the floating birds. This caused some "be kind to animals" person to call the Division Commander to complain about his soldiers being cruel to ducks. Being the combat general that he was and moving to the sound of the quacking, the CG reportedly came down to the docks and had the work crews lined up. He then proceeded to pass down the lines asking each individual in words to the effect, *"Did you throw rocks at the ducks?"* Of course no one admitted to the dastardly deed. But it became a story of some amusement about the priorities of the leadership who seemed more concerned about public relations with the local "be kind to animals" fans, than with a few soldiers who were on their way to a combat zone and who might not be coming back. It was reported the CG did not forget things that displeased him and the 1-8th was one of the units on the docks.

After I became the personnel officer, Colonel Lynch and I developed a great working relationship. He wanted a battalion, I wanted a company, and we were both dedicated to supporting troops. One day he called in all the senior rear area representatives and told us the CG was going to pay us a visit and we should be prepared. I went around with our guys from each company and pulled my own inspection. Generally, everything was in pretty good shape for a unit in combat. We were still in the stages of putting up additional tents and had work crews of recuperating, lightly-wounded and sick call guys, who were in from the field.

It was extremely hot and humid. By the middle of the day temperatures constantly fluttered around and above 100 degrees Farenheight. Being within the brigade perimeter permitted us to dress a little more casually than if we were out in the field. We were essentially in an administrative mode. Within the battalion area, helmets were not required on work details and rifles were secured in each company, with any ammunition,

grenades or explosives
ever, even to the briga
away, we were in full g

The general arrivec
Brigade XO. He had alr
XO's look told me that
confident that we would
we had made and had I
general's face. I escorted t
proudly showed him our
to make the area a more
I have always felt that se
understand when there is
when it can be relaxed.

It happened on this day
were taking a break as we
none had headgear and the
General Purpose, Medium
it taut along the sides. As
called the men to attention
of them, asking them why th
or shirts. When they answere
me in an icy tone, that we w
should be appropriately prep
at the tent that was still unfin
it was obvious the work crew
should have been completed
Uh-Oh...things were on a dov

The general proceeded into
as the company administrativ
dred degrees and the clerk had
down his torso. He also had a st
caliber pistol round as a small p

me and again
in uniform at
that did not se

It was noon
had one of th
the unit had
attention to d
ally feeding th
we were in V
the food was
The serving
ladled onto p
a small gene
refrigerator.
tribution pr
units. The
process, hov
stored and
refrigerator
into the uni
as well. He
door again
mess sergea
it was gross

When I
when he op
the battali
(meaning
tion, he to
he expecte
demoted f

I looke
me withou

Lee received the message. Colonel Lynch was a much more experienced officer than I. He recognized there was nothing to be done at the moment, except to get the silly ass out of the area as soon as possible without further antagonizing him or providing more ammunition.

Article 15 of the Uniform Code of Military Justice permits commanders to give non-judicial punishment to minor offenders. The individual is given a choice of an Article 15, or choosing a trial by courts martial. Since a courts martial gives a commander a much larger selection of punishments, including jail time for relatively minor infractions, most soldiers will elect an Article 15 and rely upon the commander to be fair. The Article 15 does not become a part of the individual's permanent record and does not follow him once he is reassigned from a unit. If the soldier continues to do a good job, the disciplinary action does not keep the individual from receiving favorable personnel actions in the future, like a promotion or desired schooling. It is used primarily as punishment for infractions less serious than felonies covered by courts martial or as a wake-up call for troops who need to be re-focused on the job at hand and more attention to detail.

Colonel Lee received both Colonel Lynch's and my reports on the matter, and had a hard time believing the CG was serious. He protested the matter to the brigade commander. However, when the matter was finally decided, he reacted as a professional soldier and recognized he did not have much choice.

He gave the mess sergeant an Article 15 and demoted him one grade. He promoted him the next month with an early promotion to the next higher grade soon after.

I was proud to be in a combat ready unit.

A few weeks later, the CG came back to the brigade area. This time he went to the field and the 1-8th's forward Command Post. The CP was on top of a tall grassy mountain with

and we were in very thick, triple canopy jungle. The single line of men now were moving at a much slower pace and we tightened up the line to only ten meters apart in order to keep visual contact with the man in front of you. There were times when the line came to a stop so the point man could cut his way through the bamboo. It was now about 10:45 in the morning and the only good thing about the thick jungle, was it kept the hot blistering sun off the back of our necks. I was thinking that it was so hard to keep an exact pace count in that terrain, because I kept tripping over vines and branches and all the thick underbrush.

Suddenly to my front a shot rang out "BANG!" then two more, "BANG! BANG!" Everyone dropped to the ground and there was silence for a second. I lay to the side of the trail we were cutting and looked all around me, but couldn't see a thing except the boots of the man that was about ten meters in front of me. He turned and said to me, "Point man spotted two NVA. They shot and ran. Nobody hit. Pass it back." I passed it to the man behind me and so on down the line went to the CO. After about five minutes went by, the word came down the file, "Move out slowly and keep your eyes open." We all got up and began to move out. We moved another twenty meters or so and again, "BANG! BANG!" from the front of the line. This time the point man and the second man return fire. "BANG, BANG, BANG, BANG, BANG!" We all hit the dirt and I still could see nothing except the man to my front. We passed the word back again, "Two more NVA. We may have hit one. They ran and none of our men got hit." We lay there another five minutes waiting for word from the CO on what to do. All I kept thinking was that "I've got to get out of here. I can't take this anymore." I put my rifle on the ground and turned my hands face up to look at them. They were trembling and wet with perspiration, as was the *rest of my body. I wiped the sweat from my upper lip and my forehead, took off my steel pot and ran my hand through my hair. "Please, God," I thought, "We only have 3 months left here. Make those NVA go away. At that, the guy behind me called up to me. "Tell them to move up a little bit and form a perimeter." That was the best news I'd heard all day. I passed the word up and in five minute the whole company was in a defensive perimeter with the CP group in the middle."*

At about the same time as the action to the front of the fourth platoon was occurring, the second platoon to the right of the fourth, also began to engage the enemy. The unit's leader, 1LT Larry Rodabaugh, later described what happened:

"We came down a little ridgeline and came across a high speed trail. I put the platoon on line on one side of the trail and as we moved into position we spotted three NVA walking down the trail. I also was told that the point heard voices to the front. At this time another NVA with a weapon showed up to our right. I used my little bit of Vietnamese and told him to "Come here!" He tried to shoot at us and we returned fire after which he dropped his pack and disappeared to the north. The other three dropped their packs and ran. Unbelievably they all disappeared into the jungle on the other side of the trail leaving their packs and blood trails. Allen wanted me to pursue, but I told him I would have to reform the platoon because we were strung out on line."

Allen then stopped the company and established a perimeter intending to check out the area further and to cut an LZ to evacuate the four NVA packs for intelligence purposes.

Renza: *"The company commander called all the platoon leaders to the CP to figure out their next move. After ten or fifteen minutes, Grandstaff returned to the perimeter and called all the squad leaders to his position. "OK, listen up,"* he said. *"Workman* (fourth platoon) *spotted three NVA in*

288

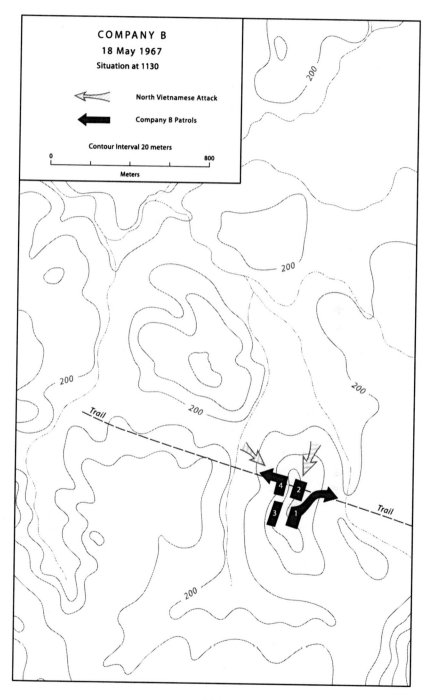

CHAPTER THIRTY ONE

COMPANY B
18 May 1967
Situation at 1130

North Vietnamese Attack

Company B Patrols

Contour Interval 20 meters

0   800

Meters

green uniforms and we don't know if there are more of them around here. Second and third platoons are going to stay here in the perimeter. First Platoon is going to recon to the south (Note: this was actually to the east, not the south) *about fifty meters and we are going to recon to the west."*

The official Combat Operations After Action Report indicates that ... *"the first platoon was then sent to the east southeast to check that portion of the trail and the fourth platoon was sent to the west and northwest to check out the trail in that direction. They were instructed to go no farther than 200 meters. The first platoon moved along the trail to the southeast for a distance of 250 meters and returned with negative findings."*

Rodabaugh, second platoon: *"Allen then said that fourth platoon would come through our platoon and pursue. The fourth platoon passed through our lines and moved down the trail (west). I started reorganizing the platoon, but held in place along the trail while LT Chuck Aronhalt's third platoon came up on our left flank."*

Renza, fourth platoon: *"Grandstaff told us, first squad, you take point, then 2d and 3d fall in behind them and 4th squad, you take up the rear. Leave your rucksacks here in the perimeter. Just take web gear and ammo. Get your squads ready to move out."* Jimmy Burch, leader of 4th squad, walked over to me and said *"We're going on a recon patrol, but this time we've got the rear."* We dropped our rucksacks and started leaving the perimeter in single file. First squad on point, 2d, 3d, then 4th and I ended up at the end of the file. In front of me was our FO artillery man. Behind me was our RTO and behind was Bob Sanzone, who was acting as Platoon Sergeant. Grandstaff was acting Platoon Leader. LT Bosch had gotten sick two days beforehand was sent to the rear. (Author note: As previously noted, Bosch had been reassigned and was an official loss. He would not return to the company.) *As we left the perimeter, 2d and third platoons tightened up and we could see first platoon moving off ... . We were supposed to go out approximately fifty to one hundred meters, look around and report back by radio, if we saw anything. I never liked it when we were in very thick jungle and the CO would split the company. It always seemed like were very far from one another and couldn't regroup quickly if we had to."*

The first platoon was on the right (east) side of the company position behind the second platoon. It was ordered to do a quick recon to the east to make sure the flank was secure. John Barclay of the first platoon was on the recon with one of his buddies and remembers it this way:

Barclay: *"It was open, dark and silent. It (the route), appeared to have a natural lane, free of impairment to such a degree, that it could have been perfect for a vehicle to glide through. It was an eerie place and I was leery of taking another step ... It was as if the jungle and all who lived in it was saying, "Go back." Every step I had taken was from one tree to another in silence, as if I was hunting deer and not taking a "look see" at just terrain. A sense that going beyond a point was possibly a point of no return. I remember making a gesture with my hand pointing back over my shoulder and whispering, "let's get the F___ out of here." The silence was deafening. As if we each knew at the same time, enough was enough. We withdrew and returned to gather our rucksacks. Some other men from the first platoon must have taken up positions for security while we were gone ... automatic fire erupted from where I had passed coming back from recon. It was on top of us. Ritchie (SGT) had been running by me and slapped me on the shoulder and said, "Follow me, kid." The fire from both sides was intense and I felt as though I had to lean way forward in my run to lower my profile ... Ritchie stopped behind a large wide tree ... the tree was big enough for the both of us, except we were both right handed. He stood up and was firing on the right side of the tree. I was kneeling and not comfortable getting a look to my front. Then I noticed SSG "Rock" Smothers was laying prone to my immediate left, only 8 to 10 feet away. Smothers yelled to me that they shot PSGT Johnson. He pointed to our front. I tried to see Johnson, but couldn't. I tried to keep my shots low, but didn't get off many rounds as the brass was shooting back toward me as I was holding it to my left. Smothers yelled that the NVA was behind a "Y" shaped tree to our front about 30 meters. I took a quick look, but it was at my 1 o'clock. Then Ritchie's rifle jammed and my rifle was pointing up in a perfect position to grab. So he grabbed it, quicker than a drill sergeant during an inspection. He gave me his rifle, like it was all a plan to keep him armed and firing and me busy fixing his weapon ... ."*

Even though Barclay continued trying to fix the weapon, he couldn't get the jam cleared. He had a Light Antitank Weapon (LAW) with him so he started preparing it to fire. Smothers told him he was going to mark the tree and did so, but Barclay's LAW did not have the range finder and sight on it. Barclay finally jumped out and fired the LAW, hitting the tree to unknown effect as far as the NVA hiding behind it was concerned.

SSG Smothers had received a wound in his right arm and was bandaging it, while Barclay found another LAW. However, it had a broken cable that kept it from firing. So he had a broken rifle, a broken LAW, and now our artillery was falling in front of him.

Barclay: "Ritchie was gone. I couldn't tell who had been on his right, but nobody was there now. Artillery was landing behind the enemy and being walked back to us .... I didn't hear an order to withdraw. I looked to my left, Smothers was gone...I was alone with artillery coming closer. I decided I wasn't going to leave until the artillery got close. Then I hear screaming from GI's..."Barclay, get back here!...Barclay, pull back!.."Goofy F...." They didn't know my fear of *withdrawing was of being gunned down from behind...shot in the back...I looked behind me and there was about 6 GI's yelling at me. I could only see their faces. They were in line, like pumpkins waiting to be purchased at a super market. They were*

Murphy's Laws:
"If you find yourself in front of your platoon, they know something you don't."

laying in a depression in the ground so that all you could see were their faces .... I decided to make a run for it. Probably the fastest 40 yard dash I ever ran. A few zigs thrown in before a magnificent ten foot jump with my helmet thunking and Ritchie's broken rifle tossed ahead of me as I flew over their astonished faces, landed and rolled. SAFE!"

In the meantime, the fourth platoon was on its way west to check out the NVA that had been spotted.

Renza, fourth platoon: *"It seemed as though we were no more than fifty meters from the rest of the company, when we were walking down a high-speed trail.* [A high-speed trail was a clear and beaten pathway through the jungle on which a unit could make very fast time, as opposed to the more overgrown game trails we often used for security reasons.] *When I saw that trail, all I could think of was, "where the hell is Grandstaff taking us?" Here we were in triple canopy jungle on a high speed trail, very close to Cambodia. It didn't take much smarts to figure out it was a very dangerous situation. That trail was not worn down to bare ground by three or four NVA. It would take more like three or four hundred to do that! The trail looked as if it were used every day, like some kind of supply route. With the tall, thick trees above*

293

it, the NVA could move freely on the ground without ever being seen from the air. We were now only about five or six meters away from each other and moving very slowly down that trail. I turned and said to Bob Sanzone, "Where the hell is he going?" Bob said, "I don't know, but I am ready to go back to the company." "He's a John Wayne, gung ho, M...F..." I said, turned and kept walking. There was no reply from Bob. I started to think that as soon as we got back to the rest of the company, I would tell the CO that I had to get out of the field. "I can't take the stress and tension. I don't care if they send me to jail. I just have got to get out of the field," I kept going over and over this in my mind. I really felt I was coming apart at the seams. "BANG!" A shot rang out in front of us. We all hit the ground and I crawled back to where Bob was with Charlie Reed, who was Bob's RTO and I could hear the talk on the radio. The CO was on the horn with Grandstaff. "Do you need any help?" the CO said. "No," replied Grandstaff. "There are only two or three of them... we'll get them!" I looked at Bob and said, "That asshole!" We got up and moved another ten meters down the trail, when the NVA opened up on 1st squad. Again, "BANG, BANG, BANG, BANG, BANG." This time 1st squad returned fire, but no one was hit. The CO again got on the horn. "fourth platoon, do you need assistance?" Grandstaff again said, "No." By now first platoon had rejoined the company and they were all sitting in the perimeter eating lunch.

Again we started to move further down the trail and again shots rang out. We dove into the brush alongside the trail and looked frantically in every direction. Being in the rear of the file, we could see nothing. Again the CO called and again Grandstaff refused any help. After about two or three minutes, Grandstaff called back to Bob on the radio. He asked him to come forward to his position. Bob picked up his rifle, looked at me and I said "Tell him to get us the hell out of here! Bob said nothing. He just kept moving toward Grandstaff with a blank, frightened look on his face. Reed, his RTO, fell in behind him and the two of them, bent over at the waist to keep a low profile. They moved quickly down the trail and I soon lost sight of them. Little did I know that would be the last time I would see Bob Sanzone alive. When Bob reached Grandstaff, Tom Sears was just in front of them and heard Grandstaff say, "I don't like this, it's too quiet."

Just then, more shots rang out to the front of us. The point squad returned fire and then it seemed like the whole hillside to my front and to my right opened up on us with small arms and automatic weapons fire. Bullets were flying everywhere, cutting branches off trees, just inches over my head. Someone from the front yelled, "Medic, Medic!" and I knew someone had been hit. The Medic who was right in front of me seemed to be frozen to the ground. I said to him, "You better get up there, they need you!" The guy in front of him turned and said "Come on — Move! Get your ass up there!" He grabbed his medic bag, dragged it alongside of him and started crawling toward the front of the file. Then we all began moving toward the front in a low, crawling position to help out 1st and 2d squads, which were getting the heaviest fire. At this time Grandstaff was on the radio with the CO and we were ordered to pull back and rejoin the rest of the company. I crawled about twenty five meters toward the front with the rest of 4th squad, all of us now well off the main trail, moving through very thick underbrush.

When Bosch left the platoon, SP4 Tom Sears became the RTO for Grandstaff. When the sergeant went to the front, Sears accompanied him. Sears told Renza:

"When the first NVA burst hit it looked like about 2–3 NVA and we returned fire. Then it looked like some of our guys

were hit and Allen was talking to Grandstaff. Grandstaff called Sanzone up forward, as well as the medic, Shultz. When Sanzone got there he crouched down next to Grandstaff, who turned to him and said "What do you think?" At that point, Sanzone didn't give an answer because the NVA opened up with a lot of shooting and you couldn't hear over the noise of the guns and grenades."

Sears lost track of Grandstaff and Sanzone at that point; because he was moving and shooting at the NVA who were on the attack. Grandstaff and Sanzone were organizing and fighting the platoon. Time elapsed. Sears remembered that he and Sanzone later were sharing a little knoll. He held the lowest end of the position while Sanzone was higher. When Sanzone's rifle took a round through the breech, it left him without a weapon, so Sears shared his rifle with him. Shortly thereafter, Sanzone took a round in the head and fell on his compatriot. Realizing he had to move, Sears started crawling toward the ditch. A burning sensation in his hip told him he also had been hit.

Sears continued crawling, dragging his M16. He lifted his head to see where he was going and saw an NVA soldier watching him crawl. The NVA took a bead on his head and fired. The bullet missed its target and struck his lower back instead. He went limp.

After most of the firing had stopped, one of the NVA soldiers sat on Sear's back to check his body and started running his fingers through Sear's hair. He put his hand down Sear's shirt to check his breathing; then rolled him over face up and stood over him...Sears held his breath. The NVA kicked him, then walked away to check other fallen platoon members.

Renza, fourth platoon: *"Suddenly I saw the guys from the 1st and 2d squads crawling toward us and they're yelling "Pull back! Pull back!" At this point it seemed like no one knew what direction to move in. We were just like thirty little ants, scattered in the grass, running in circles. To my left there was a dried up stream bed about twenty meters away and there wasn't any fire coming from that direction ... I yelled "Hit the stream bed for cover!" I started towards the stream bed ... and the streambed was about up to my chest. By the time the guy next to me got into the streambed ... the whole side of the streambed opened up on us...they were all in the trees. They were dug in. There was a machine gun emplacement and we were like sitting ducks ... . I would say the stream bed was about 12 feet wide and that was really wide open... so we were in the streambed and they opened up. Some guys followed and others just took off in different directions... no one really knowing where to go. It made a sharp turn to my left and to the right. When the third guy jumped into the stream bed, he was at my left side. I turned to him and said, "Move down and cover the other turn." Other guys piled in and started shooting. At that it seemed like the whole other side of the stream bed opened up with automatic weapons fire.*

There was a machine gun and it shot rounds right up on the wall of the streambed "TOK TOK TOK TOK TOK TOK TOK TOK!" hitting everybody in the streambed...the kid that was right next to me, a round shattered his femur bone and came right out of his leg...he grabbed his leg, the round continued on through this kid, went past and hit the kid on the other side of me...I emptied a magazine into the other side...I think this made them duck down just enough to give me a little time...I jumped up and pulled the kid who was hit in the leg with me out of the streambed. He was screaming and in a lot of pain. I said, "Come with me!" He fell across me and we both tumbled along the ground, him screaming, "My leg, my leg!" We were now receiving heavy fire from the west, north and south. I said to him "Come this way," and pointed east, which seemed to be the only direction little fire was coming from. He looked at me like he didn't understand English and started moving in the opposite direction, with one hand over his bloody thigh and the other holding his M16. At that time I just turned and started crawling east. There were guys still heading toward the stream bed and I screamed, "Don't go into the stream!" Everyone else in the streambed was killed...I started crawling away. I crawled about ten more meters and there was an old tree trunk lying in my path. I had to climb over it. Just as I got to it, a bullet ripped into the back of my boot. It made my foot snap sideways. Somehow the bullet missed my foot and just ripped open the back of my boot. I kept moving. I moved alongside the tree trunk, put my left hand and left leg over it and started crawling over the top. Just as I was halfway over, a bullet ripped through the left side of my back. As I fell the rest of the way over, I threw my M16, which was in my left hand, grabbed my back and screamed, "I'm hit, I'm hit!" I crawled up real close to the log and lay alongside it with my face in the dirt. When I threw my weapons forward it landed about five or six feet in front of me...I could see it but I couldn't reach it...My back felt like it was on fire. I started to yell, "SGT Grandstaff! SGT Grandstaff!" but no one could hear me. There was just too much noise from all the rifle fire. It now seemed like we were getting fire from all directions and I thought we would never get out of this. I then realized we were surrounded by at least a battalion of NVA. Now Sgt Grandstaff called back to the CO and asked for assistance."There's too many of them and we're being overrun! Come help us!" he said. The CO ordered the rest of the company to move west toward our position. They moved no more than fifty meters when they began receiving automatic weapons fire from the west. The NVA had set up a blocking force. They let the fourth platoon *through and they ambushed us. When the rest of the company tried to help us, they stopped them cold. Now 1st, 2d and third platoons had their own battle going on. The CO called Grandstaff on the radio and asked him about our situation and called in artillery fire and gunships to help us. Grandstaff started adjusting artillery fire within forty-five meters of our platoon location. 105mm Howitzer rounds started falling all around us. "Sssssssss, BOOM! Sssssssss, BOOM!" Rounds were ripping through the tree tops and as they hit the ground, trees were being cut in half by the red hot, sharp metal, which was flying everywhere. I was right next to two other guys and we were right behind a log...the kid that I pulled out of the stream bed was killed and the two guys were perfectly fine at that point. I told them I was shot and they kept screaming "We'll get you out! Don't worry! We'll get you out" One of them was the artillery observer, Sgt Thompson, and he kept reassuring me over all the firing that he would get me out. We were laying next to each other so close our bodies were touching. He made me feel so much better and he did that for about twenty minutes. The fire was so loud, so intense and the leaves were coming down like rain from the trees, because the NVA just laid down a blanket of fire criss-crossing over the top of us. You couldn't move, so wherever you were, you just had to try and find a target and fire at...*

Sgt Thompson went silent and I think he took a shot in the head and died instantly."

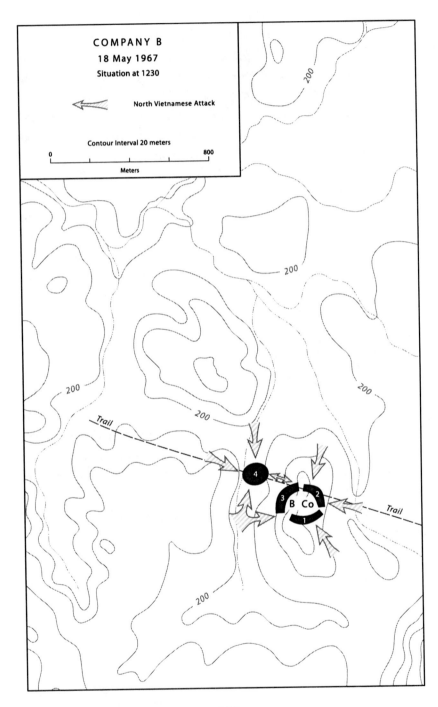

COMPANY B
18 May 1967
Situation at 1230

North Vietnamese Attack

Contour Interval 20 meters

CHAPTER THIRTY TWO

ALLEN TRIED TO MANEUVER the company to link up with the fourth platoon. The third platoon was on the left, the second platoon on the right. The first platoon was in the right rear with the CP group behind the lead platoons.

1LT Larry Rodabaugh, second platoon Leader: *"Aronhalt and I tried to move our platoons forward to support the fourth platoon but as soon as we started forward we started receiving extremely heavy fire and the front half of both of our platoons were either killed or wounded. We went into a defensive position, but we had run into a reinforced NVA battalion and we simply didn't have enough firepower to answer them. My RTO was killed in the first round of firing and I was wounded in the arm, but I took the radio knowing it was the only lifeline we had to talk to the rest of the company. I took a machine gun team of two guys and tried to flank around the right, but by this time the NVA had surrounded the entire company and all platoons were in the fight in their respective areas. As I tried to move around the right flank, we were attacked from the rear and both machine gunners were killed and I was wounded again by shell fragments.*

I found a relatively protected position and started adjusting artillery fire to the front. Sergeant Esteban Colon-Motas, one of my squad leaders, burst past me to the front and picked up Sergeant John Ingoglia, one of the heavily wounded guys and started back towards me. As he was returning, I saw enemy rounds burst through Colon-Motas' body as he was hit multiple times, still carrying his buddy. When he got to a log in back of me, he threw Ingoglia behind the log, then fell over the log and died.

Sergeant Arthur Parker started going forward and carrying wounded back inside the hasty position we had set up. I gave him covering fire but it wasn't until the 2d time that he passed me that I saw what appeared to be half of his face blown off. Yet he was still moving and saving his buddies.

The third platoon to my left was having a difficult time as well. They had moved forward when we did and run into the same fire storm. LT Chuck Aronhalt tried to rally his troops, but many of them had been killed, wounded, or were unable to move because of the incoming fire. I was busy with my own platoon and lost sight of Aronhalt for awhile, but he also apparently started carrying wounded to the rear in the middle of all the fighting. Someone said his rifle jammed, so he picked up a machine gun and started firing from behind an ant hill clearing the front. As he started moving forward I shouted at him to get his head down and he turned his head briefly, but then he was hit in the head and killed."

First Lieutenant Rodabaugh's Silver Star citation reads:

"... Immediately 1LT Rodabaugh evaluated the situation and began directing his men into a perimeter. As he moved to the edge of the perimeter he was struck in the arm by a hostile round. Disregarding the intense pain, he continued to direct

his men in defense of their perimeter. As the enemy initiated another assault, the Radio-Telephone Operator was lost. Realizing that coordinating communication was important in the completion of their mission, 1LT Rodabaugh endangered his own life several times by moving through heavy enemy fire to inform his Company Commander of the situation in his sector of the perimeter. When the order came to withdraw to reorganize, he remained behind and provided cover fire until all his men had withdrawn. While being treated for his wound he continued to call in accurate adjustments of artillery fire... ."

First Lieutenant Aronhalt's DSC citation:

"First Lieutenant Aronhalt distinguished himself by exceptionally valorous actions on 18 May 1967 while serving as platoon leader during a search and destroy mission in Pleiku Province. When another platoon of his company received devastating fire, Lieutenant Aronhalt requested that his platoon be sent to aid the stricken unit. As he led his men forward, however, the entire company began receiving intense fire from numerous concealed positions. Lieutenant Aronhalt tried to pull his men back, but they were unable to leave their cover. Since the platoon couldn't maneuver in any direction, he positioned his machine guns to strengthen the unit's defensive posture. He tried to form a perimeter, but was prevented by the hostile fire sweeping his positions. Seeing several wounded men, Lieutenant Aronhalt again tried to move his men forward. Unable to do this, he personally fought his way through the intense crossfire and began pulling the wounded to safety. He repeatedly entered the exposed area and fought his way out with wounded men over his shoulder. Seeing that casualties were mounting faster than he could carry them out, he stood and charged the insurgents alone. His rifle jammed as he ran, but he picked up a machine gun and continued charging and firing steadily to give his men a chance to withdraw. He was

mortally wounded in the successful attempt at drawing the fire from his men... ."

SP4 Tom Monahan had been brought up out of the second platoon to work in the company CP group helping to carry and operate the all-important radios. But he wanted to be promoted to SGT and be back with a platoon, so he was reassigned as a squad leader in the second platoon. On the 18th of May he was leading his squad when the battle began.

Monahan: *"We had been hit with rifle fire from the front, so we dropped behind large trees to return fire. SGT Parker's squad and mine were working together behind the trees when I was shot in the right ankle, shattering several bones. Parker shot the NVA who had wounded me and told me, 'I got him'. Parker sort of disappeared after that and I lost contact with him. I decided I needed to get back to the company area and some medical attention, so I stood up, started going into shock and got disoriented. I moved forward instead of backwards. I lost my balance and rolled down an incline into a small depression with two guys I didn't know. I asked them to use my First Aid pack to bind my ankle because I didn't want to look at it. They did, but after that they were uncertain what to do. I told them they needed to get back with the rest of the platoon and sent them off individually so they wouldn't be shot at the same time. I decided it was time for me to go as well. I figured I had gotten to where I was, so I should be able to get back to where I had been. Somehow I climbed the incline but fell after I got to the top. Someone grabbed me under the arms and took me to where there were others who were wounded and waiting attention. A medic started working on me, but I told him to work on others who were worse off. One of the guys laying next to me was obviously going to lose both legs even if he could get evacuated on time. The medic told me another guy needed a tracheotomy, but he didn't have a knife. I gave him my knife and the medic asked if I wanted it back. I told him, 'No, hopefully I won't need it where I am going'.*

When the helicopters started coming in, I was put on one of them. As the helicopter was lifting off I could hear 'Ping! Ping! Ping!' The on-board medic asked me if I needed morphine and I said, 'No, but what are those pings I hear?' The medic said calmly, 'Oh, those are bullets hitting the helicopter'. He was terribly calm about it, which I found amazing, but no one was wounded from the enemy fire."

CHAPTER THIRTY THREE

I T WASN'T JUST THE PLATOONS who were in a fight for their lives. The company CP group of 1LT Cary Allen, 1SG Victor Lopez, 1LT Larry York (the FO) and his assistant SP4 Sam Welty, SGT Don Hunter, SGT Richard Surface and SP4 Henry Kuntzler, were also heavily involved. (Kuntzler had been brought up to the headquarters section to help with the radios, and to provide Hunter and Surface with some relief on the 24-hour radio watches. He replaced SP4 Tom Monahan, who had returned to the second platoon.)

Allen was on the radio, trying to make contact with the fourth platoon, at the same time getting reports from the other platoons on how hard they were being hit. Lopez was trying to get the wounded away from the perimeter line and grouped in the center of the position. The forward observers, York and Welty, were also on the radio, trying to communicate with the artillery battalion to get artillery support. Hunter and Surface were handling Allen's radios, relaying reports to battalion and following Lopez's orders.

Surface, Headquarters Section: *As the company pushed forward to close in on the fourth platoon, we also became engaged with the NVA. At this point it became a major battle. We were receiving small arms, machine gun and B40 rocket fire from almost all directions... Because of our low location I could not receive or transmit on the radio. The communications sergeant, Don Hunter and I ran back up the hill from which we had come (25–30 yards) with the radios to contact our battalion TOC. Returning to our company area under the cover of trees, we encountered a heavy growth of jungle and got entangled in vines. Hunter grabbed the radio from me and slammed on through as I was left dangling in the vines, hung up like a fly in a spider web, with enemy bullets and rockets blazing all around, spitting bark all over me. Fighting loose, I ran on down the hill to the company area, now under heavy fire. I took shelter on the ground next to Sgt Brown of second platoon. Lying there in the prone, we observed the feet of several NVA running back and forth as the enemy was trying to penetrate our position. As they approached our position from two sides, we began firing in the direction of the NVA, spraying the area with heavy fire. Our company was now receiving casualties, both wounded and killed. We could see the guys getting shot as we lay there firing. The cry for medics started and there were blood curdling screams as more and more became wounded. Looking around and getting oriented, I spotted Sgt Hunter and our headquarters section about another thirty meters from where I lay.*

Using the cover of the trees and a large ant hill, I made my way to our group where Hunter and Henry Kuntzler lay in the prone, I slid in next to them with Kuntzler being in the middle.

There we fought the NVA for some time, firing into the trees, where they were hidden and sniping at us. Kuntzler kept raising up and I kept telling him to get down. I was expecting to get shot at any time, when Kuntzler got hit in the arm. It looked as if it was nearly ripped off his body. Hunter and I got him bandaged as we were still receiving fire from the trees. It was absolute death and destruction as more were being shot; medics were being screamed for, others for their wives. In the distance I could hear the fourth platoon engaged in heavy fighting. I could faintly hear the yelling and screaming from their location in the lull of the weapons firing around us. As this battle raged on with what seemingly was a larger enemy force than we were, I began thinking death was near. I thought about my family and friends I would never see again. There was no way we were going to survive this battle. I prayed not to suffer when the end came. So much was happening and we needed ammo and medevac desperately.

We finally started getting fire support from the artillery battery assigned to our battalion. Then 1SG Lopez ordered me to start cutting an LZ so we could get the wounded out and get more ammo. We were using ammo at an alarming rate and we were already going through the KIA's packs and getting their ammo to fight with. I took a couple of guys and went about twenty-five yards to our left and we started cutting trees and heavy bamboo.

The battle raged and bullets zinged by your face, so close you could feel the heat of the bullets on your skin. I cut and again prayed, knowing any second my life could end. The machetes bounced off the thick bamboo as we cut away. Holding it (the bamboo) while you were chopping, ripped your hands up as it split vertically.

It took us what seemed to be about an hour to get a spot big enough to get the 1st chopper in to start evacuating the WIA's. All the wounded were then brought to that location along with the dead and we lined them all up along the clearing in the cover of trees. Sgt Parker of the second platoon *was carrying bodies over to my location to be evacuated. He also had been shot in the face and his bandage was coming loose and blood was running down his neck and chest. He was a real mess and I feared his death would come soon. I told him we would soon evacuate him and he should lie there and wait. I redressed his wound and then I saw his jaw had been ripped up by the bullets. You could see splintered jawbone and teeth. After readjusting the bandage and patching him back up, Sgt Parker said he knew where the gook was that shot him and he was going back for him. I told him he should stay at my location for evacuation, but he left anyway. He returned later with another body and announced that he had killed the gook that shot him. Then I got him to lie down and wait for evacuation. I tried getting to all of the wounded and encouraged them that a Medevac would soon be coming and they would be evacuated."*

Sholly: As we were flying above, the company popped yellow smoke to help CPT Harton direct artillery fire. 1LT York, my company Forward Observer was talking to Harton on the artillery radio net. On the battalion net, LT Allen said Grandstaff was separated from the company and surrounded by NVA, as was the rest of company, but the company couldn't get to the fourth platoon because of the heavy fire and casualties.

Renza, fourth platoon: *By now the fire was so intense from all sides that there was no place to move to. Everyone in the platoon took whatever cover they could find hiding behind trees, dirt mounds, and bushes and started returning fire on the NVA, who were slowly moving in on us. The air was filled with the smell of gun powder and the only thing you could hear above the gunfire was the screams for a Medic every few minutes. I was trying to look in every direction at once, but my field of vision was limited. When I fell over the log, I landed on my right side. My head was turned to the*

310

left with the right side of my face turned to the ground and my chin was touching my left shoulder. The right side of my body was pushed tightly up against the log. Within fifteen minutes from the time I was hit, my right arm was completely numb from lying on it. I guess I had cut off the circulation, but there was no way I could raise my body high enough to get it out from under me, without getting hit again. Bullets were cutting leaves off small bushes just inches over my head. I started to taste blood in my mouth and couldn't believe it. "That's it" I thought, "the bullets must have hit me in the lung and when the lungs fill up, you're dead." I began to slide my left hand along the ground towards my face. I then put my left index finger in my mouth. I pulled it out and looked at the bright red saliva on it. I thought for sure I would die, if I didn't get help soon. I called to the two guys that were behind me. "Hey, you guys, I'm bleeding from my mouth and I need a Medic." No one answered me; I yelled louder, "Are you guys still there? I need a Medic." Still no answer. I couldn't turn my head around far enough to see if they were still there. They wouldn't just crawl away and leave me here. Maybe they went to get help and would send a Medic. Of course they couldn't answer...they were both dead... All I could think is I have to stop the bleeding. I started to turn on my left side ever so slightly and took some body weight off to get some feeling in them [arm and fingers]. They [fingers] were ice cold. With my right hand I grabbed the front of my shirt and pulled it as tight as I could across my back, then laid back down on it with my full weight. I hoped my shirt would serve as a bandage. The gunships started to arrive. They got louder and louder as they got closer to our position. I looked up through the trees and saw about five of them flying right over me, just above the tree tops. Someone popped a smoke grenade to let them know our positions. They saw the smoke, circled around and came back directly over me, this time opening up with miniguns, M16's and rockets, just twenty-five or thirty meters past us to try to hold back the NVA. Within minutes another five or six of them arrived and they all circled over us opening up with everything they had. We were now getting artillery fire all around us, gunships flying overhead giving us everything they had and from the NVA we were getting machine and B40 rocket fire from the south, B40 rocket fire from the north and sniper and automatic weapons fire from all directions and angles. If there is such a place as hell, it could not be more punishing than this. My body was trembling from head to toe with fear. Salty perspiration was getting into my open wound, which made my back burn as if it were being stuck with a red not poker. Every time there was another explosion, I waited to be hit by sharp metal. The feeling of being surrounded by the sounds of war is almost impossible to describe."

PFC Gilbert Nash had been assigned to Company C of the battalion. Shortly after his arrival, he and his new squad went out on an ambush. But he was so new that when the squad left the ambush, its members forgot about Nash and left him alone in the jungle overnight. They finally remembered him and came back for him, but after that Nash had trouble with his fellow soldiers and the company leadership. On the assumption that a change of personalities might sort things out, I agreed to his reassignment to Company B. Grandstaff asked that he be assigned to the fourth platoon. Nash joined the unit on 16 May, flying in on a resupply helicopter.

Nash, fourth platoon: *"I didn't have any C rations or ammo, or anything with me. I met Sgt Grandstaff and he told Sanzone to take care of me. So Sanzone went around and got C rations and ammo from other guys in the platoon, so I was pretty well set up.*

On the 18th we were going down this ridgeline. I was the next to last man in the column. Sgt Grandstaff had told me to take the rear guard and keep the backdoor open. That meant not to let anyone sneak up on us from the rear.

I heard a shot and then we came to a trail that was about 6 inches wide and hard packed, meaning it was used a lot. I had just used a match to burn two leeches off of me and we had to step over an NVA body to continue down the trail. We got an order to "bring up the rear," so we did. About that time we heard firing coming from the company location in back of us, then there was firing all around us. We set up a sort of ragged perimeter. I was turned away from the creek. I think most of our guys were killed in the first 30 seconds of the ambush. I heard Sgt Grandstaff say, "Listen up men... stand your ground. We are going to get all these M....F....'s for what they did!" I knew what he meant; we were going to make a Last Stand, like Custer.

Sgt Grandstaff was cursing the NVA and saying "M.....F....!" and "Come and get us you bastards!" I heard someone else say, "Drop 300!" The artillery started coming in and a round hit about 25 yards to my left. That hit me with shrapnel in my left leg. I heard somebody down in the creek area say "God Dammit! Give us a f...... chance!" I think the artillery hit in the right place and I don't think any of our guys were killed by our own artillery. I think it was the initial firing that killed most of us.

In basic training, I qualified as a Sharpshooter, so I was firing single rounds with my rifle. I hit three of them... I saw heads pop up and I turned the muzzle of my rifle towards them and opened up on automatic as they started to charge me. I saw 6 more come at me. Two grenades were thrown at me and I picked them up and threw them back at the enemy, over the heads of our guys. I don't remember thinking about picking the grenades up, I just did it. The Doctor said I did think about it, but it just happened so fast that I don't remember thinking about it. I changed magazines in my rifle. They were using our guys in the creek area as target practice. RPG's went into the creek. I had someone to my right and someone to my rear left.

I got hit in the head and lost consciousness..."

SP4 Kenneth Barker was a replacement soldier and came into Vietnam in April 1967. He was flown out to the company on one of our resupply days and was assigned to the fourth platoon. He was immediately immersed into the daily grind of learning the company and platoon SOPs and how to walk with a large pack on your back without falling over. On 18 May he was with the fourth platoon as it pursued the NVA down the trail.

Barker, fourth platoon: *"I was well back in the column going down the ridgeline. We started taking fire and were told to "bring up the rear." So when we started taking all the fire, it got so intense that we just pushed off of the ridge down the hill and there was a little flat area and then the creek. Some people had made it to the creek...and you learned real quick that that was no place you wanted to be...it was thought that if you could make it to the creek you could use that for cover... but that was well covered by the enemy. There was fire from above down into the stream bed from the embankment... they just opened up on us from the embankment and this, plus the fire from the hill caused us to draw back, but there was no place to go. There was an NVA machine gun, near a big-sized tree on the bank and it was shooting down into us. We had one LAW (Light Anti-Tank Weapon). We fired it at the tree and it took out the machine gun...there was so much fire it was cutting the trees and small limbs, it was all falling like snow...just the noise and the smoke and people yelling and men crying...*

I didn't know there were that many bullets in the world with all the explosions and rockets...

A tree fell on a person close by and I found out later it was Renza. I think the Medic Shultz (SP4 Melvin Shultz) was on my right and Nash was close by...

It gets down to self-preservation, you try to see who is shooting at you and try to take care of yourself...when the artillery started coming in...I couldn't hear Grandstaff, but I always thought there was only 3 rounds of artillery, but Renza said there was a lot of artillery. The sound of artillery coming into the jungle is horrifying...after that I must have been unconscious...I can't remember more than 3 rounds..."

Cliff Rountree was up front of the platoon when the firing started. He started returning fire, but the enemy's automatic weapons fire was overwhelming:

Rountree, fourth platoon: *"The AW fire just kept coming in, I pulled out a LAW and saw an NVA who kept jumping back and forth behind a small tree. I was laying on my side and I aimed it and fired it kind of sideways. I hit the tree and it went through and killed the NVA. Grandstaff was hollering, "Get in the ditch! Get in the ditch!" Guys were getting in the ditch...and I just thought "Machine Guns!!" but before I could shout anything they opened up into the ditch. Then the NVA started making an assault up the ditch throwing grenades...I kept shooting and throwing grenades back until one landed too far for me to get and I dug my head down with my helmet towards the grenade and it went off. I caught fragments in my left calf, a round in my right arm and two shrapnel wounds in my right arm. At that point I passed out."*

Renza, fourth platoon: *I'm giving you the short version... this went on for hours...this didn't happen in 20 minutes... this started at about 11 o'clock in the morning and this is now 4 in the afternoon...with gunships coming and rockets and artillery and the artillery fire Grandstaff kept adjusting it closer...because his radio guy was killed and he just kept bringing it in closer and closer...my friend who went up there, Bob Sanzone, he was shot in the side of the head and he was killed instantly he was next to Tom Sears who is one of the eight survivors...it just got to the point where Grandstaff knew they were just going to keep coming and keep coming...so he must have said...'Let's take as many of them as we can take.' He was like, at the final end before he died, he was screaming at them to come and get us...he was like John Wayne, all the way and they were yelling back at him 'Come get us, GI... come get us!' in English, perfect English...you could hear them and they were blowing bugles...they had bugles going, screaming and everything...so eventually Grandstaff said, 'Bring the artillery in on top of us!'"*

Sholly: In the helicopter above, we switched to the company net, and while the transmission was extremely garbled, we could make out the words. Grandstaff said, *"They are in among us now and we are getting cut up badly. I will get the men under cover, bring it in on top of us NOW!"* Colonel Gannon looked at me and with a quizzical look said, *"What do you think?"* I was heartsick at the fact that I wasn't on the ground with them, but respected Grandstaff's judgment well enough to know there probably wasn't another way to shake the NVA off if they were hand-to-hand. I said, *"He's the guy on the ground...we have to trust him; maybe the company can get to them after the barrage."* Gannon looked at Harton and said *"Do it!"*

316

CHAPTER THIRTY FOUR

WE MOVED THE HELICOPTER out of the line of fire. The artillery was called in and a massive bombardment followed. We could see bright flashes through the greenery as the artillery rounds exploded on the ground and in the trees, sending gouts of smoke up out of the jungle while trees shattered and fell under the explosions and limbs. Bits of vegetation, limbs, dust and other debris were blown into the air. It was a hellish view and I knew it would be a miracle if anyone lived through it. After the Fire for Effect, there were no further communications with the fourth platoon.

We continued to fly above the action area in the bright sunlight and to talk with LT Allen trying to keep current on the situation. From above, I took the only picture in existence of the fourth platoon's action area after the artillery's massive fire for effect. It is hard to believe that underneath this benign view of double and triple canopy forest there are U.S. and NVA dead soldiers. At the same time it was taken, U.S. wounded soldiers were being murdered one by one by the NVA

Overhead photo of furious fire

while we were flying above, unable to communicate with the destroyed platoon.

After the artillery barrage, the NVA were no longer pressing the main company in wave attacks, but they were still containing our guys in their small perimeter. Whenever anyone moved, they came under fire. Even though the company made an attempt to maneuver toward the fourth platoon, it was apparent they were opposing a larger NVA force and could not reach the platoon.

Surviving members of the fourth platoon remember their individual experiences:

Renza, fourth platoon: "*So they brought the artillery right in on our location...and you've seen the movies where artillery is fired over your heads and there is Wsssssssssshhhhh Boom! Well the closer it is, the shorter the Wssssshhhh!...and we had no Wsssshhhh! It literally lifted my body right off the ground...and every time it came in it was a total blur...it lifted me again and again and any second I expected a direct hit... and one round landed just right behind at the base of a tree and it blew that tree right up out of the ground and it came down right on top of me...so that was how, when they found me, they were saying that I was under a tree...and after they called in the artillery, Grandstaff was dead and there was no communications. All the radio guys were dead, we did not know anyone else was alive. We were not next to each other, we were all spread out all over the place and we just lay there. I could hear the rest of Company B trying to get to us, they were still firing...they had their own battle and they couldn't get through to us because they were cut off from us. So we laid there and laid there and laid there and there was no more artillery fire...it got silent and the next thing I know I heard voices and it was the North Vietnamese. They were on all sides of us at that point, coming through and checking the bodies, stripping the bodies and if they thought you were alive they put another bullet in you...*"

Nash, fourth platoon: "*A bullet hit me in the head and I was knocked out. After a while I became semi-conscious and felt the NVA pick me up by the shirt. They tied me up with* commo wire and took my dog tags, wedding band and watch. I came to when it was just getting dark but I could still see a little, but not clearly. I looked in front of me and saw a guy untying himself. I went very slowly, but I untied myself before he did. I saw him move, then I tapped three times on the bottom of his foot. I didn't see him move after that. I woke up several times in the night and heard shooting back where the main company was located."

Barker, fourth platoon: "The NVA came through searching the bodies, I was playing dead but they tied me up with a cord of some sort...they kicked me in the ribs a couple of times and they had to know I was alive...they shot other people when they moaned, I don't know why they tied me...I was lying on the ground and they pulled the watch off my arm and took my rifle...I only had a couple of magazines left and they picked up the full magazines...my billfold was in my shirt pocket but they didn't find that...my hand grenades were gone...I was only carrying C rations, a pad of paper and a pencil.

They set up around us, I guess like an ambush...if you looked through the trees you could see some movement...NVA were talking but I didn't understand any of it...sometime in the night I had a shooting pain in my leg and I slowly moved my leg...then I felt three taps on my foot...I thought it was an NVA, but after a while nothing happened, so I figured it was one of ours behind me. I knew then there was someone besides me and I wasn't alone."

Not far away, after the NVA had checked his body, Tom Sears lay there pretending to be dead. Later that night he realized that Cliff Rountree, while wounded, was not dead either. Rountree, like he had in the fight on 26 April, started taking care of people...

Rountree, fourth platoon: "After dark, I crawled over to Sears and discovered he wasn't dead, but was in a lot of *pain. I bandaged him as well as I could in the dark to stop the bleeding. I remember being thirsty myself, so I crawled around and found some canteens that still had water in them so we could drink. I don't know where the NVA were all this time, but I didn't see any."*

Sears remembers seeing NVA sitting around, but it is unclear where they were when Rountree was helping him. Sears credits Rountree for saving his life, by patching him up and giving him water, even though Rountree was wounded himself.

Renza, fourth platoon: *"After the NVA went over the bodies, about six of them sat about 10 yards from me and they were looking out towards where the fire was coming from the rest of Company B...they were just sitting there and they started eating rice...they had gone through the platoon and they stopped and they were just looking out, just waiting for someone to come help us and they were going to ambush them and they were sitting there eating...I remember I laid there, I was laying face down, watching them eat and they found me and the two guys next to me and they walked by me, they fired two shots into each of us and both bullets went right over my head into the tree I was next to...I don't know if they hit the other two guys or not, but they were already dead... and they sat there until the sun started to go down...and then they started talking, they were having a regular conversation and they finally pulled out of where I could see them and they drug off as many of their dead as they could..."*

CHAPTER THIRTY FIVE

S HORTLY AFTER THE ARTILLERY BARRAGE, our Command and Control helicopter was running out of fuel, so we returned to the firebase to change helicopters. While making the switch, we learned the company was just completing a hasty one-ship LZ to try and get the wounded out.

I asked Colonel Gannon if I could have the Reconnaissance Platoon until we determined the outcome of the fourth platoon. He readily agreed and told the S3 to start getting the Recon Platoon ready to reinforce Company B. The S3 had also requested additional aircraft to start moving people in and out of the area of action.

When Colonel Gannon took off again, I stayed at the CP and found a couple of battalion medics who were collecting their gear. I told them, *"As soon as we get a bird in, you're coming with me!"* When the first of the requested helicopters got to the CP to get directions and determine the status of the LZ, I jumped aboard with the two medics. We flew to the company location where the fighting was still going on.

Before I left, the S3 told me the Recon Platoon would follow as soon as possible.

The LZ was at the top of the western side of a minor ridgeline—a small platform of logs placed one over another like a child's Lincoln Log play set. One end of it was stabilized on the ridgeline, but from midway out it was constructed over a steep slope. Though able to hold a couple of men, it was not strong enough to support a helicopter's weight. The LZ was at the bottom of a small hole in the trees and bamboo, on the edge of the ridgeline. To approach the LZ required a helicopter to overfly a small valley from which the enemy had a clear shot at any slowly passing aircraft. In addition to worrying about enemy fire, the pilot had to put the nose almost delicately into the jungle from where the platform jutted out and hover while its occupants unloaded onto the platform. It then continued to hover while the wounded were moved onto the unstable platform and loaded. As on most of these types of log platforms, men had to balance themselves on individual logs or branches while at the same time helping to lift a wounded man or heavy body wrapped in a poncho. While the helicopter hovered, its nose and cargo bay barely on the platform, the rest of its body and tail flared out into empty space. The aircraft was extremely vulnerable to enemy fire.

As we slowly approached the platform, the NVA surrounding the company fired on us from below. The helicopter sustained hits but suffered no critical damage, and none of us aboard were wounded. One of the Company B guys standing in the hole in the forest guided the helicopter carefully to the platform. The medics and I stepped gingerly onto the log pad, and made our way to firmer ground.

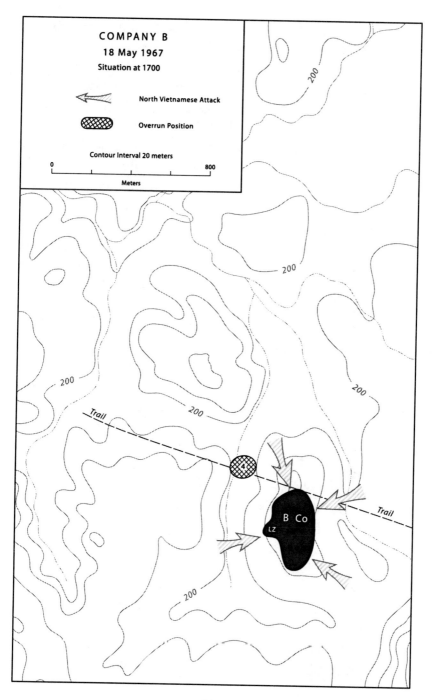

COMPANY B
18 May 1967
Situation at 1700

North Vietnamese Attack

Overrun Position

Contour Interval 20 meters

0   800

Meters

We landed at 4:55. The company had been in heavy contact for four and one-half hours and had taken many casualties. The most seriously wounded were just inside the forest wall, close to the LZ waiting for evacuation. As I passed them, I spoke to several, telling them what a great job they had done, and we would be getting them to the hospital.

One of them, lying on the ground with a field dressing wrapped around his head and left eye, plus other bloody dressings around his left leg, reached out to shake my hand and said to me, *"Captain Sholly, thank God you are here!"* I wasn't sure how to take that, since as far as I could tell, LT Allen had done all the right things, but I swallowed a lump, gripped his hand and told him that things were going to be better for him now. I could only hope the same would be true for the rest of us.

LT Rodabaugh, who had been hit in the arm and with whom I had joshed previously about seeming to miss much of the combat while he was on TDY and in Dragon Mountain, was also waiting for evacuation. When he saw me he said, *"I didn't miss this one, sir..."* Then he volunteered to remain if I needed him. I felt guilty for my previous comments because he had been there this time and I had not. I told him that he had done enough and should get on the helicopter along with the other wounded. Years later, I apologized to him for my insensitivity in teasing him on such a serious subject so many years before.

Although all the wounded seemed glad to see me, I know they were happier to see the helicopter and the medics.

I was particularly saddened when I saw LT Aronhalt's body waiting for evacuation. He was a young and valiant warrior who would have had a bright future in the military. I felt his loss deeply.

One sight that day which remains with me still, was of the nineteen wounded and the eight poncho shrouded bodies lined up for evacuation. On the ground next to the bodies was a Pabst Blue Ribbon beer can that had fallen out of someone's pack. The presence of the can, a symbol of fun and relaxation, with dead heroes at a time of such sorrow and tragedy seemed terribly obscene to me. I had the can trashed as soon as possible so no one could take a picture of it that might suggest conclusions which would denigrate the lives lost. Indeed, the sight of a Blue Ribbon beer can has reminded me of that tragic day ever since.

We were still receiving incoming fire from the perimeter, though not as heavy as earlier. LT Allen met me and gave me a quick debrief on what he knew had happened to the fourth platoon, much of which I knew from the radio calls and by being above in the helicopter. Together we crawled around the company perimeter to see what the platoon dispositions were like. He had done a good job of putting the company on the most defensible terrain available. LT Larry York, the forward observer who had replaced Bill Wilson, had done a fine job, as well. It was he who had been in most constant contact with Ray Harton, delivering the artillery as well as could be expected. He was scheduled to go on R&R in the next few days, but also wanted to know if I wanted him to stay. I felt he had done enough too, and I would feel forever guilty if something happened to him if I asked him to stay. Even though it left me without an artillery forward observer, I told him that I could handle the artillery and that he needed to get back to the rear to keep his appointment. A few hours after he had gone, I found out that York's assistant, Sam Welty had been wounded and evacuated. The next day, I discovered that his other assistant, SGT Leland Thompson, had been killed with the fourth platoon. Not really wanting to do all the artillery work alone, I asked for a temporary FO until York returned.

The terrain on the sides of the ridgeline was heavily wooded with thick underbrush. Further up, on the spine of the ridgeline, triple canopy trees permitted little sunlight to reach the ground. This had resulted in little brush but large trees. In many cases the trees were larger in diameter than a 50-gallon oil drum, large enough to protect one or two men at a time. Of course, this hindered our view of the area in front of the position and our ability to lay down clear lines of fire.

LT Allen resumed command of the first platoon, in which Platoon Sergeant Johnson had been killed, while I continued to sort out what we could do next. I worked myself back out to the perimeter.

Everything around me seemed unreal. As the sunlight filtering through the tall trees began to fade, the shadows they cast tinged the scene with gloom. Tendrils of gray smoke from small fires burning in the underbrush added to the effect, turning the trees into ominous, eerily unnatural beings more fitted to a fantasy opera than a modern battlefield. The darkening lanes that stretched between them were open and inviting, but you just knew that there were enemies on either side waiting to kill if you relaxed and showed yourself for too long. The atmosphere reeked of tension and anxiety.

With LT Aronhalt of the third platoon gone, I went out to spend more time with his men and Platoon Sergeant Morales, now the acting platoon leader. As I crawled up to the perimeter line using trees as my primary cover, the platoon continued to receive AK47 fire from NVA dodging and hiding behind the trees. Like us, they used the trees as cover and protection, then they would crawl out to the sides and shoot at anything they could see. It was like the game of guessing where the woodchuck would come out of his hole next, so you could bash him. Only in this case the woodchuck was armed and dangerous, and if you guessed wrong it could be fatal.

As the automatic weapons chattered, bullets snapped and cracked. Because of the depth of the woods there was an instant echo as the AK47s and M16s blasted away. There would be small periods of silence when no one was shooting, then a single shot with an echo, and everyone would try to determine from where the shot came. When the rounds were close, they literally cracked the sound barrier and made the resulting *SNAP!* that was becoming all too familiar. However, this distinctive noise helped you realize the enemy had missed again. The old saw that you never hear the one that hit you was true, so you just stopped worrying.

The platoon was returning fire, but I was concerned its men were beginning to get into too much of an individual defensive mindset. This natural phenomenon, after periods of intense combat, concentration and flowing adrenalin, results in a quiet but emotional letdown. An individual becomes a little traumatized and starts going into what I call "shock overload." He has time to think about his buddies and the casualties he has seen among them. Troops experiencing this effect become less alert and responsive; they only return fire when they can see a target or when they suspect something is a specific threat to them as individuals. This is a very real danger because it creates a sluggishness brought on by an inability to think clearly.

When I got on the perimeter, there were several soldiers who, from a quick glance looked like they were beginning to accept what the enemy was doing and were waiting for "somebody to do something". I knew that if I could get the men to start figuring where the enemy was located and anticipating where they might go when moving among the trees outside the perimeter, it would be a big start toward getting them more alert and active. I started firing my 40mm grenade launcher at the trees behind those where I suspected the enemy was hiding. The rounds exploded and sprayed shrapnel into the NVA using the forward trees for cover. While I didn't hit an NVA every time, there were enough of them who were forced to move or who died in place from shrapnel. I went around the company perimeter doing the same thing in all the platoon positions.

The troops got the idea. The NVA started taking wounded, which forced them to move back out of range and we started expanding the perimeter a little bit at a time. This gave the troops more confidence that we were still in control and that we could move whenever we wanted without worrying about being overrun. (At least that was what I was trying to convey without specifically saying so, but whatever the reason, the glaze left men's eyes. They had something positive to do).

When Colonel Gannon got airborne again after refueling and getting his latest operation report from the CP, he assumed that because of my bum ankle I had stayed at the firebase. In our initial radio discussion he was very much surprised to be talking to me on the ground in the middle of the fighting. I somewhat impertinently asked him where he thought I should be and he agreed I was in the right place.

As soon as I got things stabilized, it was my plan to gather up the company and go get our lost platoon. I started preparing a plan for the company to attack down the hill toward the unit. However, Colonel Gannon had already started Company A on a move to reinforce us, so he needed a protected location where he could put it. Since there was only a one-ship LZ, he needed Company B to remain in place as security, while Company A completed its move and we finished evacuating our wounded and killed. Also, because Company B was under strength, Company A could apply more force to the effort to recover the lost platoon. While I didn't like the idea of another company doing what I felt we should be doing, I had to acknowledge the battalion commander's reasoning and redoubled my effort to expand and develop the perimeter into a better defensive position.

The troops were still fighting, but they had not had much time to develop defensive positions except for using the trees as firing sites. I immediately got the platoons to start improving their positions by digging into the rocky and rooty soil, adding rocks and a few sandbags. They also put heavy branches over shallow positions to deflect shrapnel as much as possible and started setting out trip flares and claymore mines. I knew it was going to be a long night, particularly if we started receiving more mortar rounds.

As requested, Colonel Gannon had made the Reconnaissance Platoon available to me, and its men were beginning to shuttle in, one ship at a time between medical evacuations. Their last bird arrived at 5:45. I put them on the expanded perimeter to solidify the position even further. First Lieutenant Art Trujillo was the platoon leader, and he was a good soldier. I had confidence in him and his men.

About ten minutes later, the first element of Company A, which had been trying to reach us through heavy vegetation, airlifted in. We moved it into an assembly area within our perimeter. By 7:23 the unit was moving west through our perimeter to try and find our fourth platoon. We still had no contact with Grandstaff.

Since I had arrived we had taken another KIA and another WIA to bring our casualty numbers to nine KIA and 20 WIA, without counting anyone in the fourth platoon. It was dark, but even with one ship at a time, we had evacuated all the wounded we had.

Company A moved under flares and on line, prepared for a fight, with people calling out from time to time *"Company B, where are you?"* We later figured out that the unit passed about 100 meters south of the fourth platoon.

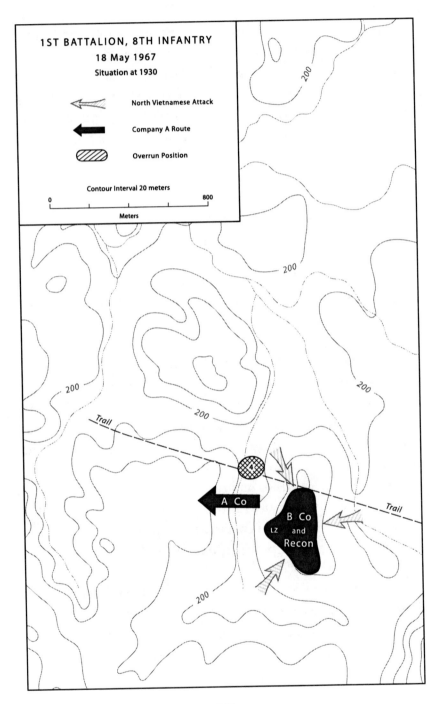

1ST BATTALION, 8TH INFANTRY
18 May 1967
Situation at 1930

North Vietnamese Attack

Company A Route

Overrun Position

Contour Interval 20 meters

0   800

Meters

With the NVA still in the fourth platoon's position, however, the unit's survivors were afraid that if they even weakly acknowledged the calls, Company A would be ambushed without warning. As a result, even though almost all of those men were wounded, bleeding and in danger of death from their wounds, they kept silent. We will never know how many died rather than make a sound that would lure Company A into an ambush. At 10:45, having heard nothing from the fourth platoon, Company A stopped for the night and established a perimeter.

Company B had fought well and for the most part had repulsed a superior force. By that time the enemy had slackened his fire and was withdrawing its main force. We did not know it, because there were still shooters firing into our main company perimeter.

We put the CP location close to the LZ, in a somewhat protected area from direct fire. I had the CP group improve their individual positions as much as possible, but because the earth beneath the topsoil was extremely rocky, with numerous roots from large trees, the ground did not lend itself to digging. We cut small trees and logs for some protection against overhead fire, but the accommodations were truly abominable. During the night, we received mortar rounds just outside the perimeter. I lost count at thirty, trying to figure if something else could be done.

Finally, in the dark, between mortar attacks, I grieved, thinking about all the good men we had lost for who knew what.

CHAPTER THIRTY SIX

THE NEXT MORNING (19 MAY) at about 6:40, four RPG rockets hit inside our perimeter, killing SP4 Joseph A. Mancuso and wounding PFC David L. Waller in the shoulder. Battalion told us, again, to stay in position while Company A kept looking for our Fourth Platoon. In addition, Company C would be coming into our small LZ to make pursuit of the enemy a battalion operation.

Still, I felt we had to make a response to the B40 rockets, so I had the company fire all its weapons in a "mad minute" all around the perimeter. I notified Company A that we were going to do this so they wouldn't mistake it for another NVA attack. I did this for two reasons. One, I wanted the NVA to know we were all awake, ready for them and were not going to be surprised by a ground attack. Two, I wanted to reinforce the idea in the unit that we were still in charge of our destiny, were still proactive, and could fire and maneuver as we desired.

Company A found the fourth platoon at about 8:20 AM. The unit was a further distance away from the company than we had initially thought. As Company A was approaching the area, an NVA was spotted in a tree, but he quickly retreated and there was no opposition to Company A as they started evacuation procedures. They chopped out and built an LZ, then began moving the wounded out before the bodies of the dead.

The survivors of the fourth platoon continue their stories:

Renza, fourth platoon: *"It was pitch black, but Company A had been airlifted into the Company B LZ and pushed out to try and find us...The NVA were still in our area, just waiting for someone to come in...Company A was maybe 150 yards from us and they started yelling...."fourth platoon! This is Company A! If anyone is alive, fire a shot!" Well, there wasn't anyone left to fire a shot, because the NVA took everyone's weapon as they came through...and if a shot had been fired Company A would have walked into an ambush and gotten all wiped out as well... nobody who was alive was saying anything that would have brought Company A down to us and the waiting NVA. So we just waited...we heard Company A calling "Company B! Where are you?" "Company B! Where are you?" But even though we were all wounded and bleeding, we were afraid to call out and say anything for fear of the NVA ambushing Company A and coming back for ourselves as well."*

Barker, fourth platoon: *"Sometime after daylight, I heard rumbling through the jungle and it was another company coming in...had no clue who or what it was, so I kept quiet...I didn't want to get involved at that point."*

Nash, fourth platoon: *"The next morning, Company A found us. I guess the NVA had left because there was no shooting when Company A got to us. When I was sure we were in friendly hands, I limped down to the streambed and saw what the NVA had been shooting at. I will never forget what I saw...*

I had been shot in the head and the round went through the helmet and ricocheted around the helmet liner and my head. Besides the head wound, I had shrapnel in my thigh. I was medevaced back to the rear and finally to the 67 Evac Hospital at Qui Nhon. I passed out three times in the hospital and they discovered I had a blood clot, which caused paralysis with my little finger...What we did was like Custer...a Last Stand. I know what he felt like..."

PFC Harry McAteer was a newbie with Company A. He had arrived on 13 May and became involved in the search for the fourth platoon.

McAteer: *"As soon as day break came we started moving again and we found what was left of the fourth platoon. It was like we walked into Hell. The bodies were stacked on top of each other, head shots and just unbelievable smell of death. We found some of the fourth platoon alive. They had had to play dead to stay alive. I had never seen Evil until then....we used our ponchos to cover the KIAs. It was the worst thing I had ever had to do..."*

Even men who had been in the big fight on 22 March blanched when they saw the wholesale destruction of men and forest. Others who had not participated in that fracas were shocked and appalled at what men do to each other.

SP4 William Dobbie, Company A: *"... it was a sight I'm not sure I was prepared for. There was much to be done. The Medics went to attend to the wounded and we set up a defensive perimeter around the area...when the LZ was completed, we had to go down and remove the dead."*

Renza, fourth platoon: *"So these guys came in, and I always thank them...but you see, we (meaning the survivors) were a part of it, but we didn't see the horror Company A saw when they came in. They found all these guys and the trench was full of dead bodies, laying on top of each other with body parts blown all over the place, arms for which you couldn't find a body...it was a terrible scene..."*

SP4 Landis Bargatze, Company A: "*I didn't see any survivors by the small stream bed where we found them...The "old timers" of Company A recognized some of their buddies. It was very hard on them....Although I had been in two firefights... this was my first experience with the reality of intense close range combat with a large force of NVA. A fight for survival ...and then death. Carrying those guys out in ponchos and loading them on choppers for their last ride home was very difficult. My life was never the same after that.*"

Renza, fourth platoon: "*I heard coming from the jungle, what I thought were voices. After listening for about one minute I knew it was voices, but was not sure if it was English. I thought, perhaps the NVA had returned. After a few more minutes I heard, "Here's one over here!" When I realized it was English, I began shouting out, "Over here!" A voice yelled back to me, "Keep yelling!" So I kept yelling and it took about five minutes for them to work their way to me through the debris and trees that were ripped out of the ground from the artillery.*

Years later I realized that it had been second platoon of Company A that had found "The Lost Platoon." The first two people who found me were "Doc" John Bockover and another soldier from the second platoon. They helped me out from under the tree. Doc sat me up and took off my shirt. He said "you have a hole in your back." Then he said, "You have two holes in your back." The bullet had come in one side of me and out the other side. Doc bandaged up both holes with field bandages. He and the other soldier picked me up and walked me out to a small clearing. I was the last survivor of the platoon that was found. They sat me down with the other six survivors and tried to make me comfortable. At that point they called in helicopters and lowered chain saws to cut an LZ for a Medevac helicopter. The helicopter had to come straight down and hover just off the tree platform while we were loaded. Company A had to get all seven of us with IV bottles onto the platform, then into the helicopter from the platform. We were a mess, two of the guys were shot in the head and others had wounds like mine in different places.

As we lifted off, I saw all the bodies of my dead friends laid out there. I was in the hospital for a few days in Vietnam and then they shipped me to Japan...I never saw any the others in the hospital and I never made contact for years."

On the morning of the 19th, when Company A found the fourth platoon, there were twenty-three KIA, seven WIA survivors, and one MIA (captured).

The totality and ferocity of all the actions of the men of the fourth platoon will never be known. There were too many killed. The story of each of the survivors is primarily one of how he survived, not necessarily of how he and his fellow soldiers defended themselves from the withering fire of the NVA. The other parts of the story were gleaned from the garbled radio conversations with SFC Grandstaff. The phrase that still comes to me clearly, with chills and tears in the darkness of night and the wee morning hours, is Grandstaff's last shouted comment on the radio, *"Bring it in on top of me, NOW!!"* Everyone who heard that knew exactly what it was going to mean to those men who were fighting for their lives. Colonel Gannon authorized the firing, but he asked for my opinion as the leader of these men and would have held off if I had asked it. How many times in the last 46 years have I relived that moment of anguish, wondering if there was something less drastic we could have done? Of course, we will never know, even though it still gnaws at my psyche during my quiet times of emotional indulgence.

The soldier Missing In Action was PFC Joe Delong who had been in Vietnam less than two months when he was taken by the NVA. I suspect that both Barker and Nash were destined for captivity as well, since both had been tied...for some reason, the NVA either forgot them, or became too busy in dragging their own dead bodies away and elected to just leave them. At any rate, POWs who were repatriated in 1973 reported that DeLong had been in mobile POW camps and had attempted to escape. His captors brought back his clothes and other items to show to the other prisoners what would happen if they tried to escape. So the loss count for the platoon went to 24 KIA and seven survivors.

Both Colonel Gannon and I agreed, that even though it appeared that Grandstaff might have been less than cautious about taking his platoon too far from the support of the rest of the company, his actions of calling artillery fire on his own position certainly qualified him for the award of the Medal of Honor. In addition, the actions of his platoon, under heavy fire and outnumbered, were certainly worthy of commemoration.

His citation reads:

GRANDSTAFF, BRUCE ALLAN

Rank and organization: Platoon Sergeant, U.S. Army, Company B, 1st Battalion, 8th Infantry. Place and date: Pleiku Province, Republic of Vietnam, 18 May 1967. Entered service at: Spokane, Wash. Born: 2 June 1934, Spokane, Wash. Citation: For conspicuous gallantry and intrepidity in action at the risk of his life above and beyond the call of duty. P/ Sgt. Grandstaff distinguished himself while leading the Weapons Platoon, Company B, on a reconnaissance mission near the Cambodian border. His platoon was advancing through intermittent enemy contact when it was struck by heavy small arms and

automatic weapons fire from 3 sides. As he estab-
lished a defensive perimeter, P/Sgt. Grandstaff noted
that several of his men had been struck down. He
raced 30 meters through the intense fire to aid them
but could only save one. Denied freedom to maneuver
his unit by the intensity of the enemy onslaught, he
adjusted artillery to within 45 meters of his posi-
tion. When helicopter gunships arrived, he crawled
outside the defensive position to mark the location
with smoke grenades. Realizing his first marker was
probably ineffective, he crawled to another location
and threw his last smoke grenade but the smoke did
not penetrate the jungle foliage. Seriously wounded
in the leg during this effort he returned to his radio
and, refusing medical aid, adjusted the artillery
even closer as the enemy advanced on his position.
Recognizing the need for additional firepower, he
again braved the enemy fusillade, crawled to the
edge of his position and fired several magazines of
tracer ammunition through the jungle canopy. He
succeeded in designating the location to the gunships
but this action again drew the enemy fire and he was
wounded in the other leg. Now enduring intense
pain and bleeding profusely, he crawled to within 10
meters of an enemy machine gun, which had caused
many casualties among his men. He destroyed the
position with hand grenades but received additional
wounds. Rallying his remaining men to withstand
the enemy assaults, he realized his position was
being overrun and asked for artillery directly on his
location. He fought until mortally wounded by an
enemy rocket. Although every man in the platoon
was a casualty, survivors attest to the indomitable

spirit and exceptional courage of this outstanding combat leader who inspired his men to fight courageously against overwhelming odds and cost the enemy heavy casualties. P/Sgt. Grandstaff's selfless gallantry, above and beyond the call of duty, are in the highest traditions of the U.S. Army and reflect great credit upon himself and the Armed Forces of his country.

(Note: The citation says that Grandstaff had thrown his last smoke grenade. This is obviously an error, and after so many years it is impossible to trace the source of this information. When he was asked to mark his position, he did so with a purple smoke grenade.)

On July 10, 1969, I was proud to be present in the Oval Office of the White House, when President Nixon awarded Bruce Grandstaff's widow, Claudia, the Medal of Honor for his actions on May 18, 1967. As one of Spokane, Washington's two Medal of Honor awardees, SFC Grandstaff joined PFC Joe Mann of World War II with a memorial in Spokane's primary cemetery. He has also been memorialized by the renaming of the local Veteran's Hospital as the Mann-Grandstaff Department of Veterans Affairs Medical Center.

After the mad minute on the ridge with the main body of the company, we spent the morning of the 19th improving the LZ in preparation for the arrival of Company C. We put more listening posts out, conducting limited patrols around the area, reorganizing ourselves emotionally and professionally, and trying not to dwell on our losses.

On the 18th the company main had six KIA and 22 WIA in the initial contact, with another KIA and WIA on the morning of the 19th. When added to the fourth platoon's losses of 23 KIA, seven WIA and one MIA, our loss for the short two-day period was 30 KIA, 30 WIA, and one MIA. Not counting the Reconnaissance Platoon, we now had only 70 Company B effectives left in the field, just about half of the company that had been present on the 18th. In my calls to battalion I asked them to clean out any Company B personnel at Dragon Mountain and make a push to get them to the field, no matter what their reason for being in the rear. Morale was coming back and I could feel a raw anger beginning to pulse throughout the unit.

We had lost too many friends now to be very objective about what we wanted to do about the NVA. Up to this point we had lost people to a relatively faceless enemy and while we mourned our losses as a whole, we had never truly blamed anyone for them. Now it had become very personal.

Colonel Gannon and COL Jackson (1st Bde CO) came in and both fussed at me for being with the company on a bad foot, but I told them there was no other place I could be. There wasn't much they could say to that because, as infantrymen, we all agreed where the commander should be located when the unit was in contact with the enemy. We discussed the situation and they told me the company had done well but we weren't through yet. I agreed wholeheartedly and told them we were ready to do whatever was necessary, as long as we could catch some of the NVA before they got back across the border.

In the meantime, Company C had been relieved of its fire-base guard duties and was airlifted into our one-ship LZ. With the exception of one platoon, their move was completed by mid-day and their last unit closed in mid-afternoon. Later in the day all three companies moved out to sweep their general area, looking for any NVA that might still be in the vicinity. As a result of the fighting, we found 119 NVA bodies that had not been carried off by the enemy. Because we knew there was still a large NVA force around, all companies stopped moving at about 5:00 PM to establish our night positions. Company A was still farther west of us, but Companies B and C linked up for the night. Around 5:30 we received about 25 rounds of 82mm mortar fire and we all hit the trees again to try and protect ourselves from the zipping shrapnel.

After Colonel Gannon had left us, he made a visit to Company A. The enemy had not mysteriously disappeared; on his departure from the Company A LZ, his helicopter took rounds, wounding three people, one seriously. It was obvious we still had work to do.

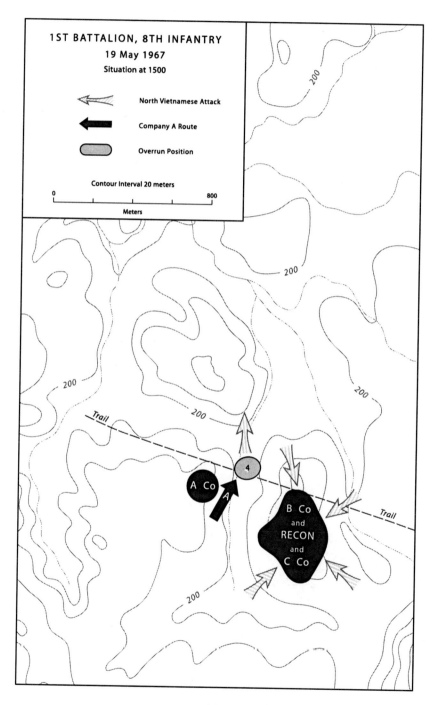

CHAPTER THIRTY SIX

1ST BATTALION, 8TH INFANTRY
19 May 1967
Situation at 1500

North Vietnamese Attack

Company A Route

Overrun Position

Contour Interval 20 meters

0   800

Meters

CHAPTER THIRTY SEVEN

THE EVENING AND NIGHT OF 19–20 May was another challenging time. We received over 40 mortar shells (I stopped counting) that exploded all around us. Fortunately they all landed outside the perimeter, but we didn't know they were going to do that and we were poorly prepared for them. The fact that we were on a rocky ridgeline negated much digging and our best defense was to be behind a tree away from the blast. It was an individual guess as to which side that was and the wrong guess could mean death or major injury. Of course, if the mortar hit in the tree above you, there was no protection. The unknown played major mental games with everybody and we were all extremely tense and anxious whenever we heard the *cough!* of the NVA mortars sending a round our way.

Before it got dark, I felt I had to capture the feelings of the moment so I would remember it clearly. Since I was already doing what I could in terms of calling for artillery and air support, I took a few moments during a particularly vicious mortar attack while huddling behind a tree, to write in my journal. I wrote:

347

"Cough of mortar, loud whack! when it lands. Sound of running feet to shallow bunkers and trees, voice on radio calling for artillery fire, delay, time stands still while more mortars come in. No return fire. Mortars come closer, finally stop. Dead silence. We get on the radio and find that counter fire artillery is being plotted in the wrong place. 25–30 minutes before round gets in area. Too late. Same drill over and over again. Rounds incoming, small arms rattling. People pushing faces into trunks of trees and others chewing ground with eyes closed and looks of wrinkled anguish and expectation on faces. Body tensed, waiting for smash of mortar shrapnel. Sgt Hunter on radio, look of surprise and a question mark on his face while radioing for artillery help and gunships. He is scrunched down with back against a tree hoping he is on the protected side. Even though he has the

Murphy's Laws:

"Radios function perfectly until you need fire support."

same fear as the rest of us, he remains calm on radio. Shows irritation when commo is bad and has to repeat same message four times. Seeming stupidity of battalion, reaction not fast enough. Still realize they are doing all they can.

I sit and wait, thinking about dead. Need to keep moving and keep busy, busy. No time for thoughts, inhibits reactions. Just act and react through intuition. Keep punching, rack brain trying to think of anything else I can do. Ask for artillery, tactical air, gunships. Remind people to sweep trees with fire. Can't talk over explosions. Scream orders. Firing stops, lull; find myself still trying to scream above racket. Shots come cracking and snapping towards sound of command voice. Trying to kill leaders. Shots tugs at harness, two holes just appear in belt. Firing starts again. Vicious cycle."

We could hear the *Thunk! Thunk!* of rounds being dropped and fired from the NVA tubes. I had a good azimuth plotted on the location. Because I had released my FO LT York to go back to the rear, I had little credibility with the artillery battalion, even though any of my men could have called the fire requests correctly.

At battalion's directive, Company A's observer (1LT Joel Fosdick) became the central fire control for the three companies to return fire, though I did not feel his unit was in a good position to identify from where the rounds were coming. We were higher on the ridge and the rounds were being fired from across the valley to our west, the same ridgeline on which Company A was located. It again took exactly 25 minutes before the first friendly response arrived in the wrong place.

The fire dance seemed to go on all night. When several mortar rounds landed in our area, we all celebrated with the "Tree Dance". We hid behind trees away from the landing rounds. When rounds started landing on the other side, we shifted our positions and tried to stay on the side away from the explosions. Observed objectively from an all-seeing eye, it must have been humorous to see us shifting around, trying to anticipate where the next rounds might land. We were all *bona fide* tree huggers that night. During some of the lulls, we continued doing "things." I kept active trying to think of what we could do to keep the initiative, including plotting artillery concentrations where I thought we might need them. I went around the perimeter to make sure I kept abreast of the situation and to let people know I cared about them and was not hunkered down in some hole waiting for rescue. I started thinking about, and writing awards statements, both for men who had been wounded or killed and those who had performed extraordinary acts.

Whenever a barrage started landing, we dove for the trees. In one instance, I scrambled for a tree and huddled against it trying to become one with its rough bark. I felt a nudge and looked over at Dick Surface, who was straining against the same tree. Trying to interject a note of humor into the situation, as if I had had a claim on any particular tree, I asked calmly, *"Surface, what are you doing behind my tree?"* I will never forget the look of sheer astonishment that came over his face as if he was being extremely impertinent by trying to save his life by hugging "my" tree. He said, *"Oh! I'm sorry, sir!"* Before I could tell him I was joking, and that there was certainly room for both of us, in the middle of falling rounds, he dashed for another tree. I immediately felt a tremendous guilt, since I only had been trying to put a little levity into an extremely serious situation. We often used humor as a coping mechanism for the fear and frustration we felt, not being able to do anything about what was happening. In this case, Surface fortunately made it safely to what became "his" tree.

CHAPTER THIRTY EIGHT

IN THE EARLY MORNING HOURS of the 20th, we received more mortar fire outside the perimeter. Later, at around ten o'clock, we received ten more, still outside the perimeter. We were grateful for the poor shooting, but since we could hear the rounds being dropped into the tube, we still didn't know where they were going to land. Anxiety city for sure. Company C fired at three NVA just outside their side of the perimeter but to no apparent effect. We continued to receive some small arms fire around the perimeter with rounds snapping through the trees, but again, no one was hit. Not all the NVA were gone, but we were by then at battalion strength, so the NVA were more cautious.

Intelligence reports indicated that major forces of the NVA 1st Division (notably battalions of the 32d and 66th Regiments) had crossed into Vietnam and were seeking out U.S. forces to create as many casualties as possible. Opposition to the war in the U.S. was growing and the North Vietnamese knew the more U.S. casualties there were, the louder would be the call for the U.S. to withdraw. Their intended strategy would also open the way for taking control of major towns in the highlands like Kon Tum and Pleiku, further clearing South Vietnamese and U.S. obstacles from the NVA avenues of approach into Vietnam.

With this background, the U.S. Fourth Infantry Division sought to cut those forces off and bring them to battle on U.S. terms. In the larger scheme of Divisional strategy, General Peers' tactic of trolling companies up and down the border as bait had succeeded. The enemy had been lured into Vietnam and was now attacking company-sized forces with larger units.

Unfortunately, Company B was part of the bait, but, the fourth platoon's experience notwithstanding, we had resisted the enemy's best efforts to overrun us and we were still fighting. We had lost many of our friends and comrades, but we were now mad as hell and more than ready for another fight.

The battalion and brigade plan was simple. We were to find the major elements of the NVA forces we had been fighting for the last two days and destroy them. The plan of action for the 20th called for Companies A and C to move west on line (side by side), with Company B behind as reserve.

The 20th dawned clear and sunny. We left our perimeter positions and headed west, down across the ravine and up to Company A's position where we linked up with them at 1110 hours. Company C slipped to the right of the formation and Company A to the left. Company B fell in behind and a bit to the left of Company A.

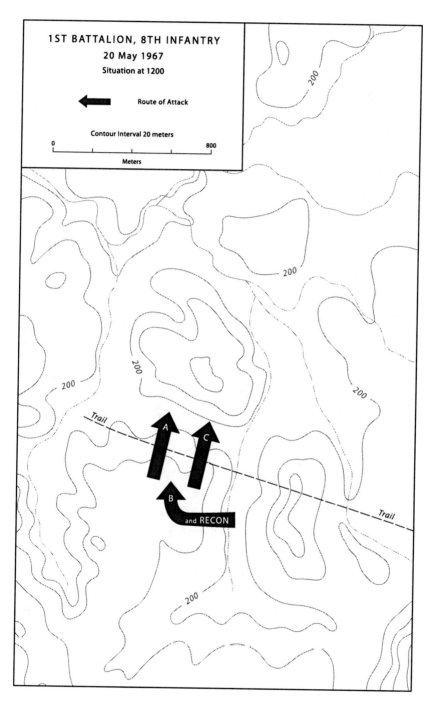

1ST BATTALION, 8TH INFANTRY
20 May 1967
Situation at 1200

Route of Attack

Contour Interval 20 meters

0   800
Meters

Our first objective was the top of the ridgeline just to our west where Company A had spent the night. Once we got to the top of the hill, we would swing the formation 90 degrees to the right and follow the ridgeline north to our next objective, a small hill-type elevation separated from the ridgeline we were following by a fairly deep gully. As we approached each of our objectives, we fired an artillery preparation at it to soften any lingering enemy.

Because of the terrain it was difficult to keep aligned as we moved west. Company B found itself more on the left flank and a little behind the lead companies, so the formation was changed tactically as we continued moving. We went west and then north up a gentle slope with little underbrush to the ridgeline where I had heard the NVA mortars being fired and where we found the empty mortar position. (I had been correct in my estimate of where they were located. If battalion had permitted us to adjust the artillery fire, I think we would have done some damage...) north of that, later in the afternoon, our second objective revealed a battalion-sized bunker complex. The complex had obviously belonged to the NVA unit that had assaulted us, but when we had started bringing in reinforcements and banging around with artillery, its occupants had moved out.

With the agreement of all company commanders, we decided to use the NVA positions as our own for the night. The S3 was not convinced it was a good decision but our rationale was sound. It was too late to be preparing our own positions, and the NVA had already prepared foxholes we could improve. The site was on the best defensible high ground around and had fair fields of fire. In addition, there was a semi-cleared area in the center of the position that we could improve to make an LZ if necessary. It made sense to use the position as our own, even though we knew the NVA were familiar with it. If they came, they would have to come at us uphill or through dense underbrush, thereby reducing much of their advantage in numbers. The only thing that really bothered me was that they had our coordinates and they had proved they were very good with mortar fire. All things considered, the battalion commander approved the location.

Using the continuing ridgeline north as our 12:00 o'clock, we oriented ourselves in the same sequence during our march. Company A took the northwest section between 8:00 and 12:00, Company C took the northeast and part of the southwest area in the 12:00 to 4:00 position, while Company B was positioned in the south with the Recon Platoon, 4:00 to 8:00. The entire battalion perimeter measured about 200 meters north to south and 250 meters east to west. I divided up Company B's sector fairly equally with the first platoon on the right, (looking south from the center of the perimeter). It tied in with Company A. My second platoon went to the left of the 1st and the third platoon to the left of the second. The Reconnaissance Platoon completed the layout, tying in with Company C to its left, and the third platoon on its right.

There was no good place to put my headquarters. The terrain did not leave a lot of room for movement. I had to choose between a spot too close to the perimeter or one too far back. Given those two options, I felt I should be close enough to the troops to see what was happening in order to be able to react quickly. As a result, I put my headquarters section in the center just behind the boundary between second platoon and Recon in a couple of holes we dug 30 to 40 feet behind the second platoon line. That we were in the direct line of fire in the event of an attack was of little importance to me. I did not think I could get a good "feel" for the situation from a position farther back in the brush. I could tell that given our somewhat crowded circumstances, if there was a fight, the internal company radio was going to be too impersonal and too slow for information to be passed quickly. On the other hand, being within hearing and shouting distance of the platoons, I thought I might better be able to influence the action personally. 1SG Lopez and SGT Surface were on my left and a little forward of my hole, which I shared with SGT Hunter and my temporary Forward Observer, 1LT Shoeck. I had not had an opportunity to chat with him at any length until the afternoon of the 20th when we were digging in and preparing our positions.

LT Bill Wilson had been my first artillery forward observer, and he had been reassigned after he was promoted to First Lieutenant. The artillery battalion sent a few temporary officers out from time to time to replace him, but I had not had an assigned observer for a while. I kept joking to Ray Harton that I wished they would send me an observer I could keep as my own and dispense with all the temporary help. Finally I received LT Larry York, who was a wizard with artillery and had done great work. I had let him go back to the rear on the evening of the 18th for his R&R and I was again without an observer. It was my own fault I didn't have an artillery forward observer, but today, given the same circumstances, I would make the same decision.

In spite of that decision, on the 19th I commented to the S3 and Harton that I did not have enough time to do my own artillery spotting, and I needed a forward observer replacement. Before we moved out on the morning of the 20th, the artillery battalion sent me 1LT William Shoeck as an officer replacement.

As we were discussing possible enemy assembly sites where we might want to put concentrations, it appeared he was a little unfamiliar with calling in fires, and with the SOPs that were required to shorten the time for bringing in fire support. I asked him what his background was and it turned out that the artillery battalion was so low on forward observers they had sent their Communications Officer to be my observer. Fortunately he had some FO experience, so calling for fires was not a foreign process. We came to a quick agreement that I would identify the targets and tell him what we needed to do and he would relay that through to the FSO and artillery battery. Though the arrangement was hardly ideal, it had promise and was the best we could do under the circumstances. As it turned out, under fire he was more qualified than I originally thought, and ultimately contributed a great deal to our overall operation in the next several days.

Company A had a rather flat avenue of approach to defend toward the west and northwest, with heavy underbrush and trees. Any organized attack would be broken up by the trees and vegetation, which would allow the unit to take on the NVA piecemeal.

Company C defended the north, eastern and a little of the southeastern avenue of approach. There was a fairly gentle slope with large trees but little underbrush, which provided excellent fields of fire that covered the entire area from the bottom of the hill on. Better still, the enemy would have to fight uphill. It was not as rocky as the ridgeline to our east and permitted actual defensive positions to be dug deep enough to do some good. In our final positioning, the companies used few, if any, of the enemy's prepared positions. They did not fit the size of our units nor our defensive tactics.

Company B, on the south. southwest and southeast, overlooked a ravine that ran between two elevations, about 50 meters apart. The one on our side of the ravine was a bit higher than the other bank, but not to an appreciable degree. We put

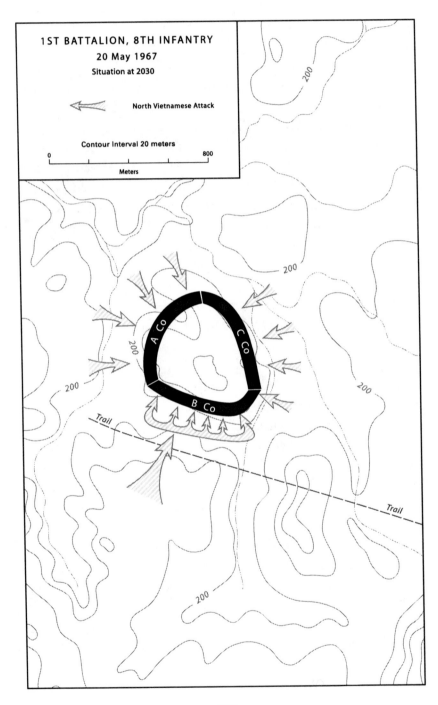

1ST BATTALION, 8TH INFANTRY
20 May 1967
Situation at 2030

North Vietnamese Attack

Contour Interval 20 meters

0   800

Meters

our positions a little closer to the edge of the ravine than the NVA positions had been in order to better cover the ravine and anything that attempted to move up, down or across it. We had a Starlight Scope (Night Vision Device) to aid us in seeing at night. I put it with an outpost about 30 meters in front of the Third Platoon overlooking the ravine.

At about 8 o'clock, we could see lights flickering through the trees to the south, near Company A's last position. (It has always been a thought of mine that we may have merely exchanged positions with the NVA for the evening.) I asked for artillery that would burst in the tree tops in hopes it would spray the lights and anyone around with shrapnel and tree splinters. We could only hear the explosions so we had no idea about the effectiveness of the fire, but the lights did go out. About an hour later, mortar rounds began coming in to our location. We took immediate casualties. Company B had 4 KIA and 15 WIA, Companies A and C each had 2 KIA and about 10-12 WIA. As during the previous nights, we could hear the *THUNK! THUNK! COUGH! COUGH!* of the mortar rounds being dropped into the tubes and firing, then a long wait until the rounds hit with loud explosions, showers of shrapnel and tree splinters. I asked for counter battery fire, but our artillery rounds seemed to dance all around the mortar positions without inflicting damage.

While we had covered our holes with branches and logs to protect us from overhead fire, it was impossible to stay in the hole all the time in order to be ready for a ground assault. The overhead cover only shielded us from small bits of shrapnel or splinters. A direct hit on a hole meant immediate death.

The outpost with the Starlight Scope began reporting a great deal of vague movement to its front and requested permission to withdraw. I told them to hold on until we got something more definite.

The next thing I knew, SFC Morales, the platoon sergeant and acting platoon leader, reported the outpost had withdrawn, leaving the Scope on site in its hurry to leave. I was furious.

The Scope, in the hands of the NVA, would permit them to see into our defensive positions and orient their attacks on our weaknesses. One of our advantages was that they did not have a night vision capability as we did with the Scope. Although I was angry that the men had returned without permission, or reporting they were doing so, I recognized I had to rely on their judgment as to when they absolutely needed to leave. We could all now see enemy movement on the far side of the ravine. We already suspected we were outnumbered, but with the Scope in NVA hands, we would be under a tremendous disadvantage. I ordered the outpost to return and retrieve the Scope no matter the cost. It was not a decision I made in anger, but I knew more men would be killed if we did not retrieve the device. Shortly afterwards I got a report the Scope was back in our hands and had been set up on the lines.

The NVA initiated a classic infantry attack. At some point, I told the platoons to fix bayonets. They continued their mortar fire and as their ground assault came close to our lines, they started targeting further to the north into Companies A and C's positions. We began taking fire from across the ravine from small arms, automatic weapons and RPGs. The NVA then started their ground attacks and were soon coming in waves. We heard bugle calls in addition to short and long blasts on the police-type whistles the enemy commanders used to pass orders to their troops.

We fought in a kaleidoscope of constantly shifting colors. The artillery-fired yellow parachute flares descended into the trees from the dark sky. They were blown by a small breeze as they came down, rocking back and forth with their light making shadows of trees and men appeared to rapidly grow and decrease in height. The shadows were shifting in one direction and then another. We had placed brightly flickering strobe lights on the perimeter so our air support could identify our forward positions. These flashed a white light hundreds of times per minute adding to the visual cacophony of confusing images; red/yellow tracer rounds from our machine guns, gunships and Spooky support, rifle flashes; and the bright red/yellow explosion of mortar and artillery rounds. From time to time, a bright explosion went off in the tree tops, setting small fires, which quickly burned out. The flickering that resulted made it appear as if the ground itself was shifting and moving.

We were firing artillery of all types into areas where we expected the enemy to assemble. We also called in helicopter gunships, USAF aircraft loaded with air to ground guns and rockets, and USAF C-130 "Spooky" aircraft firing mini-guns and dropping flares to light the battlefield.

Just before the first wave attack, I crawled forward and looked over the edge of the gully parapet into the ravine. The bushes and ground looked like they were moving. As I focused on the reality of what I was seeing, I realized it was the backs of shoulder to shoulder NVA soldiers crawling their way up the ravine wall into our position. In the moving light of the flares, they looked like slugs from a horror movie slowly moving forward to consume their prey.

Murphy's Laws:

"Five second fuses always burn three seconds."

I had a white phosphorus grenade I carried around which weighed a couple of pounds. I immediately thought this was a good place to get rid of it, so, breathing hard but being careful to get it right, I yanked it off my harness, pulled the pin and tossed it into the ravine.

The white phosphorus went off very quickly with a blinding flash and scattered burning white hot pieces of phosphorus around the ravine bottom and sides. Fortunately the grenade didn't explode as high as the lip of the ravine. Those NVA soldiers, hit by the burning phosphorus had no defense against the chunks of molten fire. While I took no gratification in their agony, I did remember that these were the men who only two days before had murdered helpless soldiers as they lay wounded, vulnerable, and no longer a threat. Their cries followed me as I jerked myself back from the edge and shouted *"They're coming over the top!"*

I barely made it back to my hole before the first wave broke over the edge of the ravine into a wall of grenades and defensive fire. They clawed their way over the top of the ridge, throwing grenades and pushing their AK-47s ahead of them and firing into our positions. There was always a few seconds of lag, from the time they appeared over the edge to the time they oriented themselves and started shooting. In that brief interval our defensive fires ripped into their ranks and pushed them back over the edge so that they fell into those still climbing. Our grenades began to have an effect on their mass. We could hear their shouts and screams as they pulled their wounded and dead off the slope and down the ravine out of our line of fire.

We could tell additional NVA troops were running into the ravine and getting organized for another push. We kept throwing grenades into the killing zone and shooting what we could see. While this delayed the next wave, the NVA reorganized themselves and came at us again. This time they made it to the top and were within a few meters of our positions where they again met a wall of fire, that threw them back all along the line into the ravine. Some of our positions were getting short of ammunition, so the platoons redistributed grenades and ammunition among themselves as we waited for the next attack. We had taken wounded and killed, but as I crawled around the company perimeter to check on weak spots and

362

morale, I was pumped by the attitude of the men, men were shouting and screaming in rage and anger. It was obvious they were acting without fear while begging the enemy to come again for more. A third wave attack did come, with the same high pitched screams and whistles and bugles. I fired my grenade launcher multiple times across the ravine into what seemed, in the shifting flare light, to be a command group of sorts kneeling on the far lip of the ravine in some vegetation. When I checked the next morning I was disappointed to find no bodies, only a small grouping of man-sized shrubs that had been shot to shreds, so...who knows?

I was popping up and down out of my hole, trying to see what the platoons and the enemy were doing. I was giving directions to the artillery observer, LT Shoeck; talking on both the company radio net and the battalion radio; all the while trying to duck unseen mortar rounds, AK47 bullets, and RPGs. I remember thinking to myself in a moment of black humor, that I should be afraid, but I would have to do it later because I just didn't have time for it right then.

Smoke from explosions and fires from artillery and mortars swirled around us. The flickering muzzle blasts of AK47s and M16s penetrated the flare light and the dark. The 3d attack got a few meters in front of our positions and looked like it might succeed, but one minute we were shooting everything we had at shadows and movement and the next minute there was nothing left in front of us. Down in the ravine out of our sight, the enemy dragged away his wounded and dead; we were still receiving fire from automatic weapons across the ravine, which kept us from coming out of our holes to fire down into the gully.

I was on an adrenalin "high". At one point when it must have appeared a little "iffy" to someone flying several hundred feet above the battle, Colonel Gannon asked me on the radio *"Can you hold?"* Excitedly, and admittedly cocky and arrogant, but with absolute certainty, I shouted into the handset, *"This is 82, and nobody is coming through us!!"*

The men were fighting their hearts out, and I was never more proud of their dedication, determination and sacrifices. This was the fighting company I knew I commanded, and the satisfaction that gave me has yet to wear off, years later. The tragedy, of course, was that we were losing troops as the night wore on. We had to shift men from one position to another to cover those locations taking casualties.

After the third wave attack, the enemy kept shooting into our lines and restarted a sporadic mortar fire. After the frenzied attacks, it was almost calm, and individuals were able to move around cautiously without setting off a firestorm of incoming. We resupplied with ammunition, moved our wounded off the line to the center of the perimeter, and tried to protect them from incoming fire.

Colonel Gannon put me in charge of coordinating the battalion defensive fires to ensure we were not shooting each other. Our 105mm artillery battery was firing in support and several times the tops of trees caught the incoming rounds intended for the outside of our perimeter; they exploded within the battalion's positions. An artillery or mortar round hit about five meters away from my CP hole and destroyed a tree. I received some shrapnel and fragments in my back but I didn't realize I had been hit until we got into the lulls between attacks. At one point when I was moving between the platoons, I was thrown against a tree from an explosion. I was only dazed however, and did not appear to be badly injured.

Murphy's Laws:

"It's not the one with your name on it; it's the one addressed "to whom it may concern" you've got to think about."

Shortly after the attacks started, we had gunships firing in support of Companies B and C, but they had trouble identifying where we were located. We put out strobe lights to mark our perimeter, but since there was tree cover, the aircraft were not particularly effective at close in support. Some of the gunship rounds came too close to our positions, so we divided up the target areas between air and artillery.

Our artillery guns from Duc Co and the 1-8 FSB were located towards the southeast, so we gave the artillery those targets that were on the east, south and southwest of the perimeter. We designated the targets to the north east, north and west of the perimeter for the aircraft. That way, the aircraft would not be flying into or under the artillery rounds.

Our air support had all kinds of weapons: a "Spooky" C-130 gunship, flare ships, F-100s, and A1E Skyraider aircraft putting ordnance around us on possible enemy avenues of approach or withdrawal. An observer flying above us that night was Colonel Charles Jackson, the 1st Brigade Commander. He was a real soldier and made it clear he was there to assist in providing whatever support we needed and not to interfere or second guess us.

Jackson and Gannon let us fight the fight without adding to the confusion by giving us unnecessary "suggestions." These men were exemplary leaders, not the micromanagers other senior officers might have been. The ground was "ours" and there was little anyone in the air could do to help us except ensure we got air and fire support, while keeping out of the way and off our radios.

Colonel Gannon had been flying above us in his Command and Control helicopter, relaying messages when we couldn't get through for our fire support. When the wave attacks ceased and the firing died down, his helicopter was running low on fuel and he had to return to the firebase. He appointed me the acting battalion commander on the ground, coordinating the defense.

We were all pretty busy, so I don't know how anyone could have counted, but someone said at least 175 mortar rounds and 43 rockets had hit within our perimeter.

After the initial attacks, Wally Williamson's Company A did not seem to be receiving the amount of fire the rest of us were, so he started improving the LZ. He did an outstanding job amid incoming fire zipping and crashing in from all sides. We had to stop close-in artillery support while trying to get aircraft in and out, starting it up again when no flights were arriving. The LZ was just a hole between the trees. As in previous firefights in dense forest, the flights had to hover over the opening, making themselves almost stationary targets, lowering themselves slowly to the ground between the trees, trying to keep the main or tail rotors from clipping the trees and brush on the way down and up. Company A personnel used ground flares as guides for the medivac helicopters in addition to the flares dropping in the night sky. In the "hot" LZ, the helicopter pilots did extraordinary things, trying to differentiate between moving shadows and real obstacles, while incoming fire added to the distractions.

CHAPTER THIRTY NINE

I CAN NEVER WRITE OR SAY too much about our medics. These were men who elected to help others, rather than destroy them. Their dedication to their trade made them special, and we were all better off just knowing we had a trained medic somewhere around. The medical personnel belonged to the battalion Headquarters Company, but were attached to the line companies for operations. Individuals usually stayed with a specific company to foster bonding and comradeship, but when medics were short, a medic might be "borrowed" from battalion or another company to help out.

Our medics put their lives on the line each time they dashed to where one of *their* guys lay wounded. They darted through the zipping bullets and crashing explosions in order to bring some aid and comfort to a wounded man and many paid with their lives. Our medics were part of us. They were the men for whom we anxiously called and for whom we searched when we were injured. Just the fact of their being there, doing *something*, was often enough to calm a soldier and make a situation more bearable.

One of the many tragic stories of the night of the 20th involved SGT Ray Borowski. With all the wounded, dead, and dying in our positions, the medics were busy men and were not holed up safely waiting for the horror to end.

1SG Lopez of Company B remembers the start of the incident: "*Ray Borowski was the senior medic who came in with the Recon Platoon, but he was the only medic we had in the whole company area...we didn't have any medics, they were all gone, all dead...so he got wounded and they brought him over to us. It was already dark and I remember he was wounded but he was talking...we carried him over to the LZ that Company A was building and that was the last time I saw him...*"

Landis Bargatze of Company A picks up the story: "*When the night attack started, Lou Macellari, who had been on one of our listening posts, moved back to the perimeter and joined some wounded soldiers waiting for aid. One of those wounded was Ray Borowski. Lou stayed with Ray throughout the night providing protection, while helping others blow trees for the LZ to evacuate the wounded for treatment. Just before he was evacuated, Borowski removed his St. Christopher medallion from around his neck and gave it to Macellari in hopes of bringing him "good luck and safety" and to help him make it back home.*

The next morning (about 1:30 AM) the LZ was hot, receiving heavy small arms fire and mortar rounds and the medivac chopper could not land. After several unsuccessful attempts it was decided to drop a cable with a life basket attached approximately fifty feet into the LZ and air lift Ray up and into the chopper. Sadly, as the life basket was being lifted to the chopper, something went wrong and the cable either broke or was shot and the basket fell outside the perimeter killing Borowski."

Years later, two of Ray's three sons, Chris and Bruce Borowski attended a Company A and B reunion and heard about the St. Christopher medallion incident. The Macellaris thought it would be a nice gesture to return the medal to the Borowski family after all those years. After several discussions between the Borowskis, former members of Company A, American Legion Post 364, VVA Chapter 267, and the mayor of Dearborn, Michigan, arrangements were made for a public presentation. The medal was returned to the Borowski family in an appropriate ceremony in Dearborn, Michigan on May 20, 2010, forty-three years after it had been given to Lou Macellari.

On the night of the 20th, after the first determined waves, the NVA back came in small groups all around the battalion perimeter. We received small arms attacks, hand and rocket propelled grenades. Most of the main attacks came across the ravine and up into Company B's area. Though it was a more difficult climb into the face of our defensive fires, the enemy had better concealment in the steepness of the ravine wall than along the other avenues of approach into the battalion's defensive positions.

The next morning we discovered their sappers had been able to inch their way up unseen in the low vegetation and unheard in all the mortar and artillery noise, to lay guide-wire up to within 5–10 meters of our positions along the front. To see the wires, even in daylight, required that we stick our heads over the edge of the ravine to look directly down onto the slope itself. At night this terrain feature provided the NVA enough concealment to lay the wires, which were supposed to guide the first attackers to their launch points. We had established our interlocking fields of fire and claymore mines to discourage this, but in a couple of instances it was a close-run thing. Without many very heroic actions on the part of our soldiers,

Company B might have given way, endangering the whole battalion.

Loading Casualties

In the early morning hours of 21 May, we fired artillery into an area from which we heard voices and saw vague movement through the trees. The first daylight helicopter came in to the LZ to evacuate wounded and bring ammunition and supplies. Wally Williamson, the Company A Commander, went out to meet it. A rocket came in and exploded, killing one of his men, wounding two other soldiers, and hitting Wally himself in the side. It made for a mind-blowing greeting for 1LT Howard Brooks, the Company A Executive Officer, who was on the bird. Wally was evacuated, and Howard immediately took command of the company.

With first light, all three companies sent out sweep patrols in front of their positions. We (Company B) found two wounded NVA. When we tried to take them prisoner, they did not want to be captured. After a period of time, we were able to bring them in without anyone else being injured, but one died before we could evacuate him to the rear. On our sweeps, all companies received mortar fire, but we were able to stop the firing by responding with artillery into the area from which the shots originated.

The helicopters coming into the area were still receiving small arms fire, so we called in artillery to dampen the NVA's enthusiasm. Even so, the enemy remained all around us, so we were never really able to stop their shooting at us or our helicopters.

Colonel Gannon came out the morning of the 21st to assume command on the ground, accompanied by Captain Terrell, the battalion intelligence officer and some of the battalion operations center personnel. Major Tausch, the battalion XO, also came out for a short time, though he did not stay long; it was not good policy for both the commander and the XO to be in an area where the command structure could be eliminated with just one explosion.

It was the first time the battalion had operated as an integrated battalion, with all three companies together, since we had come to Vietnam. Mustang felt as I did, that when it gets down and dirty, the commander's place is with the troops and you ride toward the sound of the guns. His intention of joining us on the ground during our move on the 20th had been denied by the brigade commander, Colonel Jackson, which was reasonable since it was basically a fight at company level and below. As frustrating as it must have been, under the circumstances, where there was no battalion reserve to be committed, the battalion commander could best influence the action by providing support, not direct commands.

Shortly after getting his Tactical CP established, Colonel Gannon wanted a meeting with all the company commanders. He selected the Company C CP as the location. As the battalion commander and I walked to that position, we found the company commander, CPT "Pete" Peterson, in a daze with a medic checking him out. A few moments before, he had been sitting on his steel helmet underneath a tree, looking at his map, when he was hit in the head by a falling branch that had been severed by fire from the night before but had not fallen. He had a fractured skull and had to be replaced by 1LT Donald Bullock, the XO of Company C. I was thankful that both Williamson and Peterson had only been wounded and not killed. It was strange to think that I had been in command almost five and a half months, while Wally and Pete had only made eight and seven weeks respectively. I made a sarcastic comment in my journal about wimpy junior company commanders. Both were good friends and I would have made the same trash talk comment to their faces had I been given the opportunity. I was sorry to see either of them go because we worked well together. I don't remember whether the meeting occurred or not.

I had my XO, LT George Tupa, bring everybody in Company B who could hold a rifle out from the base camp to fill in the vacancies created by our casualties. Colonel Gannon did the same for the rest of the battalion. Tupa and Cary Allen were the only officers I had left, (Rodabaugh had been wounded and evacuated, Aronhalt had been killed, and Bosch had been reassigned). My senior NCOs were in short supply also. While my feeling about the battalion commander and XO being in the same place was still valid, as short as the company was on officers, it was not a difficult decision to have George in the field with us. With the bad luck the other two company commanders had enjoyed, it was prudent to have Company B's XO nearby, just in case.

During the fighting the night of the 20th, the rear area radios were picking up reports of our big fight. Victor Renza, one of the survivors of the fourth platoon action on the 18th, had been evacuated for his injuries. Several other wounded from Company B were in the same ward:

Renza: "On the 20th, I was in the hospital and SGT Parker of the second platoon was there too, along with some others before we were moved out of country...we heard the company was being hit again and everybody started talking about going back out again. Yeah!!! Let's go!!! Let's go!!! There we were, a bunch of young guys all bandaged up, trying to get out of beds to get back out to the field to help their buddies. It must have been a ridiculous sight... However, the nurses soon took charge and started shouting "You aren't going anywhere!" After a bit I could see the humor in the situation. But while we may not have been physically capable, we were really enthusiastic about supporting our guys."

The battalion was a close knit team. We did not accept losses easily.

CHAPTER FORTY

A S WE WERE CONSOLIDATING our dead and wounded near my CP on the morning of the 21st, one of the battalion medics began cutting out the pieces of shrapnel in my back. When he finished putting dressings on the holes, he started filling out the medical treatment card that SOP required whenever someone was treated in the field. This card went back into the administrative process and was the basis for the award of a Purple Heart to the treated individual. As I was putting my shirt back on, the body of Staff Sergeant Frankie Molnar was carried up and laid on the ground next to me on the way to the LZ to be evacuated. The night before, while fulfilling duties as squad leader during the attacks, Molnar had fallen on a grenade to save soldiers in his squad. I felt extremely humbled. It is the Army's policy that each man killed in action receives a Purple Heart for the wounds suffered. I felt guilty for not being able to protect Molnar and the other men who died. Because of this I did not feel I could put myself in the same category of receiving a Purple Heart for the minor flesh wounds I had received, when men like SSG Molnar gave everything they had to save others. I had the medic tear up the treatment card, thus ensuring I would not receive a Purple Heart through a routine administrative process. I have never regretted that decision.

Frankie Molnar had a special place in my heart. He was one of the sincere ones who tried to do everything right and took his responsibilities seriously. Even though he was from Logan, West Virginia, he had gone to California to enlist in the Army and took his basic training at Fort Ord, California. After graduating from training as a communications specialist, he was assigned to Germany. When his enlistment was up, he left the Army and went to stay with his mother in New Jersey. However he liked the Army so well that he reenlisted in December 1965 before he lost his rank. In January 1966, he was assigned to the 1-8th at Ft Lewis as the Communications Sergeant for Company B. As a communications Sergeant E5, however, he was at the top of his grade structure in the company. Being a solid, ambitious soldier, he naturally wanted to be promoted, but this was unlikely as long as he stayed in the communications field and in Company B. He talked it over with 1SG Lopez and decided he did not want to leave the company. He had a secondary MOS as an infantryman, and was willing to be assigned to an infantry platoon to continue his army career.

He left the communications job and moved into the third platoon where he became a squad leader. The battalion moved to Vietnam and took to the field. If there had been any questions about his leadership ability, Molnar disabused any detractors on 3 November, 1966. His squad was on a patrol and surprised a group of VC. He immediately put his men into a combat formation and opened fire...the ensuing firefight soon spread to other squads, but Molnar's quick reaction ensured Company B's victory with only one wounded. Shortly after this action, and exactly a month after arrival in Vietnam, he was promoted to Staff Sergeant E6, the authorized rank of an infantry squad leader. As he matured in his position, I kept an eye on him with the thought that if things worked out, I would recommend him for Officer's Candidate School after his tour in Vietnam was completed.

He again showed his value as a soldier and leader on 22 March 1967. He and his squad's action took out one of the two NVA machine guns that had pinned down the third and fourth platoons, causing several casualties. For his actions in this firefight he received a Bronze Star for Valor.

He was such a good soldier and human being that when he had a family emergency in the States, after a discussion with 1SG Lopez, I expanded my authority a bit and arranged for him to return to the US for a 30-day emergency leave. While there, he took the opportunity to marry his fiancée. The honeymoon was extremely short, because he returned on May 15th, as he promised, only to be killed three days later. I felt myself fortunate indeed to be present in the White House on 10 July 1969, when President Nixon awarded Frankie Molnar's widow, Sharon and baby daughter Michelle, the Medal of Honor for his services to the United States of America on the night of 20 May 1967.

His citation reads:

MOLNAR, FRANKIE ZOLY

Rank and organization: Staff Sergeant, U.S. Army, Company B, 1st Battalion, 8th Infantry, 4th Infantry Division. place and date: Pleiku Province, Republic of Vietnam, 20 May 1967. Entered service at: Fresno, Calif. Born: 14 February 1943, Logan, W. Va. Citation: For conspicuous gallantry and intrepidity in action at the risk of his life above and beyond the call of duty. S/Sgt. Molnar distinguished himself while serving as a squad leader with Company B during combat operations. Shortly after the battalion's defensive perimeter was established, it was hit by intense mortar fire as the prelude to a massive enemy night attack. S/Sgt. Molnar immediately left his sheltered location to insure the readiness of his squad to meet the attack. As he crawled through the position, he discovered a group of enemy soldiers closing in on his squad area. His accurate rifle fire killed 5 of the enemy and forced the remainder to flee. When the mortar fire stopped, the enemy attacked in a human wave supported by grenades, rockets, automatic weapons, and small-arms fire. After assisting to repel the first enemy assault, S/Sgt. Molnar found that his squad's ammunition and grenade supply was nearly expended. Again leaving the relative safety of his position, he crawled through intense enemy fire to secure additional ammunition and distribute it to his squad. He rejoined his men to beat back the renewed enemy onslaught, and he moved about his area providing medical aid and assisting in the evacuation of the wounded. With the help of several men, he was preparing to move a severely wounded soldier when an enemy hand grenade was thrown into the group. The first to see the grenade, S/Sgt. Molnar threw himself on it and absorbed the deadly blast to save his comrades. His demonstrated selflessness and inspirational leadership on the battlefield were a major factor in the successful defense of the American position and are in keeping with the finest traditions of the U.S.

Army. S/Sgt. Molnar's actions reflect great credit upon himself, his unit, and the U.S. Army.

As I write these words, I am amazed at how many other young men from our battalion, who went on emergency leaves back to the U.S., felt the moral obligation to return to war in a far country. They knew the imminent dangers and particularly for those who did so shortly after taking on the emotional obligations of a family. I can only assume their parents imbued their children with a strong moral belief system. In Molnars' case, his parents had eight children, five of whom served in the military. Frankie Molnar and others like him were truly some of America's "best", in all senses of the word.

The heroes and bravery were not just in Company B. Company A and Company C had their share as well. At almost the same time, and just a few meters from where Molnar paid the price for his men, PFC Leslie Bellrichard of Company C performed the same heroic action. As a result of his sacrifice, he was also awarded the Medal of Honor.

I did not know PFC Bellrichard personally, but I know that his final actions speak loudly of someone who cared more for his friends than his own safety. In my opinion you cannot give a man more honor than to simply say *"He was a fine soldier and I respected him a great deal."*

His Medal of Honor citation reads:

BELLRICHARD, LESLIE ALLEN

"For conspicuous gallantry and intrepidity in action at the risk of his life above and beyond the call of duty. Acting as a fire team leader with Company C, during combat operations, PFC Bellrichard was with 4 fellow soldiers in a foxhole on their unit's

perimeter when the position came under a massive enemy attack. Following a 30-minute mortar barrage, the enemy launched a strong ground assault. PFC Bellrichard rose in the face of a group of charging enemy soldiers and threw hand grenades into their midst, eliminating several of the foe and forcing the remainder to withdraw. Failing in their initial attack, the enemy repeated the mortar and rocket bombardment of the friendly perimeter, then once again charged against the defenders in a concerted effort to overrun the position. PFC Bellrichard resumed throwing hand grenades at the onrushing attackers. As he was about to hurl a grenade, a mortar round exploded just in front of his position, knocking him into the foxhole and causing him to lose his grip on the already armed grenade. Recovering instantly, PFC Bellrichard recognized the threat to the lives of his 4 comrades and threw himself upon the grenade, shielding his companions from the blast that followed. Although severely wounded, PFC Bellrichard struggled into an upright position in the foxhole and fired his rifle at the enemy until he succumbed to his wounds. His selfless heroism contributed greatly to the successful defense of the position, and he was directly responsible for saving the lives of several of his comrades. His acts are in keeping with the highest traditions of the military service and reflect great credit upon himself and the U.S. Army."

In the city of Janesville, Wisconsin, after much perseverance on the part of Bellrichard's veteran supporters, and after much delay and reluctance on the part of the Janesville city council, a bridge was named after Bellrichard in 2004.

CHAPTER FORTY

It was entirely appropriate that the three Medals of Honor earned by the men of Companies B and C on 18 and 20 May, 1967, were presented in the same ceremony by President Nixon on 10 July, 1969 at the White House. The families of SFC Bruce Grandstaff, SSG Frankie Molnar and PFC Leslie Bellrichard received the awards, observed by some of us who were also present during their actions.

The heroism, bravery and courage exhibited by these young men and their fighting brothers was indicative of the type of warriors we knew. In their teens and early twenties, they were considered immature by many of their elders. Most of them couldn't even buy a beer when they returned home because of their age. Their willingness to give their lives for their friends and the men for whom they were responsible, however, revealed an innate maturity that their protesting civilian peers would never develop.

CHAPTER FORTY ONE

WE RECEIVED SOME FEEDBACK from the prisoner we had evacuated. In an initial interrogation he indicated we had destroyed a company of 120 men in the previous few days and that two battalions had attacked us the previous night. Just in the Company B area, we estimated about 85 NVA KIA from their wave attacks. I took two platoons out on patrols to sweep the general area and found more NVA bodies, shallow graves and weapons, and the site from where the mortars had been firing. With all the counter battery fire we had been using, we still had not hit the mortars, and they had been removed during the enemy's withdrawal.

It is not well known, but many NVA soldiers carried a rope with a hook as part of their individual equipment. During a fight, they would use the rope and hook to drag wounded or dead NVA soldiers where they could be carried away and buried, or treated for their wounds. The NVA were fanatical about recovering the bodies of their men to keep the U.S. from knowing their casualty rates. As a result, many combat after-action reports computed their NVA or VC body counts on actuals plus a formula to estimate indirect fire casualties that may have been out of the immediate firefight area.

We spent the 21st consolidating our positions, getting our dead and wounded out and tracking the direction of the general NVA withdrawal. That evening, while preparing our close-in defenses, one of our men was wounded in the leg when a claymore mine exploded. Another error round from artillery came in and burst in the treetops over our heads killing one man from Company A and wounding two others. Later that night we had more mortar rounds from a different location, some probes from small NVA units, but no large wave attacks. It appeared the major units of the NVA were trying to withdraw across the border to Cambodia. As they did, our sister battalions of the 3-8th and the 3-12th Infantry tangled with them and bloodied them even more.

Later prisoner interrogations revealed that the entire 4th Battalion of the 32d NVA Regiment, supported by the 5th Battalion of the same regiment and augmented by elements of the 66th NVA Regiment had attacked us on the 18th. The 4th Battalion had suffered so many casualties (119) that it was given the mission of protecting the regimental command post while it made up its losses. The 5th Battalion had approximately 15 KIA from artillery alone...

According to prisoner information, on 20 May, the 1-8th was attacked by both the 5th and the 6th Battalions of the 32d Regiment with both battalions suffering approximately 60 KIA each for a total of 120 KIA. I suspect the NVA casualties were much higher than that because we saw many signs indicating that bodies had been dragged through the forest. In addition, in the coming weeks, on their normal patrols, U.S. units in the area kept finding NVA mass graves close to the border where the NVA had buried their dead.

The battalion spent the 22d and 23d of May conducting saturation patrols within the area. It found additional graves, equipment and documents left behind by the NVA units. The larger NVA units with whom we had been in contact were nowhere to be seen. We no longer received fire into the perimeter, however, there were obvious movements at night that told us we were still under observation. Aircraft received small arms fire, but when artillery or gunships responded, the firing ceased.

On 24 May, Companies B and C of the 3-8th Infantry replaced the 1-8th which withdrew to Jackson Hole to reoutfit and receive replacements. My Company B was scheduled for some 58 new soldiers with a promise of more, to start the rebuilding process, enough new soldiers to form two new platoons...

If we could call the last fight a victory, it was only within the larger view of the 4th Infantry Division rather than ours. For even though the 1-8th left the field temporarily, the rest of the 1st Brigade found the retreating NVA in a series of fierce contacts. Heavy fighting ensued for the next several days. The engagement involving Company B on 18 May, continued for another 8 days, resulting in a series of firefights and contacts now known as the *"Nine Days of May"* battles.

According to CPT Ray Harton, the 6-29th Artillery Liaison Officer with the 1-8th, the following fire support was used between 18–23 May:

8300 rounds of 105mm artillery
1845 rounds of 155mm artillery
1794 rounds of 8 inch artillery
690 rounds of 175mm artillery
57 air sorties

Of course NVA mortar rounds made it an even louder, and more frightful time.

Personally, I was scheduled to depart for R&R on the 25th and flew back to the Firebase to start my trip. The night I was there, we received incoming mortars and Colonel Gannon was hit in the leg with a fragment. I kept trying to get back to Pleiku on helicopters but every time I got on one, I got bumped off for too much load, or something else. Mere captains didn't have much clout. It began to look like the U.S. Army was trying to keep me from going on leave, just like the NVA. Towards the end of the day, I finally got a ride to Jackson Hole, but couldn't find a ride back to Dragon Mountain. COL Jackson found out I didn't have a way back to Pleiku, so he had his helicopter take me all the way back; I thought it was extremely kind and I was very grateful. I arrived in good shape and took care of administrative duties based on our last few days in contact. Some of these entailed letters to next of kin, award statements, Don Hunter's application for flight school, and other general administrative matters prior to my leaving for a week. SGT Foreman, who was one of the soldiers killed in the fourth platoon, had been one of Dick Surface's best friends, so we arranged for Surface to accompany the body back to Indiana.

CHAPTER FORTY TWO

WHEN I FLEW OUT FOR A WEEK'S R&R in Hawaii, I had trouble adjusting from a combat situation to a peacetime environment. Three days before arriving in Honolulu I had been involved in a weeklong heavy firefight and was still in emotional shock from all the losses we had taken and the stress of close combat. Our first night we had a room high up in a nice hotel with a great view that overlooked much of the city and beach. It should have been perfect, except...

When I called home to speak to my children, my oldest daughter Cheron just about broke my heart. When she answered the phone, her first words were, *"OH! You're alive!!!"* The story came out...before my wife had left for Hawaii, the news media had announced there had been heavy fighting in the central highlands and that an infantry company had been overrun with all officers killed. They went on to name Company B, 1-8th Infantry Battalion of the 4th ID. Our neighbors heard this and their kids told my daughter. My daughter told her grandmother who was getting ready to take care of the family while my wife was in Hawaii meeting me for R&R. Cheron wanted to tell her mother so she wouldn't get to Hawaii and be alone when she got the news. However, my mother-in-law didn't want to say anything based on a news report and my wife flew to Hawaii in ignorance. She met me and thought everything was normal until our phone call home that night. For several days my daughter had lived with the thought that her father was dead and her mother was alone in Hawaii with the tragic news; quite a burden for a young teenager. However, it was all cleared up and it was great to talk with all of the kids in a normal atmosphere without a mortar round interruption.

After our phone call home, it could have been nice, except that it was some sort of Chinese holiday and there were great celebrations throughout Honolulu with tremendous displays of fireworks. The flares, starbursts, cracks, booms, whistles and rattle of strings of firecrackers floated up to our room and made for a very difficult night. I intellectually knew what was going on, but my body could not internalize it. I was nervous, frazzled, irritable and glad to be out of Vietnam, but feeling guilty that I was not with my men sharing whatever dangers they might be experiencing.

In Hawaii, people were too bunched together and one mortar could have hit dozens of them at one time. There was no light discipline at night and the noise would have overwhelmed even a hearing impaired person. The food was too plentiful and rich and you never knew who was following you because of all the people around. My civilian clothes had no pockets for my map and I had to leave my grenade launcher before I got on the airplane!

My wife was partly understanding, but somehow this had not been what she had been expecting either. I had lost my wedding ring crawling around in the jungle, so we had to buy another one. We shopped, explored the island, went swimming and boating and tried to pretend we were a couple again.

388

However, there was always the five-day countdown that put a sour taste in the not-so-sweet time and overlaid everything we did.

The week was too quick over, and I returned to Vietnam, feeling I had been gone much longer. On the plane, I was anxious and focused, wondering how different I would find things.

CHAPTER FORTY THREE

THE AIRCRAFT LANDED AT Cam Ranh Bay, the huge U.S. military supply depot. I was able to find a flight to Pleiku the next morning. I spent one night at the base camp getting up to speed, and it felt like I had been gone a year.

On May 24, 1967, on our return from the field to Jackson Hole, the company had only 83 men present for duty in total out of an authorized strength of 180. That number included those who were assigned to the rear area in supply and administration. Less than a week later, however, we had doubled that number with 166 present for duty, most of whom were PFCs straight from the replacement center. This created a massive job of training these men to be a part of the company, and of integrating them into the squads currently manned by the veterans who had been with the company for a while. There was no break in the combat role. We had to give them on-the-job training and hope we were able to do so adequately before any other large firefights.

Essentially it was a new company, even with new NCOs and officers. LT Allen's combat tour with the infantry was about over and he was likely to be reassigned to a Supply and Transportation unit; LT Rodabaugh had been wounded and would not return to us; LT Aronhalt had been killed and LT Bosch had been assigned to Division prior to 18 May. I still had my XO, LT Tupa, but he was getting short on his tour like many others. My six months time as a company commander was up on 10 June, so the company would be receiving a new company commander within the next few weeks. My well-oiled and well-trained company machine had lost or would lose most of its parts. However, the U.S. soldier copes well with adversity and adapts quickly. If given a little time, I knew we could bring the company back to a well-honed fighting unit capable of holding its own against anything the NVA could throw at us.

The next day I flew to the firebase to see Colonel Gannon, get the latest information on my status, and find out what the company was doing. 1LT Allen and 1LT Peter Juvet, a new lieutenant, had gone off to the 3-12th Infantry to be interviewed for jobs within that battalion. The idea was that if they were selected, the 3-12th would give us a captain who would probably be my replacement. Just like the professional sports leagues; two lieutenants for one captain, or one lieutenant and one captain for a great NCO, etc. Because of the stateside replacement cycle, battalion commanders, with the understanding of the Division personnel officer, made by-name horse trades for personnel so they could achieve a mix of new replacements with experienced officers or NCOs.

I got back to the Company in the field on the morning of 6 June 67 and started it moving. The unit had exchanged fire with three NVA the previous day, and no injuries on either side. It was always a mystery to me why so many tons of explosive and firepower were used during meeting engagements such as that, with no casualties between the parties. I had come a long way from my earlier fire eating days when I aggressively hoped for enemy contact. While I did not shirk from finding the enemy and engaging him whenever I found him, I was all too aware that when I did, we would lose good men as we had in the big fights in March and May. I did not grow more cautious, but I did remember to be thankful on a daily basis that we had not sustained any casualties for that day.

It was during this time that I realized there were only seventeen men remaining, who had been in the company when I had assumed command on 10 December 1966. Over the next couple of months I was able to find jobs out of the field for almost all of them, and I didn't go home until they had all departed as well. I am sure that did not mean much to anyone else, but it did to me.

As we moved through the days, we found the NVA were not bunching up in our area as they had in May, so the few contacts we had, provided broadening experience for many of the new replacements. These few sightings were a good way to get the new guys warmed up without getting anyone hurt. I knew we needed a little light contact to keep things realistic.

In some Montagnard villages through which we traveled, the headman insisted on our partaking of the village hospitality. This sometimes entailed listening to a village concert played on bronze or metal gongs strung on a wire, string, or rope stretched between poles or trees. The players struck the gongs with sticks or shafts with material padding the end, resembling xylophone drumsticks. Each gong had a different tone, depending on whether it was hit in the middle or the side. If there were several gongs, that many men played the tune, but if there were only three or four, the band consisted of just one player.

Then, there was the rice wine; a powerful fermented drink in a clay pot, which we sipped through hollow tubes, sometimes with more than one person sipping through their tube at the same time. After the first try, I always tried to find some polite excuse keeping the company moving without being culturally insensitive. I couldn't think of anything worse than to be caught by the NVA, woozy-eyed after even a small sip at the wine pot. The villagers were extremely poor and lived a hard subsistence life. They were old-looking and wizened while still young, they chewed betel nut, and lost their teeth early in life due to poor diet. Even so, the few times that I saw them when they, and we, didn't need to be overly concerned about the war, they seemed happy and friendly as they went about their normal activities.

In a few instances, we worked with a Military Intelligence team and searched Montagnard villages with South Vietnamese military interpreters. The villagers were segregated into groups of men, women, and children then interrogated individually about the presence or whereabouts of enemy sympathizers, and members of the VC and NVA. Some of the villages were well-to-do by Montagnard standards: wealthy with pigs, water buffalo, chickens, dogs, and everything else you might find on a rural farm except for the high technology items like electricity, gas, or running water. The houses were built on stilts and were thatch covered. They were different in architectural style from the coastal houses, where many were built directly on the ground, but otherwise used the same type of local materials. After interrogating an entire village, which sometimes took an entire day, the interrogation team and the interpreters would say if they had identified suspected NVA supporters. If so, they took those individuals away for additional questioning.

We were resupplied on the 9th in a manner that was rather haphazard. Everything came in sporadically and disorganized, putting everyone in a foul mood. While Chaplain Woehr came and held services, Colonel Gannon flew in and said that all the officer tradeoffs were postponed. LT Allen was on R&R and LT Juvet was in the hospital with the wounded foot he had received when he was with the 1st Infantry Division before coming to us. 2LT Kasey King, my new first platoon leader, was the only officer I had in the field.

My six months of command were celebrated on the 10th with an all day rain and patrolling in the mountains, where we found nothing but friendly Montagnards. That evening we moved to a brigade firebase called Combined Arms Hill, which was not far from Jackson Hole, where we were to be the security company. We provided 24-hour security, set up ambushes, and patrolled the general area to deny the enemy the ability to launch mortar attacks against the base.

Village burning after evacuation

Due to the additional encroachment by the NVA into the western part of Pleiku Province, it was decided to make more of the area a free fire zone, thus denying the enemy the support found in the villages. As part of a resettlement program, Montagnard villages were evacuated and removed to other pre-built villages outside Pleiku. This did not make the villagers happy at all. They were being moved from their traditional lands and way of life to begin new lives in the flatlands in new houses. It was a Vietnamese decision. We merely provided protection for the villagers and the transport folks.

In doing so, we usually surrounded a village and checked out the area to ensure there were no nasty surprises waiting for us in the woods or brush around the village. Then the South Vietnamese military and U.S. military intelligence teams came in to make sure there were no hideouts in the village itself. The inhabitants had been notified days earlier, but on moving day were given a time frame of a few hours to gather their important possessions and to move them outside the village proper, where they would await transport to their new homes. If the village was near a road, trucks were used. If there were no roads, everything was moved by cargo helicopters. It was an amazing sight to see the number of villagers, and the quantities of livestock, furniture, cooking pots, musical gongs, and clothing that could be put onto a Chinook helicopter. Dependent upon the size of the village, it generally took all day for the process to be completed. Then we were instructed to torch the village so that the NVA would have nothing to use when the people were gone. By the time we were finished, there was nothing left but charred ruins in a jungle clearing. In a couple of years the jungle would reclaim the entire area.

There was an intelligence rumor that both Combined Arms Hill and Jackson Hole were to be mortared and attacked soon.

...ne logical enemy assembly area would be in the mountains west of these bases, so we received the mission to check the area. We climbed into the area and set up platoon-sized ambushes.

Because we had received so many replacements over such a short period, there wasn't a lot of time to train them in everything they needed to know. This resulted in on-the-job training for some things. PFC Ralph McDermott was one of our new replacements. He posted a story on Homer Steedley's website that I repeat here because it tells what it was like to be a new guy with little time to learn what was needed. I must accept responsibility for any training that wasn't done, but we tried to give everybody as much as we could. When we moved west to spoil any NVA attacks, Ralph was a member of the third platoon. He described the experience like this:

"...When it came time to go to the boonies we humped out of there (Jackson Hole) *in platoon size units to the west toward a high ridgeline running north/south. A few days before we left I was made the M79 guy. I had fired 1 round from an M79 and that was about 3 months prior in Advanced Individual Training. I wasn't familiar with the weapon. We had started up the side of that ridge, everyone was bent over with the weight of the rucks. I was bent over, M79 resting on an ammo pouch on my web gear, my forearm was resting on the top of the stock. Somehow the lock for the trigger guard was tripped and the guard slid to the side. My forearm resting on top o the stock slid the safe to "OFF" and "BLOOP!" I watched that round bury itself in the soft dirt at my feet, WOW — what a rush!!! I'm still thanking that guy who thought of the self arming thing for those rounds. That was the first time I was to hear the word "**WHO FIRED THAT ROUND!?!** So much for noise discipline. There were about 30 other guys not happy with me right then. We traveled farther up the side of the ridge and about half way up we set up for the night. It was*

a small, tight perimeter, pitch black, monsoon rain, scared as hell — first night in the bush.

In the morning we ate breakfast and slowly made our way up the top of the ridge getting there in the late morning. At the top there was a trail following the ridge so we set up a perimeter bisecting it to eat our lunch. One M60 on the North, the other on the South. The perimeter is maybe 15 yards across. Had just started to heat some C's when the "gun" on the south end opens up with a really long burst of maybe 50–75 rounds. Hit the dirt and laid there and waited. I heard some low sounds coming from our guys over there and then my squad leader "Hurst" comes crawling over to me. "Mac, come with me!" So we go to where the M60 is setting on the trail. He tells me that he and I are going to go down the trail and check out a body that is laying about 25 yards away. I told him I'd really like to have an M16 in my hands when we did this, in fact I got a little adamant about it. So someone hands me a "buckshot round" for the M79. That round wasn't very deadly looking and I'd only shot two rounds from an M79 and one of them was the day before that went into the dirt at my feet, but I loaded it and we went down the trail. Hurst first, me after on the other side. I wasn't prepared for what I was about to see. Hurst worked his way up to the body and threw back the AK-47, he was dead. Hurst worked his way around a little bend in the trail and just a few yards more there were three more NVA, all dead. There was body matter sprayed everywhere. The gunner had killed four with that burst. We policed up their weapons and equipment and took it back up the trail. They were traveling with very little, only about 90 rounds apiece with a few Chicoms (grenades) and some water. It was said that they must have been a recon team. I wouldn't eat much for a few days but I learned a valuable lesson about growing complacent and bunching up on the trail. The saying *"let's have 5 meters or one round will get you all" made a lot of sense. So my first few days in the boonies with B-1-8 were a real eye opener for this 19 year old."*

As McDermott said, on 19 June the third platoon killed four NVA with weapons, but the rest of us made no other contact (I was traveling with the new fourth platoon). The following night we were subjected to a throwing contest with hand grenades and which lasted sporadically all night. The next morning we had one WIA and they had two KIA.

Colonel Gannon came in to congratulate us on our contact; it seemed we had the only battalion success since 20 May. He also brought some mail that officially made me an infantry officer again.(I had come back on active duty as an engineer officer from my time spent with the National Guard and h requested a return to the infantry branch but had not ' anything.) With all the infantry stuff we had bee·   ., I had forgotten all about it. It had only taken 1   .is for the Army to get the administrative details do   .as ironic that I was now being transferred back to the Infantry Branch as I completed my rifle company command.

During a resupply day, with C rations, ammunition, clothing, and mail all over the LZ, we were told to move immediately to Jackson Hole. This was a problem because we had to clean up the supply stuff, get it distributed, and throw stuff on the outbound helicopter. Jackson Hole was a good fifteen kilometers away and the time was getting late. We moved fast, however, and were able to get the LZ cleaned up and move out. We were looking forward to a shower and a cold drink of some kind.

As we moved onto the base, I reported to the Battalion CP where Major Mercer told me not to stand down, but to continue on to secure, by sundown, another firebase ten kilometers farther away. I was furious, and of course blamed it on Major

Mercer who, in my opinion, took great glee in inconveniencing my life whenever he could. I objected that my guys had been running since mid-morning, were tired and thirsty, deserved a break, and it just wasn't fair to put this additional burden on them at that time. It was not a pretty scene.

Murphy's Laws:

"If you take more than your fair share of objectives, you will get more than your fair share of objectives to take."

Colonel Gannon stepped in and made it clear that the move made sense because we were not committed in the field like the other companies. It was just the logical thing to do. I could intellectually understand the logic, of course. But I still had to instruct my guys to keep going after they had been told we would be standing down for a while at the end of a grueling march. It was already mid-afternoon and we had to have the area secured by sundown. Still muttering to myself, we moved out. Fortunately there was a relatively secure dirt road to use, but it was hot and dusty. I set a fast pace since we did not want to be moving into an area after darkness. I detailed one platoon to pick up the stragglers and charged. As we were moving out, I remembered Murphy's Laws.

While we were on the road, I was notified to release one platoon to a cavalry unit that needed more infantry for a fight. I assigned the fourth platoon, which helicopters picked up on the road, while the rest of us kept heading for the new firebase. Even after the platoon had been picked up, the company was stretched out on either side of the road for hundreds of meters. I was able to see most of it at one time, and it looked like the pictures of WWII and Korea; soldiers walking on both sides of the road, keeping about 10 meters separation so they were not as vulnerable to mortar or enemy fire. The picture is etched in my memory. It was a proud moment to me because I knew that this was MY company and that many of us had done great things together. I knew somehow, that this was a one-time event, and the image would never be repeated for me.

Company B forced march

As the column progressed, we had ten men fall out from heat exhaustion, but we kept going. We got to our destination just before dark and cleared the zone around it. The next day we started building bunkers for the security perimeter in anticipation of the arrival of the battalion and an artillery battery that afternoon. After staying there for only two days, the entire battalion picked up again and moved to Dragon

Mountain to participate in Operation Stillwell, east of Pleiku and just west of Qui Nhon. It appeared that the NVA were starting to infiltrate the areas around the towns of Kontum and Dak To to the north of us.

CHAPTER FORTY FOUR

WHEN WE GOT TO DRAGON MOUNTAIN, Colonel Gannon pulled me aside and just looked steadily at me for a moment. At this special treatment I became very apprehensive and knew I was not going to like what he was going to say. Then he told me, "*Bob, I'm sorry to tell you this because you've been a great company commander, but I have to fire you!*"

The battalion had not received a new captain replacement, so I immediately assumed the action was because of my attitude about the extended hike a few days before. Being relieved was the furthest thing from my mind and I was shocked and devastated.

Swallowing hard, I automatically came to attention and waited for more. He just looked back and waited for me to say something. Speech failed me. I couldn't say anything so I just looked at him waiting for details and condemnation. He finally smiled his mysterious little smile and said, "*I might as well find something for you to do... Mercer has been pulled up to be the Brigade S3, so you are going to have to take his place as the new Battalion Operations Officer!*"

What a rush! Sour and Sweet. My emotions were on a roller coaster...from the depths to the heights in one easy minute. I was almost as ecstatic as when I had received notice to take over Company B.

If I couldn't be an infantry company commander anymore, then I wanted to be an infantry battalion S3 in wartime. When I thanked Colonel Gannon for the trust he was showing a mere captain, he said that while he wholeheartedly agreed and approved the selection, Major Mercer made the initial recommendation. Who would have thought it? I always knew I liked the guy!

Even though I knew it was coming, I wasn't prepared for the suddenness of my reassignment, or the emotion. I had been through the fires of Hell with these guys and they were my brothers and sons, all at the same time. In some ways they were closer to me than my family, which is what shared hazards and combat does to a soldier. Knowing you eventually will have to relinquish the bonds you have developed, does not make it emotionally easier when the time finally comes.

Since we were in the Division base camp, the company had a little beer bust that night and gave me a rousing send off, which warmed my heart. I had tears in my eyes and a clogged throat when I made an incomprehensible speech. I have no idea what I said. Neither did the men, but they gave me some loud cheers anyway, probably for stopping. The truth was, I was overwhelmed that I was leaving the company so suddenly after such an intense period lasting almost seven months. I had managed to stay in command longer than many other company commanders to which I gave credit to the professionalism and bravery of the amazing warriors I led.

Colonel Gannon was present at the party and he let the company express their emotions at the news of my leaving (they were quite boisterous and loud and obviously on their 2d or

3d beers), he let me stay only a few minutes before escorting me to battalion headquarters and my new job.

It seemed we had to prepare plans for the new operation in quick time, since it was slated to start the next afternoon.

CHAPTER FORTY FIVE

THE OFFICIAL CHANGE OF COMMAND was effective on 5 July 1967. 1LT Art Trujillo, the Recon Platoon Leader was temporarily assigned to take my place in Company B until another captain arrived. He knew the company, plus the policies and the SOPs I had in place, helping him make the transition from running one platoon to four.

So...after two months as the S1 of the battalion and seven months as a company commander, I was now the Operations Officer, or S3, of the battalion.

One thing that bothered me, was that I knew the position called for a major and even though I was a fairly senior captain, I didn't think I would be able to keep it for very long. There weren't many major positions in the Division. In a combat battalion, only the Battalion Executive Officer and the S3 positions called for this rank. As a result, any infantry major worth his salt wanted to be with a combat battalion, just as I had wanted a rifle company. Granted, it was a career enhancing move, and some narcissistic officers wanted it for that reason only. For most of us, who loved to be with infantry soldiers who put their lives on the line, it was perhaps the last opportunity to be close to combat, and still be able to make direct contributions to the outcomes of battles.

I was resigned to the possibility that I would become an Assistant S3 when a major was assigned, which I anticipated would not be very long. In the meantime, I had an operations shop to run to keep the battalion flowing smoothly. My first job was to plan a move of the battalion to the northeast of Pleiku, as part of Operation Stillwell.

A battalion move was not a simple thing. Hundreds of moving parts needed to be coordinated before the helicopters landed to start things off.

First, we needed to identify an area for the battalion command post, and the artillery battery that accompanied it. This was accomplished by a map review of the Area of Operations specified by the Brigade Operations Order. We identified potential open areas that would give us sufficient room for the five or six 105mm howitzers of the battalion's artillery battery and the 4.2 inch mortars plus space for other additional weapons systems we might receive. This might be a mechanized twin-40mm Duster, a tank team, some engineers, or even dog teams. Next, the site had to be on good defensible terrain since the NVA could easily make a ground attack against a firebase as well as a moving company. The most important part of the selection process was to choose a relatively central location from where the guns could support the line companies in their operations. Once a map reconnaissance was accomplished, a flyover would be done, if possible, to see any hidden obstacles that didn't show on the map.

While this planning was underway, a request for helicopter support was made. This would mean heavy-lift helicopters for each of the howitzers and all of the artillery ammunition. Since the battalion had gotten more sophisticated, it had built its communications into a steel box, called a Tactical Operations Center (TOC). The TOC could be airlifted by a CH47 Chinook helicopter and placed as needed within the proposed perimeter of the firebase.

By this time, the artillery battery knew how many helicopters it took to move the battery and its equipment, as did the operations staff for the remainder of the battalion.

An infantry company would make either an air or ground assault into the new location, sweep the area to ensure there were no hostiles then secure the area. They would begin to make their own foxholes and bunkers to protect the perimeter of the firebase.

If the site selected was a new site, brush and trees needed to be cut to clear around the outside of the perimeter. Barbed wire would be laid, along with claymores mines. Trip flares would be rigged to provide early warning if NVA tried to cross open areas. Individual soldiers had to dig holes, fill sandbags and cut stout logs or small trees for overhead cover from enemy mortar rounds. It also entailed providing men to the battalion headquarters to help fill sandbags with the battalion staff in order to protect the TOC. Sandbags were stacked and piled around and on top of the TOC to provide added protection from mortar blasts. It was doubtful the TOC would survive a direct hit, but it was fairly well protected against flying shrapnel and air bursts.

The firebase moved in two phases, for even though the battalion headquarters was moving, it still had companies in the field to control. It had to be able to maintain contact with them and provide support. A portion of the headquarters went first—about half of the operations staff and half of the artillery tubes and 4.2 mortars. This left half of the battalion headquarters with an indirect fire support capability, still active in the old location in the event the companies needed help during the move. Once the new firebase's tactical operation center was up and running along with the first phase artillery and mortars, it assumed operational control, the remaining staff and indirect fire support began their move.

The Assistant S3 (Air) was responsible for the control of aircraft involved in the move. In its initial stages, helicopter gunships circled the new area and patrolled the general region hunting for NVA forces that might disrupt and attack the movement. Once the area was announced as secure, large crane helicopters or CH-47 Chinooks, flew out of the old location carrying heavy lift items. HU1-Bs, the ever-present Huey slicks, brought in people and equipment.

It was like moving a small town, with all the infrastructure requirements. The guns and mortars were the priority, along with the fire direction control and the battalion command and control facility. Communications were mandatory, so radios and antennas had to be set up in the most efficient manner. Net loads of ammunition for the guns were swung into place. Sweating men, stripped to the waist, did the work, red dust adhering to their bodies and getting in their eyes. Some wore bandanna sweatbands, or T shirts over their faces to filter out the dust blowing from the helicopter rotor wash. Water trailers were airlifted into the logistics area of the firebase. A small kitchen also arrived to feed the firebase occupants at least one hot meal a day. With the infantry company on the perimeter, the artillery battery (almost the size of an infantry company), the battalion headquarters staff, the Reconnaissance and 4.2 Mortar Platoons, all possibly augmented with engineers and additional support elements, the firebase might contain 500 or more occupants.

The move was executed with the precision of an opera or ballet, but also with a huge commotion. The extremely loud engine noises of the different helicopters were a constant background chorus as they brought in their loads to different parts of the firebase. The overall ambience was augmented by the shouts of men directing where things were to go. Blasts of dust with flying pieces of dirt, branches and small rocks were everywhere. After depositing their loads, the aircraft added screaming power to their engines to take off and do it all over again.

Tents couldn't be erected until all the helicopter loads for a particular area of the firebase had been delivered. To do otherwise, might blow away the tent canvas, possibly into a helicopter rotor blade, thereby creating casualties. The only people to have any kind of physical or noise protection were the infantrymen on the perimeter who had completed their bunkers and those out beyond the perimeter on patrol to keep any NVA off-balance during the move, and those few men on operations duty inside the TOC. Even so, during the normal four to six hours it took to relocate this constantly swirling behemoth, the firebase was a miserable place.

Control was a misnomer. We had plans that called for what should be moved in sequence, and we identified who was responsible for what, but Murphy was a soldier and helicopters sometimes broke, or were pulled out for a higher priority. There were small things that delayed moves, or threw sequences out of order. Slings of artillery ammunition were misplaced next to the mortars, causing manual double handling once the helicopters were released. You could never have too many eyes on the multiple choke points. Supervision and oversight imposed a constant strain on all concerned.

Radio conversations were at a minimum because the TOC operators had difficulty hearing anyone, even though this was one of the most vulnerable periods for a company in the bush. The artillery and mortar support was cut in half, radio communications with the battalion was sometimes difficult, and people were focused on getting moved in and operational.

Fortunately, the NVA never figured this out, and so never placed us in a position where we had to support a company in contact, while at the same time, moving the entire support base. Never, during my time, at least, was a moving firebase ever attacked while being set up.

All of the planning for my first battalion move as the S3, occurred and was disseminated to the companies in one night. The next day we moved all three companies and established a firebase northeast of Pleiku.

The area for Operation Stillwell had seen a great deal of NVA movement, but the NVA was avoiding contact. It turned out they were getting ready for a big push against Dak To and Kon Tum. Since they were assembling a large force, they wanted to avoid contact until they were ready for their big attack. As a result, we patrolled aggressively, but saw little contact.

On 14 July, the division terminated the operation and the battalion was airlifted back to Camp Enari at Pleiku. The next day, on 15 July, our battalion moved into an old firebase to continue patrolling operations.

The following week was quiet, but on 20 July, Company B made contact with an NVA patrol of approximately 15 men. This was the first major contact for the company since it had received all its new replacements...the baptism of fire resulted in one U.S. killed (PFC Michael Menchise) and six wounded.

The next morning, as the company was leaving its overnight site, one of the soldiers (SGT Paul Domke) was killed by his own grenade. Apparently he had straightened the pin in the grenade in order to make it easier to pull when he needed it. This was a dangerous technique some soldiers used when they anticipated getting involved in a firefight, and felt the need to pull and throw their grenades without the added delay time the bent pin created. In this instance, the grenade was hooked onto his web belt by its spoon handle. As he moved through the brush, the straightened pin was pulled from the grenade, allowing the spring in the handle to flip the grenade from his belt and arm it. The grenade exploded and killed the sergeant. PFC Robert "Bone" Hemminger was about 15 meters behind him and still remembers the "beehive" that whizzed past his ear when the grenade went off.

There was another item of significance to me...a new major was assigned to the battalion. However, Colonel Gannon told him that since he was new to Vietnam, it would be better if he watched what I did until I left country. He assured the major that he would get credit for his full tour as an S3, but that for all practical purposes, I would remain the S3 for the rest of my time. I was extremely pleased; I would be able to finish out my tour in a position that would enable me to plan and develop operations for the battalion.

The major was a former marine but had gotten a commission in the Army, so he had some additional experience that could assist him in operations. He was a great guy and we made a good team in identifying potential problem areas and developing solutions for them. It wasn't that I was the S3 and he was my assistant, it was that we recognized each other's strengths and collaborated together on the problems. We both spoke Spanish, so when we communicated on the radio with each other, we were fairly certain the NVA were not understanding our transmissions. With both of us working together instead of in a superior/subordinate relationship, we provided a stronger operations capability to the battalion. Having two experienced officers in the TOC, albeit with different backgrounds, Colonel Gannon was extremely pleased with the situation; it left him more time to oversee the entire battalion, including the rear areas.

On August 12, three more soldiers of Company B were killed, again by an artillery short round. SP4 Tom Healey described it this way:

"We had a minor conflict on August 12, 1967. We called in air support and artillery and we threw out smoke and the NVA threw the same smoke back at us...when the artillery landed, it landed on top of us. I was a little higher up the hillside, but three other guys were below me. I got hit in the legs and they got hit in the upper body and died.".

The results were more than minor. In addition to the three KIA, (SGT George Alvarez, SP4 Leonard Ludwig and PFC Edward Randazzo), there were 14 wounded besides Healey, more than fifty percent of the platoon's fighting strength. The explanation I received was murky, and I have been unable to obtain a clear investigation result. One soldier said that the new company commander had a marking round fired, and instead of firing two more to validate the first one, he fired for effect based upon the one smoke round. The rounds fell on the first platoon.

A second story was that another unit was working in the same general area, and had called in a fire mission at the same time as Company B. The Fire Direction Center was supposed to ensure that fires requested by the units did not conflict, but apparently the two smoke rounds fired by the artillery were too close to tell which belonged to whom. As a result, whoever was calling fires for Company B oriented on the smoke round fired by the other company, and adjusted from it. The fire for effect hit the first platoon in a single moment. It was a sad fact that sometimes we hurt ourselves just as much as the enemy did.

The battalion continued patrolling operations and search and destroy missions, but made no contact with the NVA.

We moved the firebase several more times, but there were no significant activities.

As we all knew must happen at some point, Colonel Gannon gave up the battalion to our new battalion commander, LTC Gail Wilson.

Colonel Wilson was a good officer. He understood when he didn't know something and should listen to the staff. As with our previous battalion commanders, he liked to visit the troops, and, as he became known throughout the battalion, he became well respected.

He had an idiosyncrasy that took me, being a coffee drinker, a little while to get used to; he was a tea drinker. My memory may be at fault, but as I recollect, Wilson had been an exchange officer, or had some other assignment in the United Kingdom and had developed a taste for tea. Since tea was not in the supply system like coffee, it was difficult to find the right kind of tea for him to drink. It being important to keep the battalion commander happy, we stretched our resources to discover where the right kind of tea might be found. Even though Vietnam was a major exporter of tea, it wasn't available to us during the war. At last we discovered a kind he liked at a resort named Vung Tau. This was an in-country R&R station in the southern part of Vietnam that the Australians and New Zealanders secured. They seemed to like the same kind of tea as the commander.

We commandeered a helicopter one day, and with the connivance of the two helicopter pilots, sent one of our trusted staff to Vung Tau to obtain tea for the colonel. As might have been predicted, the helicopter developed engine problems and had to spend the night in the R&R camp, before returning the next day with a load of tea. Colonel Wilson was most appreciative, but we never told him from where it had come, nor how we had obtained it. A happy commander makes better decisions, so I considered the use of the helicopter an official supply run.

I was informed that my new departure from overseas date was 5 September, which gave me a 30 day drop from my original date of 5 October. On 2 September I arranged to fly back to the division area to prepare for my return to the US.

On the morning of the 2d, Colonel Wilson had a meeting at the Oasis and he and I left the firebase at the same time. We waved to each other as our respective helicopters took off and flew in opposite directions. When I landed in Camp Enari and got a ride to the battalion area, I was met with the news that during my flight back to base camp, Colonel Wilson's helicopter had developed engine trouble and crashed, killing all on board. There was no evidence of enemy fire. Had I not returned that day, I would have been on the same helicopter. Chance affects each life in different ways. With my last days marred by tragedy, I was as glad to leave as I had been to arrive.

I returned to the U.S. to another company command assignment at Fort Bliss, Texas, teaching basic trainees how to work and survive in Vietnam. I used all the experience and techniques I had learned to try and prepare them for combat. I received letters from some who returned safely and who gave me much of the credit. I had outstanding Drill Sergeants who did their jobs, so as is the usual case in the Army, it was a team effort.

Back in Vietnam, as I indicated earlier, the NVA was avoiding US troops so they could build up their forces in the region. Finally they were ready to move on the cities of Kon Tum and Dak To.

General Peers, decided that he would flood the area with U.S. troops to spoil the intended attack;, he did so with elements of the 1st Brigade, 4th Infantry Division, the 173d Airborne Brigade and units from the South Vietnamese Army.

The resulting battles in late October and November 1967, stopped the North Vietnamese from destroying U.S. forces prior to their country-wide effort in TET of 1968. The 1-8th Infantry was heavily involved, and A and C Companies were awarded another Presidential Unit Citation for their participation in the costly battles.

them for over forty years, we still have that bond, created in those moments of crashing artillery, hornet's nests of bullets and cemented in mud, sand and blood. Many men have said that they never felt so alive as when they were closest to death. Nobody expects someone who has not experienced this feeling to understand it, so they come to reunions to remember those times with others of like spirit and to remind themselves that at one time they were part of a Great Event.

I attend two reunions associated with my military career: one is with my classmates from my OCS class of 2-60, a traumatic and stressful event in its own way, and the other, far more emotional, with the former members of the 1st Battalion, 8th Infantry Regiment of the 4th Infantry Division, Class of 1966/67. The latter provides a closure of sorts for many of us and for others it provides an opportunity to vent their angers and frustrations on behalf of those who didn't come back. For all of us it provides the ability to connect with kindred souls who have survived our own Valley of the Shadow of Death.

The difficulties of transitioning from combat to civilian life experienced by some Vietnam Veterans have been publicized time and again. Those now returning from Afghanistan and Iraq have similar stories. I believe the antagonistic attitude of our citizens and leaders in the Vietnam era shamed the American people and have now encouraged more programs to help our current veterans. There can never be too much help for those who return from wars. They should all be treated with dignity and respect and shown appreciation for the time out of their lives they have given to their country.

Those who join the military sign a contract with the nation—they promise to support and defend the Constitution against all enemies, foreign and domestic. In return, the nation agrees to provide certain services. We must take care of those who take care of us. It cannot be a one-way street. For those who go in harm's way to protect the nation, those services must be maintained or we will soon find ourselves bereft of our amazing warriors.

The men and women of America's military deserve the best the country can provide...people can help through their vote for rational and responsible government representatives who understand that only a strong military can defend our nation.

This book is my way of passing on the story of what happened to some of us when we were young. I have no fantasies that the stories I have told will have far-reaching effects on the general populace, but if one person reading this, reaches out to a veteran and thanks him or her for their service, it will have accomplished something worthwhile.

I salute those of you who served with me for your sacrifices at home and abroad. In the hard times of battle, I was seldom fearful because I had my God and my men with me. Thank you.

APPENDIX 1
4th Infantry Division

THE ORGANIZATION OF THE division in 1966 was similar to other US Army infantry divisions of the time. It started with the individual soldier as the basic building block and then consisted of small unit organizations to which the soldier was assigned. There were variations in actual numbers and specific weapons, but the overall organization followed a basic pattern.

Infantry soldiers were formed into teams and squads. A rifle squad was approximately 12 men and a team was half that. They were led by the team and squad leaders, who were supposed to be junior Non-Commissioned Officers (NCOs in the rank of corporals and sergeants), but in combat this could turn out to be the most senior private or private first class.

An infantry platoon consisted of three rifle squads and a weapons squad. The weapons squad carried two machine guns, which were positioned in a firefight by the platoon sergeant or the platoon leader in a spot where they could provide the best fire support to the platoon. A second or first lieutenant was usually the platoon leader, while a platoon sergeant was the second in command.

A company was made up of three rifle platoons and a weapons platoon. The weapons platoon was armed with the company's indirect fire support, the 81 millimeter (mm) mortar.

The company was the first level of organization that had a dedicated administrative and supply function in addition to combat troops. It was commanded by a captain (CPT) who had a first sergeant (1SG) and who was the senior NCO in the company, to assist him in organizing and overseeing all elements of the unit. There were generally six officers in the company...the commander, his executive officer (1LT)), and four platoon leaders (1/2LT). When a second lieutenant was promoted to first lieutenant, he was not reassigned from his platoon but rather continued his duties until circumstances offered other opportunities. In the 4th ID, because there were few roads where the companies operated, the company mortars were found to be too bulky to carry. The weapons platoon became the company's fourth rifle platoon, albeit armed with only a single machine gun.

When the Division deployed to Vietnam, there were three rifle companies (A, B, C) in each rifle battalion, which was commanded by a lieutenant colonel (LTC). Another rifle company, Company D, was added to the battalion after the first year. The battalion also had a headquarters company to provide administrative and logistical support to the battalion staff, and other elements that might be attached or assigned to it. There was also a Reconnaissance (Recon) Platoon for various tasks having to do with security and surveillance. It also served as a small reserve.

A Brigade, commanded by a colonel (COL), had three battalions plus support troops and was the primary structure around which combat troops were deployed. In the 4th ID, there were three brigades, as well as armored cavalry, artillery, engineers, military police, aviation, maintenance, transportation units and other support and service, or combat organizations, which could go under the operational control of the brigades, or the battalions, depending upon the needs of the operation. The overall division was commanded by a two-star, major general (MG).

When all positions were filled, a rifle company might have 180 men. A battalion could have upwards of 800 soldiers. Depending on attachments, a brigade could have around 3,500 troops.

APPENDIX 2
Training and Preparation

THE "TRAIN AND RETAIN" METHOD for filling the division to combat strength, meant that the Division officers and NCOs accepted recruits fresh from civilian life. They put them through eight weeks of Basic Combat Training (BCT), and another eight weeks of Advanced Individual Training (AIT) in their respective Military Occupational Specialties (MOS). Following that, the men remained in their units where they learned their unit and organizational duties.

Basic Combat Training moves an individual from civilian life to the military. It involves developing the soldier's physical body, while cultivating a mental outlook that will make him capable of working as a member of a team focused on a goal. Physical training is stressed throughout the entire period in order to prepare an individual for the stresses of combat. The recruit learns drill and ceremonies, unit traditions (an important aspect in developing individual loyalty to a unit and fellow soldiers). He also learns how to march, which not only teaches him the most efficient way of moving from one location to another but also develops teamwork and instills mental alertness so that he will obey orders instantaneously, essential in combat for survival. The soldier learns core skills: how to handle a weapon, and how to operate as a member of a team. As time goes on, training is provided in hand to hand combat, the use of the bayonet, map reading and land navigation, first aid and obstacle courses. Toward the end of the BCT phase, Chemical, Biological, Radiological and Nuclear training is conducted to prepare the soldier to fight in a contaminated environment. He/she also spends time firing the rifle, throwing hand grenades, general weapons training, and always the constant physical training...

Advanced Individual Training is focused on individual Military Occupational Specialties, determined after a series of tests administered the first day or two of entering the service. If there is an aptitude for medicine, the service member might go to Fort Sam Houston in Texas for medical training to become a medic. If you were an administrative person you might go to the former Fort Benjamin Harrison, Indiana for schooling in military administration...if you indicated an interest in mathematics, you might receive artillery training at Fort Sill, Oklahoma, or mortar training at your home base where you would learn everything about the weapon, how to determine azimuths, and how to adjust fire, among other complicated computations. Other specialties required in an infantry unit included supply and logistics personnel, communications, mechanics and heavy weapons specialists. Then there was the regular infantry squad that had machine gunners, anti-tank gunners, grenadiers, and riflemen. They had to learn and practice fire and maneuver infantry tactics and of course the know-how to use everybody else's weapon, even the enemy's.

Everybody else in the U.S. Army existed to support this small element. Even tanks and artillery needed infantrymen to accomplish their missions.

Unit training took the individual's basic and advanced training to a higher level. There the squads and platoons learned how to operate as part of a company, while the companies operated within the organization of a battalion. The unit training fused the disparate and individual components together until the platoons, companies, and battalions understood their roles as a cohesive whole.

The 4th Infantry Division was filled with men from varying walks of life, different social, financial, racial and educational backgrounds. Friends in high school dared each other to join the army, then joined with them when they found others called their dare. Men knew they were to be drafted, so joined or volunteered for the draft so they could control the timing of their training and service. For the 1-8th, men came mostly from the heartland...Indiana, Illinois, Iowa, Ohio, Wisconsin and Michigan. Others came from the east coast...New York, Pennsylvania and Maryland. There was a sprinkling of a few southern boys, but not many. The timing of the draft and the numbers assigned to individuals controlled who was finally to become a part of the unit. A number of these men knew each other before they were enlisted, while others were as strange to each other as different species. The training developed bonds, however, and when the unit shipped out, many close friendships had been established.

The "train and retain" technique ensured that there would be a great deal of bonding and team-building among the soldiers, which in turn fostered better tactical efficiency and mutual trust among individual soldiers. However, the development of close ties also had the disadvantage of creating personal uncertainties, when close friends began to die in combat. Because losses were emotional events, survivors established cliques and shut out new men because they did not want to establish new emotional ties to someone who might be killed. The men who went through training and deployed together labeled themselves "originals" and it became difficult for replacements to break into the cliques unless they were mentored or sponsored by one of the older hands. While this method of recruiting and training military organizations has proved to be the fastest way of creating and preparing a large organization for war, it has had the same advantages and disadvantages since mankind first began fighting in organized units.

The "train and retain" technique also presented a difficulty to the Division in that tours were for a year. Rather than have to retrain an essentially new division every 12 months, individual tour lengths had to be staggered in order to provide a healthy rotation that did not simultaneously denude the division of combat experience. Some men found themselves able to return to the U.S. in less than a year, while others found themselves extended for a month or two in order to balance the replacement schedule. In the case of the 1-8th, however, large combat losses during the first year ensured that the unit received sufficient replacements to refresh the companies while maintaining experience levels.

The NCO pre-deployment situation in the 1-8th however, was not good. Sergeant Major Ritchie was the senior NCO of the battalion, First Sergeant Stanley (Pappy) Holland had the Headquarters and Headquarters Company, and First Sergeant David McNerney was already the first sergeant of Company A, while First Sergeant Drexel Finley was the senior NCO of Company C. All of these men were top notch experienced personnel, and for the most part, their platoon sergeants were in good shape...however, the structure below platoon sergeant relied upon newly promoted personnel who were as inexperienced as the soldiers they led.

Several NCOs elected to retire, or to leave the service, rather than spend their last year or two in a war zone. They were hardly to be blamed. After a lifetime of military service and approaching retirement, the concern to the family was that the soldier might go to Vietnam and be killed. This was of great concern to a family, or spouse, who had endured years of hardships following the soldier around the world. To lose him just as a safer life beckoned, was not an attractive option. While these NCOs were undoubtedly as patriotic as anyone, there is a life after the military. Wives and families were instrumental in encouraging some of these retirement applications. What this meant was that when the battalion deployed, there were many NCO positions that had to be filled by younger and less experienced personnel.

When the first sergeant of Company B announced his immediate retirement, the company was fortunate in that Platoon Sergeant Victor Lopez had just arrived in the battalion from Germany. Lopez had been selected for first sergeant rank after his last tour but was sent to Fort Lewis before he could be assigned to a company. When Company B needed a first sergeant, Lopez was available. He remembers that out of the 48 NCOs he was supposed to have, there were only eight experienced NCOs assigned when the unit was scheduled for deployment. The Division solved this with a stop-gap measure; authorizing PFC's to be assigned in acting NCO positions (fire team and assistant squad leaders). Naturally, this resulted in a less-experienced NCO structure, impairing effective training and operations.

But while the experience level of the mid-level ranks was initially low, it was made up for by common sense and a work ethic on the part of the team and squad leaders. The senior sergeants taught everything they knew, and the junior NCOs absorbed all the information they could retain. It was then polished on the battlefield. Halfway through the tour, the 1-8th's NCO experience status was fine and the battalion proved it in the crucible of combat.

Acknowledgments

THERE ARE THOSE over the years who have encouraged me to tell the story of our time in Vietnam before we all fall prey to old age. The survivors of Company B have been the primary pushers, so it has been our story from the beginning. I have expanded it to include others — you will see that the men of Company A played a large part in our experience — but the journal I kept as company commander told the actions mainly of Company B.

In a story that has taken over 46 years to finally put on paper, it is difficult to identify all who have helped bring it to fruition. In the narrative proper, I have included the names of those who shared their perspectives but others went beyond contributing to the text. Several of those individuals I have pointed out at the end of the book.

As far as the collection of stories, John (Doc) Bockover of Company A is the champ. He and I discussed the writing of this book years ago at one of our reunions and the next thing I knew he had gathered many great stories from A and B guys. He printed them off and he had a book of stories.

433

Landis Bargatze and others cleaned up his first efforts and a more complete edition evolved. With Doc's permission, I have used his narrative and other perspectives printed in his collection. Where possible I obtained individual permission for each story, but since John's manuscript has passed into the public domain, I used several quotes to augment the perspectives of our experiences. John passed away in 2007, but left such a patriotic legacy with us that he will not be forgotten by those who knew him or who have read his collection of war experiences. RIP, Doc.

George MacGarrigle (LTC, USA Ret.) is the author of *Taking the Offensive, October 1966 to October 1967* in the Vietnam series from the US Army Center of Military History and co-author of *Black Soldier/White Army: The 24th Infantry Regiment in Korea*. George interviewed me for his Vietnam manuscript in 1978 and used my journal to flesh out the official reports on some of the 1-8th actions. He encouraged me to use the journal as a basis for a future book. I told him that was the plan, but it might take a while. In 1990, when I was assigned as the Chief of the Histories Division of the Center of Military History, I was surprised to discover George still there and now one of my colleagues. His Vietnam volume had been postponed due to other commitments and priorities, so I was able to confirm my journal entries and see the bigger picture that had been unfolding in 1966 and 1967. George's volume, by necessity, was focused on a higher level of command than my battalion and company level journal. So, upon my retirement from the Center in 1992, George again encouraged me to do something with the journal...and now I have...thank you, George. I hope you like it.

Another former colleague at the Center was Dr. Bill Hammond, author of three major books on the role of the media in Vietnam. *The Military and the Media*, a major

434

two-volume series and *Reporting Vietnam,* an Organization of American Historian's Leopold Award winner, as well as a co-author of Black Soldier/White Army along with George MacGarrigle and William Bowers, a successor at the Center. Bill was known at the Center as "The Book Doctor" for his aid and assistance in helping authors remain focused on their themes. In my case, his lightly-worded suggestions, expertise and edits were always improvements over my original efforts.

Thanks must also go to Mike Boren, Bill Wright and Lynne Royce, friends who read the early manuscript and were kind enough to make many relevant comments.

Victor Lopez was my steady backup and advisor when it came to suggesting solutions to personnel problems within the company. As my first sergeant, he was a professional's professional; he never gave me bad advice and always had the men's welfare at heart. In service and out, he is still a good friend and supporter.

Richard Surface got off to a rocky start with me. A week after I assumed command, Surface and another soldier took off for a seven-day R&R. They managed to parlay that into a 29-day break, delayed (allegedly) by bad weather and lack of air transportation to get back to the company. Over time, however, he was able to prove he was worth the wait. By position, Surface was the company commander's driver, but he became far more than that. Lacking a vehicle in the field, he became my primary radio operator and lugged his radio, spare batteries, a weapon, ammunition and household goods every day. He was right with me when we moved to the sound of the guns in firefights and like all radio operators, was a constant target with his radio antenna flying above his head. He acted as my surrogate in giving directions to the platoons when I was too busy, and in spite of the dangers to which I exposed him, still maintained a positive outlook on life. He had little control over the combat conditions in which we found ourselves but reacted with quiet bravery under all circumstances.

Don Hunter rates meritorious mention as well. When my communications sergeant (Dannie Ballinger) was wounded in the ambush on Christmas Day, 1966, Don Hunter moved up to take his place. He became my communications sergeant and battalion operations radio operator. He was responsible for communicating with the battalion headquarters, though he and Surface were interchangeable in that role. He filtered out what was important to me at the time and answered on his own cognizance, if it looked like I didn't need to be bothered. Together, he and Surface were my "go to" guys when I needed something done immediately, without worrying about whether it would be accomplished. While the entire company was a team of young warriors, led by platoon leaders and their Non-Commissioned Officers, the first sergeant, the two radio guys, and I, were the inner core of the team. They were major contributors to the genesis of this work and keepers of the faith that I would finally get the manuscript completed.

Victor Renza had the beginnings of immersion foot the first time I remember him on a trail in a misty rain the day after I took command. He was a brash young man with a New York accent and wasn't going to admit he had a problem. I made him change his socks, and from then on, made it a special point to ensure he and others kept dry socks with additional pairs as necessary. It stopped his foot problems and he was one of my barometers for how things were going in the company. Even though like many GIs he was constantly muttering about the Army and the current situation, you could rely upon him to do his job. He always seemed to be in the hottest fire, and was one of seven survivors when his platoon was overrun. This event marked the rest of his life. He has done well and has been one of my strongest friends and supporters for writing this book.

Bill May has also been a strong advocate for the book over the years. He has been kind enough to tell me that he and a few others thought I did a pretty good job as company commander for which I am grateful. He is a past president of the Fourth Division Association and has continued to query me on how the book is coming. Bill, if you read this, we finally got'er done.

To those who contributed their stories to Doc Bockover's manuscript, and permitted me to use them for this narrative, thank you. To others who were interviewed and shared your deeds and experiences, thank you as well. All of the stories make up a piece of American history that is now forever.

Acknowledgements would never be complete without mentioning my family. My children, Cheron, John, Susan, David and Mark paid the price of my absence during the days I was living this book. Cheron and Susan have been more than supportive of my efforts to talk about events I could never share verbally. Kids, if you ever wondered what I was doing on that first tour, here she be.

My wife Peggy has been my strongest inspiration and supporter in finally getting the book completed. It took a long time, but she was instrumental in getting me to the Vietnam Wall with some of the guys and helped me come to grips with what is still an extremely emotional time. Her loving kindness and patience, as well as her suggestions and ideas have made the final version far better than it would have been otherwise. Thank you for the support and marrying me, my love.

About the Author

ROBERT SHOLLY spent 35 years in the U.S. Army as a combat infantryman and Middle East/South Asia specialist. He served two tours in Vietnam, the first of which is described in this book. Command and staff assignments included a five-year period with the Defense Intelligence Agency while other special assignments took him to the deserts of the Middle East, the mountains of Afghanistan and the plains and jungles of Africa. After Desert Storm, his last military assignment was with the Center of Military History involved with the writing of the official histories of the U.S. Army. Upon retirement from the military, he worked fifteen years in the corporate world again on special projects supporting military operations around the world to include Iraq and Afghanistan. He now consults on Middle Eastern affairs and writes for publication. He and his wife Peggy live in Texas.

CPSIA information can be obtained
at www.ICGtesting.com
Printed in the USA
FFOW04n0921110314
4160FF

CHAPTER SEVEN

"*T*ELL THE S1 TO BE HERE *first thing in the morning to take over the 82 element!*"

This enigmatic and terse radio message from the Operations Section was handed to me about 6 o'clock in the evening on 9 December 1966. After two months as the Personnel Officer, I was apparently going to get my wish for a company. Company B's call sign was "82", but I could not think of what might have happened to the former company commander. In the rear, we had no indications any of the companies had been involved in a firefight and I could think of no other reason for my summons to take over on such short notice. All of the line company commanders had several months to go before their six-month command tours were complete. This was obviously not something to be discussed over a radio in the dark of night. I passed everything I had been working on to my senior sergeant, packed my rucksack, loaded up with M79 ammunition, slept little and caught the first morning flight.

As in the case when the CG had visited the battalion in the field, the battalion CP was located on another grassy hill overlooking a broad river valley. This made direct radio communications easier with the units and provided a certain amount of isolated ground protection for the command group. Each company was given its own area of operation to search for VC or NVA. The battalion commander usually overflew or visited a company each day for a few minutes when it was operating in an area where a helicopter could land.

In this instance, the battalion reconnaissance platoon was adequate for the command post protection force. A small hexagonal tent had been erected on the hill by the side of some protective just-in-case fox holes and this was the CP. It had room for two or three people in the tent at any one time, a radio operator with his radios and the Operations Officer (S3) or his Operations NCO.

When I landed, I headed straight for the CP and Colonel Lee walked out and met me enroute. Since we did not salute in the field as a security measure, we briefly stood looking at each other and he radiated a controlled anger. He said curtly, *"You said you wanted a Company, so now is your chance. 82 is on its ass and I want you to straighten it out! Tomorrow I want you to link up with Company A and the next day both of you will make a combat assault into a possible hot LZ and then we will see what happens. Can you handle it?"*

After all my lobbying for a company, what else was there to say except a confident *"Yes sir!"* He replied, *"Operations will give you the details"*. With that, he stalked to his helicopter and flew away to visit the battlefield.

Unable to fully comprehend what had just happened, and more than a little apprehensive, I made it to the CP tent. Major Ritvo, the S3, was looking at the map. I reported to him and asked him if he had some details for me. He began to show me where Company B was, where Company A was, where we would link up the following day and when we would be picked up by helicopter. He mentioned that not much was known about the area, but the Landing Zone (LZ) would be prepped by artillery and gunships prior to our landing. He pointed out where the two companies would form a blocking position in a valley and evacuate all Vietnamese from that area. Other units would be pushing towards us and we would pick up any locals who tried to escape in our direction. We covered the dividing line between Companies A and B, call signs, radio frequencies and other important information. All this I obviously needed to know, but he still had not said anything about why I was taking over Company B. Finally I stopped him and said, "*What happened?*" He knew I was talking about the change of command.

Company B's commander had commanded the company during the training phase at Fort Lewis and as far as I knew, had done a fair job of transitioning from Washington State to Vietnam. However, the unit had difficulty keeping men in the field because of foot fungus, immersion foot, illnesses, and other health problems. In the last few days Company B had sent in 10 men with immersion foot, taking them away from combat duties and reducing the unit's effectiveness.

Jim Burch commented upon it in a letter home: "*We are loosing (sp) men out of the company by the dozens. Most of them are because of feet trouble. We have about 100 out of 170 men.*"

The command structure cannot control all health and hygiene difficulties. However, it can minimize them by making sure the NCOs and platoon leaders focus on keeping men healthy by providing supervision and information. In addition, when I had walked with Company B, the commander's lack of empathy with his men had been apparent and he treated the men he led with contempt. I felt there was a definite morale problem and I had not been impressed with his leadership skills.

41

However, as an observer, it was not my place to comment upon the situation. I did, however, tuck his lack of leadership into the back of my mind determined that it definitely was not the way I would do it if I had the opportunity.

Years later I learned the internal company situation had gotten to the point where some of the men were actively harassed as individuals and were deliberately placed in dangerous situations by the company commander. These men were seriously considering direct action against him for fear of their own and their buddy's lives. One soldier, upset over PFC Grow's death due to deliberate inaction by the commander, had pointed his rifle at the captain and almost pulled the trigger. The First Sergeant (1SG) intervened and calmed the situation, but it was indicative of the strong feeling against the captain. Fortunately nothing came of the direct action threats, but I am told it was a near thing.

According to Major Ritvo, it had become obvious to the battalion commander that the captain had a difficult time with the health of his men as well as reading maps and determining his actual spot on the ground. 1SG Victor Lopez did a lot of map confirmation, keeping the company where battalion thought they were located. Knowing where you are is an extremely critical skill, particularly when you have to rely upon artillery to provide you indirect fire support or when you need to coordinate fires from other units.

On the day before I arrived, unknown to the company commander, the company had wandered outside the effective range of the artillery. Colonel Lee had to help them get reoriented. Major Ritvo said the battalion commander had been furious with the captain and his lack of overall leadership skills and his inability to determine where he was. The cumulative effect on the battalion commander had resulted in a radio call to me.

Also years later, the 1SG told me the battalion commander quietly had asked his opinion of the captain a few weeks before the change of command. Torn between his feeling of professional loyalty to the captain and the safety of his men, the first sergeant told Colonel Lee the captain should go.

After talking to Major Ritvo, I felt better about my being thrown into a situation when I didn't have many facts. I was still a bit apprehensive about taking over a company of men who had been on the line while I had been a staff officer dealing with paperwork. However, I was excited about finally being able to put my leadership training into practice.

My basic leadership approach was the product of my reading military history and the biographies of great soldiers. One of my favorite generals was General George S. Patton. I had read as many of his writings as possible. While I didn't approve of many of his actions and attitudes, he articulated many of the better basic philosophies in which I believed. In addition, my father was a leader, mentor and role model and passed on his common-sense approach to human relations. Between my father, Patton and formal leadership classes, I had developed a set of principles in which I believed and by which I lived.

1. *Know your men and look out for their welfare.* Leaders must protect their men as much as possible. If you do this, the mission will take care of itself.

2. *Never ask your men to do something you have not already done or are not willing to do.*

3. *If you pick subordinate leaders, do so by merit and give them authority and tools to do their job.*

4. *Don't tell your subordinate leaders HOW to do their jobs, tell them WHAT to do and let them do it.* If they

do the same thing wrong more than once, make sure it isn't your fault for not training them properly. If you are not to blame, replace them and make sure they know what went wrong so they can do it right elsewhere.

5. *Always try to find out what you don't know.* Many wrong decisions are made when the answer to a simple question might have made the difference.

6. My father had a personal one which he passed to me and which I have always cherished. *Always try to get your boss promoted.* That thought has nuances and depths dealing with many things including loyalty, character, personal best and ensuring your subordinates do their jobs well.

With these philosophies, I was ready to take command.

After my little briefing by the S3, it was almost mid-morning and I knew I had to get to the company. I asked Major Ritvo if he had an extra map and he said to get the previous company commander's from him.

I rode into the company on a logistics helicopter providing supplies and tried to say *"hello"* to my predecessor and get a data dump. Not unexpectedly he was bitter and professionally embarrassed about being relieved and had little to say. As he strode past me to the helicopter on which I had arrived, I asked for his map. He tossed it at me and as it fluttered to the ground between us, he got on the helicopter and flew away. I never saw him again. Not much of a change of command ceremony and certainly no overlap briefing. However, this was where my previous trekking with the troops paid off. At least I knew 1SG Lopez and the platoon leaders and some of the men by name.

By November 1966, it became obvious the weapons platoons of all infantry companies were too restricted to road networks and were unable to support companies operating cross-country in the hills and jungle. Artillery had a much longer range than mortars, so terrain dictated it should be our primary indirect fire support. Therefore, after a short time in the field, the mortar/weapons platoon in each company stored its mortars and converted to a straight infantry platoon.

The weapons platoon became the fourth platoon. It had fewer men than the other line platoons and only one machine gun, but Company B's fourth platoon was fortunate to have 2LT Bernardo Bosch as a platoon leader. Bennie was from Cuba, had fought in the Bay of Pigs, been captured and finally released. He joined the U.S. Army to fight Communists and obtain U.S. citizenship. Assisting him as the platoon sergeant was Sergeant First Class (SFC) Bruce Grandstaff, an extremely tough professional career Noncommissioned Officer (NCO), who also had been a drill instructor for the company during the basic and advanced infantry phases. Fortunately the weapons platoons that underwent this transition were able to refresh their rifleman and small unit infantry skills under light opposition prior to moving to the central highlands and an entirely different war.

While the company was distributing the supplies that had been brought in, I called a quick meeting of the platoon leaders and platoon sergeants. I told them I wanted to move out to our rendezvous point with Company A the next morning and asked who had been the point platoon on the last march. I then gave them a different platoon sequence of movement. I had noticed previously that some of the companies always moved in a set sequence, with one platoon generally being the point platoon. It was my opinion this established a dangerous mind-set that detracted from the company's flexibility and mental alertness. Instead, each platoon would have the opportunity to be the point platoon, with a different one adjusting to the situation each day.

Breaking trail through thick growth or underbrush was a tough job. A man tired very quickly, with a decrease in mental alertness, while in hot weather he tired even more quickly and became dehydrated. As a result, his platoon leader had to be constantly aware of the physical condition of the men, especially the point.

When moving on trails, the point man would be out perhaps 25–50 meters, followed by another soldier who kept him in sight, followed at a distance by the remainder of his squad or platoon. The point man's responsibilities in this situation consisted of checking for signs of recent enemy tracks, booby traps, ambushes, and the possibility of running into an enemy force. In dense jungle, the point man might be only a few meters ahead of the squad. When there was thick growth it didn't take long to lose the man in front of you if you didn't keep alert. If the point man got too far in front, moreover, he became too vulnerable to provide early warning to the company.

That first evening I made the rounds of the perimeter checking basic skills. I wanted to ensure everybody had dug their foxholes, identified their lanes and fields of fire and had sticks firmly in the ground on each side of their holes to mark those boundaries. The sticks assisted the soldier when he was moving his rifle from side to side at night. If he felt his rifle hit the stick, he knew he had gone as far in that direction as he should and that his lane was between the two sticks. This technique also ensured overlapping fields of fire with buddies on either side.

I randomly checked out weapons cleanliness and knowledge of the assigned weapon, machine gun emplacement by the platoons, flare and claymore positioning, password procedures and other normal infantry operating procedures. There were a few corrections required, but on the whole, for such a quick check, I was pleased with the overall result. Not having taken the unit through training, I needed to know what the soldiers knew, had forgotten or didn't know. I was a believer in ensuring simple basics, before moving into more advanced knowledge and techniques. For example, normal stream crossing techniques called for a swimmer to tie a rope around himself prior to entering the water, with the remainder of the rope being held by someone on the shore for safety. If the swimmer lost his footing, he could be retrieved by the rope. I did not know why this procedure had not been followed three weeks before when PFC Grow of the Second Platoon had been swept away as he tried to swim a swollen stream with a rope. I still don't.

Studying the map carefully helped me identify what route we should take for the next day and what type of terrain we could expect on the march. I wanted to be able to envision the terrain in my mind's eye at all times. I noted possible ambush sites and ensured the platoon leaders understood what I expected of them on the march and at these potential contact sites.

After my hurried meeting with the platoon leaders, LT Bill Wilson, my Artillery Forward Observer (FO) and I went over the map in greater detail, so he could preplan artillery concentrations on potential trouble spots. This became routine. We never had to wait for the artillerymen to go through their computations before they could fire a supporting mission.

CHAPTER EIGHT

IT WAS A FAIRLY ROUTINE six-kilometer walk the next morning, though it rained on and off. (The military uses the metric system, so a kilometer equals .62 miles and a meter equals 39 inches, 3 inches longer than a yard. In this case, six kilometers, or clicks for short, equaled six times .62, or 3.72 miles.) We all had waterproof ponchos, but the sound of rain hitting the garment overpowered any other sound. Most of the time we just slogged in the rain without the protection, getting thoroughly soaked.

Murphy's Laws:

The worse the weather, the more you are required to be out in it."

We had all learned the lesson of not wearing undergarments as well. Because undershorts and T-shirts were made of cotton, they did not dry quickly. When worn wet they were uncomfortable, tended to bunch up and contributed to rashes and blisters. As a result, very few soldiers continued to wear underwear after the first few times moving in the rain. The light fabric of our jungle fatigues absorbed water rapidly, but also dried quickly.

One of my letters home described the conditions under which we were operating..."*On the east coast of Vietnam it is the monsoon season and it rains every day. If it doesn't rain in the morning, it does in the afternoon and vice versa. Oftentimes it rains all day, or else is overcast and cloudy. We are seldom dry...the only good thing is when it stops raining for a few hours, the sun comes out and we get dry until the next shower. As long as we are moving, the rain is a constant nuisance, but we can overcome it. However, at night, when we stop and set up our soaked poncho shelters with our air mattresses and our soaked poncho liners* (a lightweight nylon cover), *the wind bristles through our clothing and it becomes as cold as winter somewhere else. We carry field jackets when we can to provide a barrier to the wind, but they become very heavy after they are soaked through, and unless we are operating at the higher elevations where it gets really cold and wet, many of us elect to be miserable rather than carry the extra weight.*"

During this first march I instituted my first basic changes. I insisted we put out local security (guards out on both flanks and to the rear for early warning) and take a 10-minute break for each hour on the march. This had not been a previous SOP but troops needed refreshing, even if it was only a quick stop on a trail to recharge their mental and physical status. During the few breaks we took, I walked the line in the rainy mist checking for dry socks and seeing if everyone had extra pairs.

As mentioned before, the battalion was beginning to have too many soldiers with fungus, trench or immersion foot or blisters. These injuries were caused by never allowing the soldier's feet to dry and exacerbating the problem by continuing to hike in the same pair of wet socks. The skin on the feet became soft and started wrinkling. The rubbing of wet socks against the softer skin caused blisters and bleeding. Then the soft skin started sloughing off in patches, leaving boils and sores where new skin attempted to grow. Fungus got a small foothold *(pun intended)* and then slowly increased in size. Infections created pain and soon the soldier could not walk or put pressure on his feet and had to be evacuated for treatment.

One would think that taking care of your feet would be common sense for a foot soldier. Unfortunately, after monotonous hours trudging through rain, streams, mud and wet ground without a break, soldiers became so mentally numb they didn't feel like taking care of themselves. They just pulled into themselves and became like automatons, concerned only with taking the next step and following the guy in front. Needless to say, this did not enhance mental alertness when on the lookout for bad guys who hoped your guard was down.

Having studied military histories about foot problems in World War I, II and Korea, I knew that drying and rotating of socks would begin to cut down the number of bad foot problems.

During that first day of command, as I was walking the line during one of the breaks, I saw a soldier massaging his feet through his waterlogged boots. His name was Renza. As I recall, the general conversation went something like:

"Renza, how are you doing?"
"Fine, sir..."
"Why are you massaging your boots like that?"
"They always itch a little bit after walking for awhile."
"Take off your boots and socks and let me see..."
"They're OK, sir, just a little itchy..."
"Now, Renza."
"OK, but they're fine..."

As he took his boots off, I could see his socks were not in good shape, his feet were white and wrinkled and there were several red spots where blisters were starting to form.

"Do you have any dry socks?"

"No sir, and the other pair I have are just as wet as these..."

"I want you to take your other pair and wring as much water out of them as you can...then put them on. I want you to wring out the ones you have on and put them inside your clothes next to your skin to warm and dry them as much as possible. Every other break, alternate the pairs on your feet. We'll get something for your blisters as well."

"I'm doing fine, sir...I can take care of it."

"I'll be checking, Renza...just make sure you do what I tell you..."

As I recall, there was an exaggerated New York sigh, but the squad leader said he would make sure it got done. I told the squad leader that he needed to make sure every man in his squad did the same thing...

That evening I made it company policy for the platoon leadership to get reinvolved in ensuring their men changed socks during the breaks and at night and to start giving personal attention to foot problems. I also directed the company medics to check everyone's feet each night and requisition enough foot powder and foot ointment to take care of blisters and fungus.

In my mind, just about everything in Vietnam was against us...the enemy, the terrain and the weather as well as Brigade and Division...my judgment was still out on Battalion...not many junior officers knew that all companies were judged by their seniors, according to the enemy body count they racked up, versus the number of friendly casualties. Also included in the statistics account was the number of healthy fighting men they could keep in the field, the number of Article 15's, an indication of morale problems, and other indications that purported to show a good, bad or lackluster company. These units were arbitrarily placed on a winner or loser list by higher headquarters to provide an understanding of not only how were the companies performing, but how the battalion commander was doing his job. I knew all of this from my staff time and had decided I would be damned if we were going to be placed on a list of losers by sheer neglect on our own part...

It took a couple of weeks, but the foot problem was minimized a great deal, the troops started feeling better and we started having more men in the field instead of sitting back in the rear area waiting for their feet to dry out and heal. It wasn't planned, but it also gave me an opportunity to show the men that I cared about their health and welfare and would go to extremes to make sure we had done all that was possible to keep them healthy. In later years, Renza told me that for the first time in the military he really felt someone cared about him as an individual and that I would do my best to protect them as I could. While I would have appreciated the positive feedback at the time, it was gratifying to hear about it at all and to know I had been on the right track in building morale, promoting good health, and taking care of my men.

In the weeks to come, when quiet movement was not necessary, I took the opportunity to do a little extra training during the breaks. Sometimes I would stop with a platoon and quiz squad members on individual skills on land navigation, map reading and quick reaction responses to unanticipated enemy threats.

After the death of PFC Grow a few weeks earlier, the company was understandably cautious about crossing flooded streams. That first day, our route took us to a stream about 50 feet across and boiling down the mountainside. I moved up to the front of the column to assess the situation and decided it was an opportunity to show a little leadership other than looking at soldier's feet.

Fortunately the company carried ropes for just this situation, but there were no instant volunteers to take the rope to the other side and tie it off. Having accomplished this exact scenario in Ranger and Jungle Warfare School numerous times, I decided to take the plunge myself. This would do two things; it would show I wouldn't ask someone to do something I wasn't prepared to do, and it would show I wasn't going to let a little obstacle hold us up while we dithered around. Of course, there was the possibility that I would fail and drown, in which case the morale of the company might drop for a couple of hours, but that wouldn't mean much to me at that point. I figured the plusses outweighed the minuses, so I tied the rope around myself and waded into the stream...the current was strong and the water came up to my chest. I was able to hold my own until about three quarters of the way across; then my feet were swept out from underneath me and I was sucked under. I started tumbling below the frothing surface. I boiled to the top, flailed and struggled against the current towards the far shore. I held on to the rope, which gave me a leverage point, got my feet under me again and launched myself again. I was carried several meters below my aiming point, but managed to grab some brush and pull myself out of the streambed.

I tied the rope to a tree and the rest of the company was able to cross safely while holding onto the rope. My gear, (my helmet, rucksack, weapon, etc.) was brought over piecemeal as the rest of the company came across. Richard Surface, my company radio operator remembers thinking *"Oh, my God... This man might be crazy if he is going to be the first man and I have to escort him with a radio."* Fortunately it worked out all right and after having set an example, it was not necessary to do it again.

We linked up with Company A about mid-afternoon and formed a large two-company perimeter. Captain Bidd Sands and I had an opportunity to talk about the next day's operation. All of the battalion first sergeants were experienced NCOs and were largely responsible for getting the battalion as well trained as it was for combat. Company A's First Sergeant Dave McNerney was of the old NCO school and demanded his troops be as good as possible. That night, the two first sergeants and Bidd and I, talked late about "what ifs" for the morrow. My respect for the two sergeants and their substantial experience and knowledge grew. (McNerney already had two previous tours as an advisor to South Vietnamese units.) Sands and I had several common acquaintances and some similar previous assignments. He had been a part of the battalion at Fort Lewis, and had even been the commander of Company B for a short time, but he had wanted a company in combat. He was promised one by his old unit, the 1st Brigade of the 101st Airborne Division, so he had transferred to them and gone to Vietnam as an individual replacement. The 101st had been part of the allied buildup in Tuy Hoa and its base camp was at the region's airfield. Fortunately for us, Sands was still waiting for a Company when by chance our battalion was posted to Tuy Hoa. When Nick Romaine, the former Company A commander, was transferred to the battalion staff, Colonel Lee asked for Sands back. He became the new company commander.

I had my first real opportunity to talk with my platoon leaders and senior NCOs about the company, what they would change if given the opportunity and my perspective of how we were going to handle the next day's operation. I only had two platoon leaders in the field with me (2LT Alan Wilder, first platoon and 1LT George Tupa, second platoon), of the other two, 2LT Larry Rodabaugh (third platoon) had been sent on temporary duty (TDY) three days before, to help develop a training course for newcomers. Second Lieutenant Bernardo

Bosch (fourth platoon) had stepped on a booby trap and been evacuated the morning of my assumption of command. However, I was impressed with the two platoon sergeants who were in command of the two platoons without lieutenants (SFC Felipe Morales and SFC Bruce Grandstaff). The 1SG told me they were good NCOs and could handle the platoons with no difficulty. First Lieutenant William Woodford was the XO providing support for the company from base camp.

The next day's operation for us was part of an overall plan to deny the enemy the rich rice harvest this area produced. We were scheduled to go into a blocking position to police up any VC/NVA that might come into our area trying to escape other U.S. units.

The extensive use of helicopters in warfare was a relatively new tactic. As every person who has ever watched the TV show "Mash" knows, small helicopters were used in the Korean War for medical evacuations, for forward observers and to move senior commanders around the battlefield. Research continued in designing helicopters capable of carrying larger numbers of troops. By the late 1950's designs had been improved and concept models were constructed. Military tactics using the helicopter as a medium for force extension were being developed, but it wasn't until the early 1960's that sufficient numbers of helicopters had been manufactured to fill the military's expectations for newly organized "airmobile" units. Except for a few times when I used helicopters for transportation or skydiving, I had little experience with them. The 1st Cavalry Division had been the first fully airmobile combat unit and was posted to Vietnam in 1965, the year before. My previous training had all taken place in units where you got to work by walking, riding on tanks, armored personnel carriers, trucks or by parachuting. If anyone had known how apprehensive I was on this, my very first air assault or mass troop movement of any size by helicopter, I suspect they would have found some reason not to go with me. In the Infantry Advanced Course, we had planned all sorts of heliborne operations on paper, but many of us had never actually participated in one.

Under classroom planning conditions, you identified how many men you had that needed transport. Then you requested the appropriate number of helicopters through channels, assigned a number of them to the platoons, and figured how you would take care of any leftover troopers. In Vietnam, we were seldom asked how many helicopters we would need because the S3 knew how many men we had in the field. He requested a certain number and the aviation battalion would provide as many towards that number as they could, based upon the priorities of the day and the status of maintenance. We were usually told how many helicopters we had for the move and had to plan around that figure. If there weren't enough helicopters to move everyone on a single lift, double and even triple trips occurred to move everyone else.

I started thinking about how we would split up the company into the number of helicopters we were given for the move. There were several personnel variables with which I was unfamiliar, so I was uncertain as to exactly how all this was going to take place. Finally, I mentally slapped myself on the forehead and remembered my NCO background. I realized the company had done this before and had far more experience in planning this sort of thing. I asked 1SGT Lopez *"Top, who normally does the planning for the move?"* He said *"The NCOs generally do the details once you give the platoons the order of move."* So I said, in my most knowledgeable and professional voice, *"OK, I think we will move the platoons in WXYZ order, with the two radio guys, the FO and me with the lead platoon and you with the rear platoon."* At the evening meeting with the platoon leaders and the first sergeant, I outlined the move. The platoon leaders and NCOs then organized their parts without any additional guidance from me.

Whew! Nothing like asking the right question and then delegating to get things right with no one the wiser concerning my anxiety and ignorance...

CHAPTER NINE

OUR HELICOPTERS ARRIVED the next morning looking like a huge flock of birds descending upon a newly mowed wheat field. We watched Company A get picked up and then we moved into position for our turn. After depositing Company A, the helicopters returned.

We were in a large enough open area that the entire company could be lifted at one time. Looking at the number of helicopters as they flew in to pick up their squad "stick" was the first time I really comprehended that I was in charge of over a hundred men who were about to fly into combat. It was a sobering thought and I vowed to do my best for them.

In a flash of fantasy, I saw the company's potential as a well-honed elite unit, spearing into the ranks of the enemy and spreading confusion, death and destruction by use of superbly trained skills. I saw us as being the "company to be feared" and the enemy melting away rather than meet us in combat on the battlefield. I felt positively euphoric with this vision and knew that Mars, the Great God of War, was watching over us.

Then a cloud of dust from the helicopter rotor wash flew into my face and eyes and I had to clear my mind of everything else to get on with the job. My mental meanderings were great aspirations, but this was only my second day in command, and there was a long way to go before my "vision" could be realized.

Jolted back to the present, I joined the two radio operators (one for the battalion net and one for the company net) and the artillery Forward Observer and his radio operator and loaded onto the second helicopter. 1SG Lopez went with another platoon so he could assist LT Tupa (the senior lieutenant) in assuming command if something happened to me.

Riding in an open helicopter was exhilarating. The speed and height thrilled me and it had an exalting effect in which I thought I was literally on top of the world and prepared for anything. All the seats were taken out to make room for men or loads to slide in and out quickly. As the wind rushed through the open area, the crew chief/door gunner was busy scanning below looking for any muzzle flashes that meant we were under fire. Looking out the door to the rear I saw the entire company in 15 or 16 helicopters flying in formation, an awesome and thrilling sight. We flew just below the gray cloud ceiling, then dipped down to follow the nap of the earth in our approach to the landing zone (LZ). We streamed over green hills covered with trees that looked like giant broccoli plants that followed the contour lines of the valleys and hillsides. Momentum and gravity pushed and pulled at our bodies. Coming up over the last ridgeline, I saw flashes and smoke as our LZ, a large clearing, and the forest around it, exploded. Flashes of light reflected off the rotating blades of gunships as they raked the areas around the clearing with tracers and rockets.

Somehow I thought we would wait until the gunships were finished and the artillery rounds stopped falling before we made our approach, but we kept drilling directly into the gouts of dirt and fire ahead of us. LT Bill Wilson, my FO, suddenly shouted in my ear over the roar of the wind and explosions, *"Last artillery rounds in the air!!"* I was scanning the area and had little time to think, but I remember feeling I had been born to do this and that I was in the perfect place for me, in my life at that time. There was no fear, no concern for death, only a need to get on the ground as fast as possible to come to grips with any enemy who might contest our right to be there.

The timing was perfect. As the last artillery round exploded, our aircraft flared and barely touched its skids to the earth. As we all tumbled out onto the ground and ran toward the edges of the clearing, gunships roared by still firing on the three forward sides of the LZ. When we cleared the ship, our helicopter rose into the air to make room as the remainder of the company landed. Meanwhile, soldiers streamed away from the LZ to its sides and front forming an immediate defensive perimeter. Small fires were burning around the LZ from the artillery and gunship "prep". A heavy quiet settled on the ground as we maneuvered into position and waited to see if there was a VC or NVA challenge.

My decision to go in with the lead platoon was not a normal procedure for Company B. Its previous company commander had always waited until the company was on the ground and in a perimeter before he landed. Dick Surface, one of the radio operators told me: *"On other air assaults, because we were with the previous commander in the rear and he waited to land until things were safe, I didn't think that things would get too bad; but that first day, when you started going in with the first attack platoon and we had to go with you, it was pretty scary and I really wasn't sure you knew what you were doing!"*

There were several schools of thought on where the commander should be in an air assault. Some felt he could affect the battlefield better if he was above the fray and was able to oversee the action of the platoons. I understood this concept, but felt it was more appropriate for a battalion commander. I always felt I needed to assess the on-ground situation myself. In this way I could make any immediate adjustments to the landing pattern before the entire company was committed to one location from which we might not be able to extricate ourselves. In addition, it was my personal conclusion that at company level, soldiers needed to know their commander was willing to take the same chances they were being asked to take and wasn't afraid to be out in front. I am a firm believer that leadership means leading and by definition, in order to lead, one has to be in front to see and be seen. You can manage something from the rear, but you can't claim to have led anything except the cheerleader's section. I have always been a great admirer of General Patton's leadership philosophies though not necessarily of all of his actions. One of his quotes helped develop my personal leadership style, *"A piece of spaghetti or a military unit can only be led from the front end."*

We landed in a broad valley in good order and spread out. There was little opposition. The third platoon came under some distant automatic weapons fire, but no one was hit. We responded with some rifle fire, called in artillery to show we didn't have time for such nonsense and moved out to our designated blocking positions. This move established a standard operating procedure that continued throughout the remainder of my tour as company commander. The company command group would be located near the front during any air assault or ground attack.

We were now operating in a coastal mountain range that paralleled the coastline. In comparison to the highlands in which we later operated, I would classify these elevations as high hills. But while they may not have been particularly tall, because of the amount of rainfall in the area, there was vegetation everywhere.

In the valleys there were the ubiquitous rice paddies. On the sides of the valleys there were terraced rice paddies or thick grass or bamboo forests. On the top of the elevations there were large trees that morphed into rain forests with double and sometime triple canopy jungle. Interfacing these different zones were areas that displayed a mix of all sorts of vegetation. It made for slow going.

There were broad valleys bisected by rivers thirty to fifty meters across and there were smaller, steep-sloped canyons with rocky, tumbling streams at the bottom. A few villages were established in the more open valleys with rice paddies stretching out from the riverbanks to the beginning of the hills. In some cases there were isolated huts where families tended their own rice fields. There were trails on top of the rice paddy dikes connecting all of these, but we had to be careful using them because of potential booby traps and ambushes. In order to avoid them, we chose our own way across country where possible. While this was the safest way to travel, it was also the hardest and slowest. Elephant grass fields, a tall, razor-edged tropical plant, grew taller than a man on the open mountainsides, obscuring our forward vision. Sawtoothed edges of leaves cut at our clothes and skin, delaying our movement. Small cuts became infected quickly if they didn't received immediate care.

To someone raised in the deserts of the US southwest, Vietnam was a beautiful country. The waterfalls, running streams, greenery and wonderful landscapes made it seem a magical place. On the other hand, the exertion required to hump the hills sometimes blinded us to nature's beauty all around us. SP4 Tom Monahan had an experience, which is one of his favorites...

"It was a wet and rainy day and I was miserable and climbing a mountain. I was grabbing elephant grass to help me up the next step and getting my hands cut up by the leaves. At one point I grabbed for a handhold on another type of plant. As I pulled on it, it came loose and I got a face full of beautiful orchids. I was sopping wet and miserable but I remember thinking, 'Everywhere in the world there is some beauty.' I still remember that moment."

We moved from the grass fields to bamboo stands that bounced even the sharpest machete. Trying to struggle between bamboo stalks barely a few inches apart in the rain on a steep slope with a rucksack and weapon, made walking a difficult chore.

Sometimes the terrain was more of an enemy than the Vietcong or NVA. We could not avoid all the trails all the time. When we had to use them, we were gambling we could avoid the traps, obstacles and ambushes.

On some of the creeks and small rivers, there were few fords or crossing places. On the trails and approaches to these locations, the NVA or VC put punji stakes as obstacles and booby traps. Punji stakes were sharpened bamboo stakes set into the ground, hidden in the grass or shrubbery or on slopes to deter movement. The sharpened ends of these stakes were often dipped in human feces so penetrating wounds would become infected. If someone tried to walk between them and slipped, they would invariably get punctured by another one unseen. There were also camouflaged pits or holes set into trails filled with punji stakes into which a man could fall or step. Once you were wounded by a punji stake, immediate action had to be taken to clean the wound to deter infection. This often necessitated evacuation to the rear, thereby lowering morale and depriving the company of a soldier in the field. Of course that is what the enemy wanted.

Other booby traps were more lethal, consisting of large swinging spiked branches or tree deadfalls activated by pulling or tripping over a small vine, string or wire camouflaged on a trail. In some cases there were sophisticated explosive devices created out of mortar or artillery shells that could go off when a soldier stepped on something that closed an electrical circuit. A hidden VC, of course, could also set it off with a pair of electrical wires and a battery.

As a result of our blocking position in the Ky Lo Valley, we picked up 182 detainees, several of which were later determined to be VC; 5,000 pounds of rice; and 600 pounds of peanuts. It became obvious to the Vietnamese that we were blocking the valley. Foot traffic into our positions dwindled to nothing and we received orders to move into the hills above the valley. Because of the small-sized VC units we generally came across, usually two to ten personnel, I gave our platoons their own routes and areas of operation in order to search as much ground as possible. Since a platoon could be as much as a couple of kilometers or more away from any of its supporting sister platoons, this was an excellent way to train platoon leaders and NCOs for independent movement and action.

As each platoon took a different route and moved higher into the hills, automatic fire from the heights hit the first platoon while its men were climbing a grassy slope in the open. Unable to maneuver without taking casualties, they were soon pinned down. I was moving with one of the other platoons, heard the firing and received a call about the action. I moved to a small ridge overlooking the platoon's position. With my binoculars, I could see the platoon and the general area of the VC above them, but was in no position to provide immediate or direct assistance from the other platoons. The first platoon leader, 1LT Alan Wilder, was wounded in the foot in the initial exchange and while not too mobile, was still very much in charge and had gotten his squads down and in concealment on the grassy slope. A squad leader, Staff Sergeant James Smothers, had gone to ground closer to the enemy. He directed the platoon's fire upwards towards the suspected enemy positions, but still could not get a good fix on them. Even though we were several hundred meters away, I had a fair view of the action and acted as an additional spotter for my FO, 2LT Bill Wilson. We called in artillery and with the calm assistance of the two platoon radio operators (SP4 Theodore Kohn and PFC James Bloom) relaying information from Wilder and Smothers, we walked the artillery down the hill to about 35 meters from the platoon. The platoon started getting pieces of bursting shrapnel around the men, but this effectively stopped the enemy fire. The platoon maneuvered its squads upward while the enemy broke and ran.

We got a "dust-off" helicopter in to evacuate Wilder, but as the helicopter settled into the grass, the VC started shooting again. The rest of the platoon returned fire, while Kohn, who was helping Wilder hop to the aircraft, fired his rifle back one-handed. He didn't drop Wilder and defended his platoon leader while in a very vulnerable position. As the helicopter took off and the platoon maneuvered towards the VC, the VC disappeared into the tall grass and up into the hills. I had lost another platoon leader (Bosch was still gone because of his punji stake wound) but the first platoon had proven capable of handling business. SFC Clifford Johnson, the platoon sergeant, was an experienced NCO and had good squad leaders to support him.

The next night we were probed on the perimeter and exchanged grenades and rifle fire with the enemy. No friendlies were hurt but the next morning we saw no evidence of VC casualties either. I began to wonder about our night response capabilities.

The next day we received some resupply. A battalion supply clerk, who came out to accomplish our direct exchange on clothing had to spend the night in the field with us because we were unable to get a helicopter out before dark. It was suggested he might want to dig a hole for the night, but being quite the combat soldier he replied that he really didn't think he needed to dig a hole for just one night. (We all dug holes whenever we could, whether it was just a tiny trench, or an actual foxhole. All of us knew that bullets keep going until something stopped them and it was not pleasant to be that something.) His attitude was aggravating and I was about to order him to dig one for his own good. But based upon the previous night's activities, I thought that if we got a few random shots into the perimeter, it might give this guy a better appreciation for field duty. About midnight we started getting probes on the perimeter with a lot of firing from both sides, grenades going off while neither side was able to see anything except muzzle flashes. When the shooting started, the supply type rolled out of his poncho hooch and just lay there with his face into the ground. When everything got quiet, you could hear the *"Thunk! Thunk!"* of his borrowed entrenching tool (a small shovel) digging a hole. He didn't sleep much that night he just kept digging and had a nice hole by morning. We were able to get him out the next day before he suffered from too much combat fatigue.

Similar probes occurred the next night and again, no one was hurt on either side. I began to realize that perhaps we needed some additional target practice if we were going to hit anything. Somehow I had assumed that if a soldier went through basic training, advanced individual training and unit training, marksmanship had always been a part of the curriculum. If that was so, then why weren't we hitting anything?

After analyzing what happened in our short firefights, I realized we were ignoring a basic rule for fighting at night and in the jungle. When we were shooting at night, we seldom had a good idea of where the enemy was located. We were always in a reactive mode and when the enemy fired into the night perimeter, he didn't necessarily have a hard target. He was trying to trigger a response. Plus, like all good soldiers, he moved quickly to another position after shooting. We might see his muzzle flash, but knowing he was no longer in that position, we just sort of sprayed an area with multiple bursts hoping we would get lucky. This often resulted in giving away our more static positions, which was the purpose of the enemy's probe. Now that he knew the boundaries of the perimeter and a few individual locations, he could be more effective with his shooting, grenades, and mortars.

Murphy's Laws:

"Never draw fire; it irritates everyone around you."

During a discussion with my platoon leaders/sergeants, I reminded them again we needed to get back to basics. We knew the VC had to come close to the perimeter to sense where we were before identifying actual targets. This put him within hand grenade range. A hand grenade is an area weapon. Its effective radius is far more than a small 5.56mm M16 bullet and unlike a muzzle flash, it doesn't mark the thrower's position. So my instructions were that, unless there was something specific at which to shoot, our first response should be a grenade.

Our basic marksmanship skills still bothered me. I discovered the men had trained mostly on the M14 rifle and had only received the M16 just prior to deployment with little time for familiarization. In addition, many of them had not fired their weapons much since they had arrived in Vietnam, a period of over three months. Given the lack of enemy contact for many of them, this was understandable, but the situation needed to be fixed. The company leadership, officers and NCOs, insisted on clean weapons at all times, so I never found that to be a problem, but hitting a target like the VC was altogether different. Marksmanship skills degrade if not exercised, so I set aside time for each platoon to do familiarization firing to refresh themselves with their weapons. Not surprisingly we started hitting things after that.

During this period, we were still climbing out of the valley and into the mountains. Considering we had started at sea level, the mountains presented physical challenges. They were covered with grass, double canopy trees and lots of brush. Since we essentially carried our homes on our backs, a loaded soldier might be carrying 60 or 70 pounds of weight, sometimes more, while trying to clamber up a rain-slicked slope, or maneuver between trees and bamboo. When combat loaded, nobody moved very fast.

The whole combat kit was a carrying system called Load Bearing Equipment (LBE). This consisted of a combat harness which had several pouches for ammunition, grenades, canteens, a first aid pouch and anything else the individual felt he might need in a hurry. Our rucksacks carried things you wouldn't need immediately, like a quarter-pound of C4 explosive, a poncho and poncho liner, an air mattress, C rations, a field jacket, a mosquito net, maybe a small hammock, letter writing materials, maybe a paperback book or magazine, and lots of spare ammunition.

In a firefight of course, 'rucks were shucked to gain mobility, and the fighting was done primarily in the combat harness. Of course you had to contend with Murphy's Laws: "*Whenever you drop your equipment in a firefight, your ammo and grenades always fall the farthest away but the one with the loose pin lands at your feet.*"

Canned C rations were our primary food. C rations had 12 boxes of food in a case, along with plastic bags called sundry packs. Each box made a full meal. It had an entree-type can, with a dessert, crackers and a sundry pack. The pack contained plastic knives, forks and spoons, salt, pepper, sugar, chewing gum, matches, instant coffee and cream, sometimes cigarettes, and other small items. The C's themselves consisted of a variety of canned, prepared foods that just needed opening to eat. Some of them were better if heated, but all of them could be eaten cold. There was beef stew, ham and eggs, ham and lima beans, boned chicken or turkey and other laboratory-prepared and dried delicacies. Everybody had their favorites and everybody had their not so favorites...there was a lot of trading among the men when their randomly selected boxes turned out not to have what they liked. The pressurized pound cakes, cinnamon-nut rolls and the mixed fruit were prized bartering materials and were hidden away to be enjoyed at special moments or used as a form of currency or barter. In a somewhat morbid but nevertheless humorous manner, these sweets were sometimes bequeathed to buddies. If a man were wounded and about to be evacuated, he might "leave" the cinnamon-nut roll he had been saving, to a friend. Or if his friend knew he had a pound cake he had been hoarding and they were going on a patrol or into some action, the buddy might ask, *"If something happens to you, can I have your pound cake?"* Small things often took on great importance in our small world.

A basic punch can opener called a P-38 was included in the ration case, but most people carried one attached to their dog tags for convenience. The different sizes of cans were labeled with a B-something designation and could be used as containers. A 15-ounce B3 can originally carried crackers in it, with a small tin of peanut butter or jelly. When the lid was cut about 90% and lifted back and away from the container, it could be bent further back and folded at the sides to become a handle. The can then could be used to boil water to brew a most excellent cup of coffee or hot chocolate.

We made stoves out of a flatter 5-ounce can. We cut the top off and punched air vents into the bottom sides. We were issued heat tablets—small dry chemical lozenges that were placed in the bottom of the "stove" and lit with a match. This produced enough heat to boil water or to warm a can of stew or even to cook rice mixed with some boned chicken or some other ingredient for a sumptuous repast. As time went on, when we didn't have heat tabs, we could take a pinch of C4, our explosive material and light it. It would burn as well as a heat tab without exploding. This was an old trick, known to most GI's, but I am not sure I would have been the first one to experiment to see if it worked.

Since we usually got resupplied every three to four days, we had to carry enough food in cans to fill the gap. C rations and ammunition were our heaviest loads and I knew we needed to cut the weight to increase our mobility and reduce the frequency of supply helicopters.

In the valleys there were always rice paddies and hidden small villages. The people had been terrorized for so long by the VC that none had any desire to help us find anyone. For the most part they just wanted to be left alone. The VC, of course, hid in the villages or else were actual villagers during the day and part of the VC at night. They controlled the villages simply by terrorizing and killing headmen and their families if anyone told a U.S. unit that a particular village had VC in it. We participated by providing protection for people who were being moved out of the area in order to cut off any indigenous support the VC might count upon. We provided protection for rice harvests and their movement to market to keep it from the VC and NVA. In some isolated areas, we had no choice but to burn the rice to deny it to the enemy.

We continued our climb up into the mountains. I jokingly noted in my journal that we were indeed in an amazing and strange land because there was only up, never down.

Murphy's Laws:

"No matter which way you march, it's always uphill."

Finally, we received orders to move back into the Ky Lo Valley. This move was unprecedented because US units had not operated in that region before. It was also a little different in that we did not go by helicopter, but moved in on foot. The tactic worked fairly well at first since we found small bands and groups of VC who did not expect us to come in over the mountains. We found a group of five with weapons, two for which we accounted, with three getting away. Since one of the dead had $200 on him, we speculated that perhaps he had been a tax collector or a paymaster. As the days went on we picked up about 20 more men we suspected of being VC, and destroyed approximately 2800 pounds of rice, thereby denying it to the VC and NVA who were trying to salvage it.

The fourth platoon caught some VC trying to cross the river on a boat and called in artillery fire on the entire group. Other platoons had smaller firefights in which the enemy came out worse than we did. It was obvious the firearms refresher was beginning to pay off.

A new officer, 1LT Chuck Aronhalt was assigned to us on the 20th of December and LT Bosch returned to us on the 24th of December, having recovered from his punji stake injury. I had been told that LT Rodabaugh would be gone for an indefinite period, so I assigned Aronhalt to the third platoon. SFC Johnson was doing a fine job in the first platoon but I expected a new lieutenant to replace LT Wilder. Even though the NCOs were doing a great job, I felt that the more men assigned to bring us up to full strength was a good thing... This gave me an officer for each platoon except the first platoon.

After two weeks in command, I was beginning to feel very comfortable in my new role and the unit was starting to come around in their opinion of me. In a letter to his family on the day I took command, Jim Burch commented: *"We got a new CO today. He's starting out worse than the one we had. The other one raised all kinds of hell..."*

However, a few weeks later in another letter he said, *"We have a new CO and he is a lot different from the other one we had. He lets us take a bath about every three days. We get clean clothes and socks more often. Also we get hot chow more often. Everything is better..."*

So while nobody was going to tell me I got an A on my report card, at least some of the troops thought things were improving...

CHAPTER TEN

A CHRISTMAS TRUCE WAS declared between North and South Vietnam in 1966, so we were ordered to find a spot to sit it out. On Christmas Eve day, we set up on the northern side of the swollen Ky Lo River in a spot that would give good protection from a ground attack and all around fields of fire for the entire company. As a matter of course, we always pre-fired our protective artillery fires in the evening. Using this technique in the event of an emergency, all we had to do was call the artillery and request they fire Concentration Number 672 or whatever the number was with the target coordinates available. They could then provide us fire quickly without our having to adjust rounds in preparation for firing for effect. Unfortunately, the artillery battery did not let us range in our rounds because their commander thought it was too dark to adjust the rounds. Lieutenant Wilson took issue with this, but it did no good. We were unable to get our artillery fires adjusted for the other side of the river.

The following day was Christmas Day. The sun was out, the grass was green, we were next to a nice running river and it was truly a beautiful day without a hint of the normal rain we had been experiencing. Many of the company had had an opportunity to take a bath in the river and wash some clothing all the while guarded closely by security. We got our resupply helicopter with Christmas mail, clothing and supplies and it was a relaxed atmosphere. The mail had been jammed up in the system, so there was much that had to be returned because the men did not have room to carry all their well-meant gifts. SFC Grandstaff got a small Christmas tree that had to be returned to base camp and others received gifts that while meaningful to the soldier, were too large or inappropriate for the field. (I remember someone received a large teddy bear from a loved one.) The helicopter also had our hot Christmas meal (turkey and dressing and other trimmings). It was a good day.

When we finished the meal, the mermite cans, vacuum containers used for transporting and serving food, were stacked at the side of the LZ in preparation for removal by the next helicopter. We were in the process of adjusting our protective artillery rounds when we were asked to hold up the process, as a helicopter was enroute. I had sent the first and fourth platoons to patrol our side of the river to ensure we were not surprised by an attacking ground force. The river was running too high to cross it without a major effort, so we stayed on the north bank.

The inbound helicopter turned out to be Colonel Lee and the new battalion sergeant major, who were visiting each company on Christmas. As they got off the aircraft, 1SG Lopez and I moved out to greet them. Just before we shook hands, I saw puffs of dirt popping up between us and we heard the crack of rifle rounds coming from across the river. I shouted *"Incoming!! Get down!!"* We all hit the ground and all of us managed to make it back to the CP area without being hit. The platoon we had on the riverside for security laid down a field of fire. The helicopter immediately took off, but before it could get out of range it took several hits and one of the crewmembers was wounded. It managed to make it back into the firebase at Dong Tre for medical attention and repair. We could not get across the river because of the swift current, and it took about fifteen minutes before we could obtain any artillery support.

Fortunately none of our people were killed, but two were wounded, recently promoted communications Sergeant Dannie Ballinger and one of the temporary radio operators, SP4 Robert McKissick who was substituting for SP4 Surface, still on an extended R&R. While rounds were zipping all over the place, 1SG Lopez got the wounded into a shell hole we had used for our CP. While I was maneuvering two platoons towards the river threat and reminding the other platoons this might just be a diversion, Colonel Lee used his authority as a battalion commander to get us some air support. One of the machine gunners, SP4 Bill May, managed to get a machine gun to a location where it had a good field of fire on the enemy. Lieutenant Tupa was able to get to May over the open ground without being hit, started directing fire against the enemy machine gun, and finally silenced it. By that time gunships arrived to strafe the far side of the river, and the enemy broke.

Even though we were all still pumped up with adrenalin, Colonel Lee looked at me and said with a straight face, "*What was that all about? Didn't you give those guys Christmas presents?*" Not knowing exactly what to say, I responded weakly, "*We did, but they said Made in America!*" This was the first time the battalion commander had an opportunity to see close action on the ground with one of his units and I think we developed an even closer bond because of it.

Lopez called in a dustoff for the wounded. It arrived as the firing was ending. Later, we figured we had been a target of opportunity for some VC who were passing by on their way home for Christmas dinner and stopped to exchange presents. After some sustained firing from protected positions across the river, they broke contact when the gunships arrived and moved out. We also got some soldiers on the far side of the river, but it was too late, the VC had disappeared.

All in all, Christmas of 1966 had enough of the Fourth of July thrown in to remember it. It also showed me that even if the North Vietnamese agreed to truces and cease-fires in North Vietnam, not everybody was going to get the word down in South Vietnam. While it was part of the learning curve, I promised myself we would not get caught like that again.

The day after Christmas and the broken truce, we moved further down river with orders to destroy any rice caches we found. By this time the civilians had been moved out of the region, and authorities did not want any rice left lying around to feed VC.

We were doing well...over the previous 10 days we had destroyed almost 7,000 pounds of rice, another 600 pounds of peanuts and had detained almost 300 people with many VC among them.

When we finished our project, we were airlifted further back up the Ky Lo Valley in case some of the VC might be returning because we had left and gone downriver. We made it in two lifts. The first landed in our planned location on the south side of the river, but as the second was coming in, one of the pilots saw several VC we had surprised on the north side of the river.

Reacting to the sighting, I put the fourth platoon on the north side of the river to take the enemy under fire. We killed three and captured two. We picked up the platoon and moved it onto our side of the river and sent the captured VC back to the rear. As we continued our sweep we ran across several more and killed two. We managed to wound and capture another VC and detained eleven others. By the time we were able to get the wounded and detained VC ferried back to the rear, it was getting time for the New Year's Day Truce.

We moved south into another valley. I had learned my lesson about setting up too close to a river, we selected an open area away from the base of the overlooking mountains that gave us good close-in protective fields of fire and visibility.

On 30 December we suffered another casualty...the first Company B man killed since the drowning incident of LeMoine Grow...sadly, it was another senseless loss. As it was reported to me, our mess sergeant, Sergeant First Class Guy Huey, who generally stayed in the base camp, was visiting the Tuy Hoa Airbase to pick up rations. Before individuals could go to different locations on the airbase, they had to clear their weapons for safety reasons. The process consisted of an individual pointing his weapon (rifle or pistol) into a bucket or barrel of sand, removing the magazine from his weapon and ejecting any round in the chamber. The trigger was then pulled to release tension, which resulted in a *click* as the firing pin went forward and hit an empty chamber. Sergeant Huey was standing near the clearing barrel when a non-Company B man stepped up to clear his weapon. The individual failed to clear the round from his chamber and failed as well to keep the weapon pointed at the sand. When he pulled the trigger, it fired, killing Huey instantly. When I heard the news I was saddened that the rear area appeared to be even more dangerous to our men than looking for the enemy in the forward operating areas. It was tragic that the first two men killed in both Companies A and B were killed by fellow soldiers.

Since New Year's Day was going to be a Truce, it was a good time for resupply and visitors. Chaplain David Woehr came out to conduct services and was puttering around our perimeter. He saw a wire and pulled it, setting off a trip flare. It startled him quite a bit which gave us all a little amusement at his expense. Fortunately it had not been an explosive device or booby trap. At any rate, he was going to spend some time with us, as he had in the past with little or no excitement. He set up a poncho lean-to and started cooking a C-ration lunch. About that time we started receiving sniper fire from the hill above us. Chaplain Woehr dove into his hooch, shouted that Protestant services were in three minutes and everybody had better hurry because he was leaving the area. We had no helicopter in the area at the moment so I wondered where he thought he was going. We fired a few rounds of artillery in the general direction of the sniper so he wouldn't think he was completely ineffectual, but we mostly ignored him since he didn't seem to be hitting anything. According to a letter written home by Jim Burch of the fourth platoon, one of the rounds hit the ground near him, but no one else seemed to be affected. Things quieted down, including the Chaplain. The rest of the day was uneventful, but we held our record of not going through a truce period unmolested.

The Chaplain held a special place in the battalion. Not being in the chain of command or an authority figure, enabled him to be a spiritual guide to our soldiers as well as a personal friend to many. He was often used by soldiers as an unofficial conduit to inform commanders that something was amiss with individuals or even the junior leadership. A very likeable and generous man, he was always held in high esteem by officers and men alike. In addition, he, like all the commanders, performed the sad duty of writing letters of condolence to the families of those who were killed.

On 2 January 1967, the truce ended and we moved north for another airlift. We sent one platoon back to check the area we had just left. Five VC were digging up the trash dumps, looking for misplaced ammunition and discarded C rations. When discovered, they broke and ran. Three were killed, one was wounded, and one was captured. The wounded one got away without a trace.

CHAPTER ELEVEN

WE LINKED UP WITH Company A again so I had a chance
to work with Bidd Sands some more. We stayed in the Ky
Lo Valley for another five days, linking Companies A and B
into a single perimeter during the nights. Bidd and I got to be
even better friends, with great philosophical discussions in the
evenings about a myriad of topics in which our first sergeants,
Lopez and McNerney, sometimes joined us. I am sure they
considered these pleasant times as continuing the professional
education of their young officers. Both Bidd and I appreciated
their experience and were glad we had them with us. During
the days, we saw little action.

War is not an amusing event, but the average serviceman
must find humor in day-to-day events in order to survive. We
picked up three individuals one day, which for various reasons
we knew had to be VC. We were due for a resupply, so we kept
them overnight with the intention of evacuating them to the
base camp for the intelligence people to question. Our logistics
helicopter arrived the next morning with various items for the
companies. We blindfolded the prisoners and tied their hands

behind their backs, but left their feet free so they could walk. When the helicopter was emptied, the prisoners were walked to the helicopter and placed on the floor. All of our helicopters had door gunners, crew chiefs who manned their side-mounted machine guns during flight, and the doors were never closed. Of course this was the first time the Vietnamese had ever been on an aircraft and they were terrified. The helicopter took off and started across the rice fields towards the tree line gaining elevation with each second. When the aircraft got about fifty feet in the air and was beginning to get some forward momentum, one of the prisoners decided he had just about as much fun on this thrill ride as he could take. He surprised everybody and jumped out of the still climbing helicopter. We all were standing with our mouths open as he fell with legs kicking through the air, hit a dry rice paddy, sort of bounced up onto his feet and disappeared into the forest.

It took a few seconds to recover from the surprise and give chase, but it was too late. He was GONE and not to be found. I hope he survived the war and at night tells the story of his miraculous escape during his Great Event to the open-eyes of his grandchildren.

When the helicopter returned from delivering the remaining two prisoners with another load of C rations, the pilot had affixed a cardboard poster made from a C ration case to the back of his seat. He had written a paraphrase from a popular airline commercial, *"Two out of three VC prefer to fly with us"*.

If you lose your sense of humor in the midst of chaos you can easily lose yourself in the chaos.

CHAPTER TWELVE

WE WERE LIFTED OUT OF the general area of operations on 14 January 1967, with the mission of guarding the 1st Brigade forward CP at North Tuy Hoa airfield while also serving as the Brigade Reaction Force. This was a mission rotated among the battalions over a period of time. While I disliked it, it gave the troops a chance to wind down and get a rest from walking every day. I had to send one platoon to a resupply point at the village of Dong Tre to provide a security force. Resupply facilities were positioned at various locations throughout the country to provide logistical support to Special Forces advisory camps, and other US advisory elements. They also supported South Vietnamese regular troop organizations and civilian irregular defense groups (CIDG) that patrolled their home areas and assisted in protecting villages and critical points such as bridges, roads, and small ports.

The brigade CP was on top of a sandy hill near the outskirts of the town. With transient companies moving in and out as the protective force, there was little development in the security of the area. I felt the condition of the fighting positions was ineffectual and that a good push by a determined enemy force would be able to penetrate the wire. The wire on the perimeter itself was such a joke that I wondered at the professionalism of the people on the brigade staff who were responsible for oversight of the security of the command post. The local ladies of the night (affectionately known to some as boom-boom girls) were permitted to come up to the broken and bent wire obstacle to solicit the soldiers inside the wire and entice them out. The first evening we were there we almost shot some people from the brigade staff who had gone out to the wire after dark.

The second day we were there, the Brigade Commander invited VIPs for lunch, but someone stole his 15-pound turkey while Company B men were on guard. I was pretty sure it was an inside job because I really didn't think my guys were guilty. We were all in fairly close quarters and there was no good way to cook a turkey and eat it without someone in the company seeing or smelling it. However, I was never really sure. These guys were very innovative and imaginative and had been in the boonies for a long time. One thing I did NOT do was line them up and ask if they had stolen the turkey, like the CG had done with the ducks at Fort Lewis. They may not have lied to me. Over the years no one has come forward to admit to the deed, so I suspect my initial suspicion of an inside job was correct.

I put the company to work improving the area's defenses with properly placed concertina wire, bigger and stronger bunkers with sandbagged overhead cover in better locations, and more and deeper trenches. We put trip flares in front of our positions to provide early warning, ran landline communication wire to the platoons for more positive control at night, and denied the brigade staff access to the wire. We also made them more sensitive to passwords and challenges when they were wandering around at night.

The brigade S2 (Intelligence) was the officer in charge of security oversight, so I had to explain to him as well as the brigade commander that they had minimal security in the event of an attack. As senior officers they needed to support me when we stopped the staff from taking unnecessary strolls around the interior of the perimeter. To most of these staff NCOs and officers, the enemy was primarily a theoretical entity represented on their maps as red arrows and symbols. They were intelligent people, but my security measures were considered "inconvenient" and unnecessary in their "safe" rear location.

It was true that the security at Brigade headquarters was never tested in the Tuy Hoa area. However, after our move to the highlands, it was not uncommon for the brigade head-quarters, staffed by many of these same personnel, to receive 50–100 mortar rounds within their perimeter in one night. Learning quickly, individuals moved from place to place while always knowing full well where the nearest protective bunker was located so they could take cover when the mortar rounds started to fall.

After we had improved the defenses, the troops got bored and started getting fiddle foot to return to the field away from all the people. (This feeling probably did not apply to everybody, but it certainly did to me.) It was never good for the troops to be too inactive, because it nourished an environment where small slights, imagined insults, looks and gestures took on unintended meanings between naturally competitive platoons and individuals. Several times I had to mediate or take other action to resolve conflicts.

I also had to deal with normal administrative matters that did not stop wherever we were. Some of the troops from the platoon at Dong Tre were caught in off-limit bars and broth-els, so I dealt with them. One was an NCO, who should have been more responsible, I recommended him for a Special Courts Martial. Two soldiers received oral reprimands and fines under Article 15 while others received extra duty based upon the individual situation. It was difficult for me to take these actions because I completely understood the situation of being in the field, subject to combat week after week with no recreation or stress relief. Being given a job close to temptation made it seem natural to take advantage of opportunities, even though it was prohibited for hygiene, health or security reasons. Whatever the reason for the off-limits restriction, breaking it was prohibited and discipline had to be maintained.

In spite of our brief respite at the Brigade Headquarters, we were reminded on 19 January that there was still a nasty shooting war in progress. One of Company A's platoons encountered a tough, professional North Vietnamese Army unit of some 35 soldiers. Of the nine men in the U. S. squad that made contact, four were killed, with an unknown number of enemy dead. This was the first major action in the battalion that resulted in multiple friendly casualties. The word soon spread. It was a tragic reminder for everyone that we were in a dangerous business and we needed to be on the alert at all times. The enemy was not always moving around in small groups, and he was capable of inflicting a lot of damage.

CHAPTER THIRTEEN

WE WERE RELIEVED BY Company C and moved to the field northwest of Tuy Hoa on 20 January. Airlifted to the battalion CP overlooking another broad valley and moved out on foot from there, the fourth platoon surprised a VC while he was resting. He got away with his weapon, but we did find his ammunition, web gear, and gas mask which verified he was a soldier.

On another evening I personally briefed a squad leader who was going to put in an ambush on what looked like a well-used trail. I particularly wanted a prisoner, so I made this very clear to the young NCO. I asked him if he knew any Vietnamese and he said all he knew was *"di di"* and a couple of other words that had nothing to do with our current situation. The term *"di di"* had been shortened by GI's from the phrase *"di di mau"* that when loosely translated meant to bug out, to move quickly or to go somewhere quickly. It had become a verb of action as in, *"We saw the Sergeant coming so we thought it was time to di di."* Or, *"The mortars were hitting all around us, so we di di'd out of there."* I didn't know much more, but I had a small phrase book that had proven useful in the past, so I taught the squad leader a new word, *"dung lai"*. As far as I could figure out it meant *"stop."* I had him practice it several times until I thought he had it cold. Off he went, muttering, *"dung lai, dung lai, dung lai"*. The next morning he and his platoon leader reported back to me on the results of the ambush.

When I asked him how it went, he said shamefacedly, *"Well, sir, we got set up on that trail in a good position where we could see both directions, and just before dark this guy came bopping along with his weapon over his shoulder. I was a little excited and was practicing "dung lai" to myself so I would do it right; but when I stepped out in front of him with my weapon leveled I got a little confused and couldn't think of anything to shout, except, 'Di Di'! AND HE DID! I was so surprised that I just let him run off down the trail and he got away. We moved our position of course, but nobody else came down the trail all night."*

This of course proved another of Murphy's Laws correct. *"If your ambush is set correctly, the enemy will never come close to it."*

Many of us have been in situations when we intended to say something under stress in English, but something else came out of our mouths. When you try it in a foreign language, it is even more difficult. Even though I was aggravated, the visual description was funny to me. In addition, the incident was past, the squad leader would never forget something like that and a lesson was learned. There was no need to berate him. As a training point we went over his disposition of the ambush to make sure he had done it correctly, and I asked what he would do differently next time. He said, *"I'll let somebody else do the Vietnamese!"*

We conducted normal field operations with one platoon working at night on ambushes and another working on day sweeps. The other two platoons worked on their own. I felt this gave the platoon leadership good training in being away from the centralized company effort, and helping them address routine decisions they generally did not have to make when we operated as a consolidated unit.

I had come to the non-original conclusion that helicopters hovering over us all the time gave our presence away and may have been one of the reasons why we were not more successful in finding larger units of the NVA or VC. With this in mind, I ordered each platoon to start carrying 9 meals per man so we could operate for at least three days without relying upon air resupply and that from now on, only medivac aircraft would be permitted into the company area. (Of course I had no control over the battalion commander, but he understood my concern and agreed to limit his visits.)

I was told the 4.2-inch mortar platoon was going to be placed under my operational control because it was anticipated we would be moving out of the artillery's 105-millimeter howitzer range. The battalion mortars would provide our indirect fire support.

After waiting three days, I learned the 4.2 mortar platoon would not come under my control but would remain with the artillery guns. This annoyed me because I had been pushing the platoons out to the edge of the artillery fan in anticipation of getting the mortars, which would have extended our search area.

Then, on the day I selected for resupply and a hot meal for the company, I told the third platoon to secure a landing zone and begin accepting supply loads. They did this, to include the hot meals in mermite cans for the rest of the company. The remainder of the company was converging on the third platoon location. I was traveling with the first platoon. In keeping with my standard procedure, I tried not to interfere with the internal workings of the platoons, which included, when possible, avoiding telling them exactly how to do their jobs. In this case, it was to find the third platoon area. The first platoon point man (whoever the poor guy was) couldn't find anything except the thickest woods and brush to go through. I received a radio call from the second platoon that they couldn't figure out exactly where they were, and the fourth platoon was way off course as well.

I finally got disgusted with the whole mess. We had not seen any bad guys for over a week. If there any VC around they were probably laughing so hard they wouldn't be able to take advantage of a small group wandering around by themselves anyway. So I took the company headquarters section—myself, two radio operators, the forward observer, a medic, and the first sergeant—and struck off. It was not a particularly smart move, but I was curious to see if we could move cross-country to the rendezvous point faster. I remembered this made the radio guys a little nervous, but I was so aggravated I actually hoped we would find someone to beat on.

We arrived at the third platoon two hours before the first platoon arrived. The second platoon finally made it, and it took the fourth platoon four hours to waltz in. In reaching the landing zone, I determined the third platoon was 1,000 meters off from where the platoon leadership thought it was. The hot meals and mail had been dropped off and it was getting to be evening. We tried to fire a protective artillery mission but we were out of range. I had had such a bad day I decided not to tell battalion, since they would have wanted us to move back within the artillery fan. It would have been a night move; we had all the paraphernalia that went with resupply and I was sure it would have been another disaster on top of the one we had just experienced.

Supply day

Literally, I was not a happy camper that evening. The following day battalion moved the artillery guns towards us, which put us back into the fan, so we became legal. However, they couldn't send us any aircraft until later in the day to collect the mermites, the mail, and the other stuff that had to go back to the rear. We had to hump everything about three miles over a mountain to another LZ where all the excess paraphernalia could be extracted. At this point we were instructed to keep moving to another LZ where we would be picked up for an insertion into another area of operations. This further convinced me we should not be burdened with extraneous equipment on a daily basis and we should be self-sufficient for as long as possible.

All in all, it was a very frustrating couple of days. I was peeved that the platoons had all become disoriented on the same day, since I thought we had worked out all the map reading and orienteering bugs. I blamed myself for not training the troops harder in those elements in which we were obviously weak. I immediately started focusing on map reading skills for the entire company, to include the NCOs and all platoon members. I wanted everyone to be able to read a map and tell where he was independently of anyone else. I knew there would come a time when all of our squad leaders would be asked to set up ambushes away from their parent platoons. I wanted every individual in the entire company, no matter his position, to be able to call in and adjust artillery fire. The incident with

Creek Crossing

the first platoon, where the radio operators had to adjust fire (even though it had been done through our forward observer) told me that everybody should know the basic skills.

Map reading was not just a good thing to know, it was a matter of real survival in combat situations. As it turned out, the problem may not have been as bad as I had originally thought. My platoon leaders had been training their subordinates in map reading techniques in periods of relative calm and had permitted them to make a few mistakes to impress upon them the need for good location skills. For whatever reason, this wholesale disorientation never happened again, so we either fixed it or were very lucky.

The next few days were busy. We continued searching our assigned area for anything out of the ordinary, but found little. At one point we climbed down into a canyon that was close to 300 meters deep with a creek at the bottom. Halfway across I lost my footing and fell in. I was with second platoon and I thought, "*What the heck, we ought to stop and take a bath*". I had just taken my shirt off when the S3 called and said, "*Find an LZ for your entire element in 40 minutes!*"

The first platoon was already on top of the ridge in a good place for an LZ, so they were told to secure it for the rest of us. Second platoon and I started up the hill. third and fourth platoons were still in deep woods, so they started for LZ's closer to them. Fourth platoon ran across what seemed to be a VC base camp with fires still burning. However, we were told not to delay and keep moving, so we had no time to search the area. The third platoon had to go up a hill against hundreds of punji stakes. One soldier passed out from exhaustion and one fell and cracked his head. There were no places to land a helicopter, so the platoon had to continue with its injured.

The first and second platoons with the company headquarters were airlifted exactly 45 minutes after the first notice, in spite of the hard haul to the LZ. The fourth platoon got to an LZ right after we did and was picked up immediately as well. The third platoon had the most difficult route to follow and couldn't get to an LZ until after dark. The helicopters had changed frequencies and didn't have ours, so it made coordination that night a little tough. However, we all made it back to base camp at Tuy Hoa and closed in by 2000 hours on 25 January.

A humorous story came from SP4 Cliff Rountree of the fourth platoon: *"We were all being picked up by the helicopters and I was the last man getting on the one my squad was on...all of a sudden I was booted off because they shouted they were overloaded and I made the load too heavy! I looked around, there was one bird still loading on the far side of the pickup zone, so I started running towards it. It had been raining and the grass was wet with little puddles and ponds so I was splashing through trying to get to the chopper. All of a sudden I was submerged in a hole completely filled with water with my rucksack and weapon...I was too surprised to stop, so I kept moving my legs and just ran myself up and out of that hole! I just made it to the helicopter and they had room for me, otherwise I would have been left by myself on the LZ in enemy territory!"*

This never happened, but the platoon leadership was responsible to make sure no one was left on the LZ. My instructions were that if there wasn't enough room on a helicopter, then that man's squad stayed with him until there was enough transport for everyone.

After arriving at base camp, we found that all of the battalion's companies, minus base camp personnel were scheduled to leave for Pleiku the next morning by C-130. The battalion was to be placed under the operational control of the 2d Brigade to provide additional combat power. An estimated three NVA regiments were massing in Cambodia with the intention of entering the Fourth ID's area of responsibility and General Peers was determined to stop them.

CHAPTER FOURTEEN

O N 26 JANUARY 1967, we flew from Tuy Hoa on the coast
into New Pleiku Airfield in the highlands. We trucked out
towards the border to a firebase called the "Oasis," which, at
the time, was the 2d Brigade's headquarters. Since we were
operating a long ways away from the 1st Brigade, still on the
coast, we were now under the operational control of the 2d
Brigade.

The red dust was about three inches deep all around and
it was extremely hot. The weather in Vietnam was always a
puzzle to me. In the highlands it was the dry season, while
only a few hundred kilometers away, the coastal areas were
in the monsoon season. In Texas we might have storms in
different parts of the state, but not entire different seasons! It
just didn't make sense to me. But then we were in Vietnam!

We camped in the Oasis for a couple of days and I took
the company for a walk into the area for some acclimatization
to make them understand the importance of salt tablets and
lots of water. Salt tablets have since gone out of style, but for

a number of years they were the staple for replacing body salt lost by perspiration in dry climates.

We company commanders took terrain orientation helicopter rides with Colonel Lee over the general area. The Oasis was located a few kilometers north of the Ia Drang River Valley that had seen a large battle on LZ XRAY between the 1st Cavalry Division and the NVA in November 1965, just a little over a year before. This was the battle commemorated in the book *"We Were Soldiers Once...and Young"* by Harold Moore and Joseph Galloway and was the first major battle between U.S. and NVA forces.

We also flew fairly close to the Cambodian border and thought we could see smoke rising from where the NVA regiments were allegedly located. We were told that US troops were not allowed closer than one kilometer to the border to forestall any international incidents that might occur if we accidentally operated in the next country. This seemed rather ridiculous to me since I figured we would be in a fight for our lives and everybody knew the NVA were using Cambodia and Laos as safe-havens. I thought we had learned something from Korea about letting the enemy have sanctuaries where they could rest, resupply and assemble without fear of punitive action. Obviously there were elements in the Big Picture that were not visible to my limited viewpoint and those of my soldiers.

On 27 January, Company A moved by air from the Oasis to secure a bridge on a route north. The word was that we would be heading to a place called Kontum, about 40 kilometers north of Pleiku, and that we would be going by truck. The next day we learned that we would be going to a small Special Forces (SF) camp near Polei Kleng, a little west of Kontum. Colonel Lee, CPT Al Treado (Company C commander) and I flew up for a reconnaissance. The mountain ranges of the highlands made the hills of the coast very small indeed. It quickly became obvious we were in for some strenuous exercise just to get from one place to another even without considering the NVA.

We stopped by the Special Forces camp located just inside Vietnam on the Laotian and Cambodian border for a briefing. The "A" Detachment Commander was Captain Don Enloe, one of my former OCS classmates. After bringing each other up to date on what we had been doing for the last six years, he told us that Intelligence indicated there was an estimated 1,500-man NVA regiment moving toward his area with about 200 VC supplementing the force. I arrogantly thought, "*We might be able to get in some good licks yet.*"

We flew back to Pleiku that afternoon. I had a chance to get to the Division Headquarters to see old acquaintances from my short time on the staff. I had an opportunity to chat with Major Vancil in the G1 section and also with Lieutenant Colonel Rosell, the Division G3. Colonel Rosell was interested in my viewpoints as a company commander, even though the battalion had just arrived and had seen no action in the highlands as of yet. He and Major Vancil were interested that I carried an M79 grenade launcher instead of an M16, and I explained my rationale. We then discussed the possibility of fielding a new fleschette shotgun round for the M79.

Colonel Lee arranged for his company commanders to get together with some of the company commanders from the 1-22d Infantry. They had been working in the area for the last several months and had some useful information to share about fighting in the area. Our operations on the coast had been primarily against small NVA or VC elements that we generally outnumbered. The coastal terrain had broad plains as well as mountains interspersed with broad valleys that were dotted with villages and possessed a fairly large population base. The vegetation along the coast consisted primarily of rice fields, bamboo, some mountain forests and tall grasses.

In the Central Highlands, by contrast, our enemy were well-trained, main force North Vietnamese Army divisions and regiments that attacked in waves with mortar support. They preferred to find U.S. companies and attack in superior numbers with one or two battalions ensuring large American casualty numbers without regard to their own losses.

The vegetation in the highlands was double and triple canopy forest, bamboo and extremely steep slopes on the higher mountains. In some areas, herbicides had been sprayed to denude the forests of their leaves and branches to deny the NVA cover and concealment.

Since open areas were not always readily available, landing zones often had to be cut out of the jungle so helicopters could provide resupply or medical evacuation. As far as firebases were concerned, we heard that 500 rounds of enemy mortar fire in one night were not uncommon. After shelling a firebase, or attacking a unit, the NVA ducked back across the borders to Cambodia or Laos. We were told that it was just common sense for a company to stop early in the day to dig foxholes with overhead log cover to protect against mortar shrapnel in the event of an attack. It was even more important to fire artillery defensive fires around your perimeter when you stopped and you never wanted to get outside your artillery fan range. The guys of the 1-22d were extremely helpful and we took their comments to heart. It was obvious we still had a lot to learn about war in the highlands.

Murphy's Laws:

"The enemy invariably attacks on two occasions:

a. When they are ready and

b. When you aren't."

As usual, things didn't work out as the plan indicated. We were awakened at 0130 on 31 January and told that instead of going to Polei Kleng, we were moving west of Duc Co, another small, but important intelligence-gathering US Special Forces camp with a force of Civilian Irregular Defense Group (CIDG) Montagnards. Montagnards were an ethnic group native to the highlands and worked well with U. S. forces. These were local inhabitants who were armed and supported to defend their local villages. We moved out by truck at 0730.

Someone tried to put me into the cab of a truck, but I elected to ride in the back of the uncovered truck with the troops. I figured that if anyone hit us with an ambush during the move, they would aim most of their initial fire on the lead cabs, which meant I would have to deal with getting out of the door, thus delaying any reaction time I might have to respond to the ambush. I figured most of us could bail out the back and over the sides a lot faster. As our move progressed, however, I had occasion to rethink my decision. In the end, though I could have changed my decision, I decided to suffer along with the troops. I had thought the dust was bad when we first arrived but it was nothing compared to what we endured this time. The road was traveled so much, with no rain, that the surface now consisted of several inches of powdered red dust. It hung in the air...we couldn't see the back of the tailgate and it clogged everything. Eyes, ears, nostrils, skin, weapons, uniforms and web gear were covered with a fine red color. I was almost hoping for an ambush so we would have an excuse to stop and breathe.

We finally arrived at Duc Co where Don Hunter took my picture. I felt a sorry sight and I was! I told him I wanted a copy of the picture and he agreed. In 1986, almost 20 years later, he showed up at my house in Vienna, Virginia with several other members of the company and presented me with my copy. Even after long years in the Middle Eastern deserts, I can still taste the dust on that one trip in the central highlands. The picture has become the symbol of my time in Vietnam and it occupies a place in our house in Houston to remind me to be grateful for air conditioning, clean rain and paved roads.

We were told to set up a perimeter and dig in. About an hour later we were told to stop digging and get back on the trucks. We moved further west into the drainage basin of the Ia Drang River with more dust settling on us. We rode into a large area that had been cleared by one of our escort tanks going around in circles and knocking down the underbrush and tall grass. The area had once been the location of a village on the border, but the huts had long since been burnt. With the inhabitants gone, vegetation had reclaimed the area. This was the new battalion CP and firebase.

Our web gear never recovered from the dust however, and retained the reddish patina that marked those of us who had been the "dust route."

Author after red dust ride

CHAPTER FIFTEEN

THE NEXT MORNING WE LEFT the firebase and moved west towards the Cambodian border along the northern edges of the Ia Drang Valley.

The day was bright and hot without a cloud in sight. The terrain was open and rolling with broad-leafed trees fifteen to twenty feet high and small green leafed shrubs below. Dry grass stretched between the trees and dust puffed up wherever we put our feet. The dust, the heat and the grass combined to make a musty smell that was not unpleasant, but the combination made our noses itch and eyes water. Visibility was good out to about a hundred meters.

I had two platoons leading in column with the other two following and deployed outwards to the sides. The command group was behind the right lead platoon. We had flankers and scouts out to provide early warning, something we weren't always able to do.

We found a cleared area surrounded by trees for a company position and dumped our rucksacks, leaving the first platoon as the reserve force. The rest of us continued west to a CIDG outpost.

We found the outpost on the old road that led directly to the border. I found it strange that we were able to find them so easily and wondered why the NVA hadn't done so as well. They were from Duc Co, and Duc Co was under constant threat of attack since it sat on a main avenue of approach from Cambodia into Vietnam.

I put the three platoons into the brush around us and settled down in the shade of a little copse of the broad-leafed trees to chat with the team chief. The Montagnards were small, wizened little brown men with wrinkled faces, constant grins and teeth blackened from chewing betel nut. Their haircuts were bowl style and their eyes were black and constantly moving as different things about us caught their attention. Of small stature, it was obvious they were at home in the forest. A couple of them had short-sleeved shirts but all wore loincloths. The others were dressed for the weather in just loincloths and some had leather necklaces with small bags around their necks. They all looked straight out of National Geographic.

I saw two small crossbows, probably used for small game hunting, but they also had old WWII M1 .30 caliber carbines. The rifles didn't look well maintained, but I didn't ask to look at one. The team chief and I tried sign language and what little French I knew and what little English he knew. He rattled on for a while and then started puffing on his long slender pipe looking serious and worldly. I rattled on for a while with big expansive gestures and drawings on the ground while he looked inscrutable. We finally started laughing at what we were doing squatted down on our haunches, making motions but passing little information.

I finally saw a radio antenna sticking up and got the message across to him to call his bosses at the Special Forces camp at

Duc Co. After much difficulty, I finally got an American on and explained to him that I was trying to find out about trails in the area that were not on our maps. He said he would send me an overlay, so that finished my business with the outpost. As I was leaving, I noticed one of the Montagnards looking at the latest issue of Playboy. I am sure the articles intrigued him. Somehow it seemed a little out of place, but there were always small moments of humor in between periods of boredom and fright.

The next morning we were instructed to standby to accept guests before we moved out. We acquired two tracking dogs and their handlers to help us find traces of any NVA activity as we worked our way west and down into the Ia Drang Valley. I moved the whole company, but got a late start waiting for the dogs. We made only about ten kilometers when we found a great spot on top of a small hill for an LZ and position. We spent about an hour and a half clearing trees and making an LZ. To us, the spot was better than Dulles Airport. We dug bunkers with sturdy overhead cover around the top of the hill with visible fields of fire that made it into a great defensive position. It definitely commanded the surrounding terrain.

Murphy's Laws:

"If your positions are firmly set and you are prepared to take the enemy assault on, he will bypass you."

The next morning we left the fourth platoon as the CP guard for our rucksacks and moved out with the dogs to an area where our intelligence said there was a lot of enemy activity. We swept through and found a carbine with magazine, but no people. We continued toward the Cambodian border, got a little closer than one kilometer, and started back. Our new S3, Major Warren Mercer, became concerned because we weren't supposed to be that close, and we had already diminished our firepower by leaving one platoon as our rear security. He also was concerned by the fact that I was planning on spending the night in the same place twice. Both were valid concerns, but I felt I had compensated for them by sweeping the area around our perimeter for several kilometers out and saw no evidence of enemy activity, even by a watcher. The overnight position was away from the natural avenues of movement, so it was less likely that a casual enemy passer-by would identify our specific location. The other concern about spending two nights in one place, in my opinion, was overcome by the fact that we had time to improve our positions even that much more... deeper holes, better overhead cover, clearing better fields of fire, more time to fire in artillery concentrations, etc. I didn't list these items over the radio, so I just listened to the S3 make his comments. I responded by saying I thought it would be fine to stay one more night.

We got back to our little hill about 2:30 PM and Colonel Lee flew in to see us. He looked at our LZ, took a trip around the perimeter, checked our defensive positions, asked a few questions, seemed pleased and flew out. We brought in hot chow and sodas with mail for the troops. We had to hurry the chow call so we could get the mermite containers out before dark. When we got the mail sack open, one guy had a package with a hole in it. He opened it up and found a bullet in a can of peaches. I suggested to the pilot that he not return by the exact same route on his return. He agreed. I also received the trail overlay I had been promised by the SF guy in Duc Co.

I realized we had a lot of adjustments to make from the coastal war to the highlands, but I felt we were making a good start. Even so, I was apprehensive about working in the Ia Drang Valley after the Cavalry's big fight the year before. As one of my tactical instructors used to say *"You can change the people variables in a tactical situation, but you can't change the terrain!"*

Since the Ia Drang Valley was a major avenue of approach into Vietnam from Cambodia, I was sure the NVA would not stop using it. We were just the latest obstacle in their way and only time would tell how successful we would be in stopping and eliminating their forces.

CHAPTER SIXTEEN

THE HEAT WAS OVERWHELMING and dry. It was obvious we had to adjust more quickly to the weather and operational tempo. Due to the heat, we sent our field jackets and other non-essential items back to the battalion rear area at Dragon Mountain.

I started thinking again about what we absolutely had to carry in order to survive and came up with ammunition, explosives, food and water. As on the coast, I wanted to be able to work for at least three or more days at a time without a helicopter coming in to our position. Since it appeared we were going to be in the general area for a long time, I did not want the company to become predictable. My goal was for us to become jungle-wise and more like ghosts who were able to hit hard and fast without giving ourselves away. I wanted to "out-injun" the NVA and I felt fewer visits and resupplies would enable us to maintain higher levels of security and secrecy, which would give us a better chance of surprising the NVA.

Since we had some moonlight, I thought it might not be bad to get the troops used to making night moves. If the enemy could do it, why couldn't we? I started with a little bit of practice, so we got up early and started moving by 0530 while it was still dark. I figured if there was someone out there watching us he would not expect us to be moving before daylight. We were all a little edgy; but either there was no one around or we took them by surprise. We caught the S3 shop by surprise as well, we had to report twice we were moving that early. That led to the inevitable discussion with them about the dangers of movement in the dark.

It was 5 February, and we still had not had an opportunity to get clean from our dusty move the week before, so we moved north to a beautiful little stream with clear, clean water and small rapids. We set up security, took baths, washed clothes and in general took the morning off for in-country rest and relaxation.

That afternoon we moved out to check some of the river trails on my new overlay. We found one large enough to have been used as one of the routes leading east from the Ho Chi Minh trail across the border. However, it did not look like it had been used recently. An Air Force Piper Cub spotter plane was shot at about 5 kilometers away, out of our area of operation. He obviously had no idea where the sniper was, but he must have had a spare air strike loitering because he used it on the area as well as some artillery. I thought it was a lot of money to spend on one sniper, but also thought it might make the culprit think a little longer before he shot at the U.S. Air Force again.

We moved to the top of a hill for the night. It had good defensive positions, big trees, and little undergrowth. That the weather was cool and pleasant was all the better.

We were instructed to check out the sniper area the next morning, so we came off the hill. Unfortunately, the unit had two cases of food poisoning overnight, so we had to carry the men to an LZ to get them airlifted out. Then we set up ambushes throughout the area around a region that covered about four square kilometers. Nothing came of it.

The next day there was another Air Force Forward Air Controller (FAC) Piper Cub aircraft flying in the area. I got the pilot on the radio and talked to him about what we were doing. I asked him if he would mind flying low over our area so someone would shoot at him and we could then get a fix on the sniper.

There was dead silence on the radio while the pilot considered what I was asking. One must remember that these guys were not used to spending their time getting shot at; they spent their evenings at base camps with hot showers and cold beers. They worked mostly during the day flying over terrain helping ground guys like me get explosives on the ground where they were needed, but theirs was a completely different military culture.

After a short while, this guy came back and said, *"Let me get this straight. You want me to fly around down there, so somebody will shoot at me, so you can shoot at him. Is that it?"*

I said, *"Yes, but the sniper is not a very good shot and there is hardly any danger in him hitting you, besides, you might even see him from up there."*

He responded, *"Do you think I'm crazy?"*

I said, *"Well, you are in the Air Force and that says a great deal about it, when you could be down here on the ground without having to worry about falling out of the sky at any time."*

He chuckled and then finally said something like *"Ohhh Kayyy... but this is definitely not in my job description."*

With that, he tumbled down out of the sky, leveled out and made several passes over our area. The sniper shot at him several times and missed, but we got a fix on the enemy location, which was about 2 kilometers towards the Cambodian border.

Of course the platoons were in the wrong places and we had to move quickly to try and apprehend the fellow. The aircraft stayed with us trying to identify where the sniper was, but no luck, even though we moved all the way to the border against all regulations and policies. I felt fairly secure since we had our own overhead spotter and there did not seem to be any NVA units in the area. The pilot finally had to return for fuel but made sure he had our unit identification since I told him I owed him a beer or maybe even two.

He was definitely more cheerful when he was at a higher altitude heading back to Pleiku airbase and thanked us for a most interesting afternoon. I thought he had gone beyond normal duties with no safety guarantees and passed on the incident to battalion to make sure his squadron knew about his assistance, even though we were not successful in catching the sniper. After his departure, we moved smartly back east where we were supposed to be, and found a spot for the night.

The next day we moved into the battalion firebase to become the "palace guard". Since we had moved to the highlands, a battery (six guns) of 105-millimeter howitzers was always co-located with the battalion headquarters to provide fire support for the battalion's line companies. This also provided extended and additional fire coverage for other battalion's units if they were within range. In order to secure the battalion headquarters and the guns, one rifle company was always present to secure the firebase while the other two were out working the areas. Since the firebase moved every three to five days, we could expect to provide security for the firebase every two to three weeks or so. Of course, operational requirements sometimes required us to be in the field for longer than a couple of weeks, but at least there was an attempt to balance out the time spent in the field versus the firebase.

When we came into the firebase, Company A moved out into the same area we had just left. I remember thinking they would probably find the sniper we could not. They found him, but he was able to wound one of their soldiers before he got away from them as well. We once again improved communication trenches and bunkers, received mail, got resupplied with clothing and Captain Pat Mantooth, my replacement as the personnel officer came in and set up an airmobile PX. The facilities and inventory were limited, but the troops truly appreciated the effort.

We stayed several days at the firebase, but even there it wasn't completely safe. Again, Company B had a casualty from an avoidable accident. It was a sunny day and guys had their shirts off and were sitting on their sandbagged bunkers taking care of housecleaning matters and writing letters. There was no contact in the Area of Operations and the artillery was quiet. It was one of those beautiful and peaceful days that made you glad you were alive and enjoying the moment. We shared the firebase with the battalion Recon Platoon. One of the Recon NCOs was standing next to his bunker, with his tools on the sandbags cleaning his rifle. I was standing about 20 feet away from him just looking out from the perimeter wondering what we had done to deserve a day like this. I heard a sharp BANG! and jerked around to see the NCO looking at his rifle as if it were a snake. Further down the line I heard immediate cries for a Medic. I knew immediately what had happened and ran down to where the soldier had been shot. I shouted for someone to get a dust-off and heard a reply that it was on the way. When I got to the soldier I saw he had been shot in the neck. A medic was trying to staunch the blood flow but it looked pretty bad.

A resupply helicopter was in the firebase and we got SP4 Robert Earl Gabbard onto it accompanied by one of our battalion medics, and they flew to the hospital at Jackson Hole, the 1st Brigade headquarters and the closest hospital located northeast of Duc Co. The Command and Control helicopter had just been refueled and I asked permission from Colonel Gannon to let me use it to see how my soldier was doing. He OK'd the flight and when I arrived at the hospital I was able to talk to the medical personnel. They had just stabilized the soldier and told me he would live. I transmitted that back to the firebase so his friends and the rest of the company would know. He was later transferred to Japan and the US for medical treatment.

Jim Burch in his letter home commented: *"This may be short as I feel pretty bad this morning. Robert Earl (Gabbard) was shot about a half hour ago. We had just come back from taking a shower. Just received word that he will live. He was shot in the right side of his neck. The bullet came out the left side. An E-6 Sgt from Recon was cleaning his rifle when it went off."*

As I recall, the Recon NCO was a good soldier and this was taken into consideration, but he was still fined, reduced in grade with some other punishments and transferred out of the battalion. If Gabbard had died the punishment would have been much harsher.

On 11 February we were split up for other duties. I had to attach the third platoon to the 1st-69th Armor for road security between Pleiku and An Khe, while the first platoon was attached to the 1st-10th Cavalry to protect the engineer quarry west of the Oasis. The other two platoons and my headquarters went in to Dragon Mountain to form a reaction force to defend the division base camp. This was a duty that rotated among the Division's line companies so no company would become complacent in its duties. It also provided the companies with a little break from humping the boonies.

The Division units and staff sections permanently located at Dragon Mountain provided personnel to man the base perimeter at night and to conduct limited patrols. But their firepower and training were limited, so they were at a disadvantage if they had to engage any sizeable NVA force. For that reason, the defense was supplemented by a rifle unit.

One of my non-infantry friends, who was assigned to the base camp told me about one time when he was picked to lead a short night patrol a few kilometers outside the perimeter. It was dark and he had six or seven inexperienced young men with him. At any rate, they heard muted noises coming from a wooded ravine and convinced themselves the NVA were sneaking up on the perimeter to recon for an attack. My friend the patrol leader called for mortars and flares, but the noises continued and nothing could be seen down in the ravine. The mortars kept missing the target, so the patrol was ordered to make contact to clarify the situation. The patrol quietly moved to the lip of the ravine, rifles at the ready. When they got to the edge of the drop off, in the light of the flares, they saw brush and trees moving as if men were trying to get away and out of the target zone.

The patrol leader shouted *"Open Fire!!"* and an explosive and withering fire poured down into the killing zone. There was constant thrashing about, trees and shrubs were bent and knocked over and after a while all was still except for an occasional moan. The patrol was ordered to stay in place in the event there were other NVA elements. When daylight came the patrol looked into the ravine and counted the bodies. It was an adrenaline rush for the rear camp commandos. However, the bodies were not NVA, but water buffalo from the nearby villages that had gotten too near the perimeter. It was an exciting night and those that participated, in a parody of the famous black soldiers of the western frontier campaigns, became known as "the buffalo soldiers".

We received two tanks, two flamethrower equipped armored personnel carriers (APC) and two regular APCs for carrying troops to augment our reaction force. As a result, I had my own mechanized and armored teeny weenie task force. I rotated one platoon on and the other one off on a daily basis. The division base stayed on a mortar alert for three days expecting some sort of attack. It was difficult to see how anything very large could get too close to the perimeter with radar on top of the mountain that reached out eleven kilometers (almost 7 miles) and the internal division artillery and mortars that discouraged any night movement around the perimeter. One night we launched one platoon into the dark to check out some suspicious movement based on radar reports, but found nothing.

The platoons conducted daily patrols and put ambushes out in the evenings. There really wasn't much for the company headquarters section to do, since most of the real work fell to the platoon on duty. One good thing about the assignment was that the camp had a hot water shower unit set up for us. Of course the weather was cold and you froze in the wind when you got out to dry off. (No idea what happened to the hot and dry weather we had in the field!)

The food folks from the division had not planned on two platoons being assigned as the reaction force, so there weren't enough A rations (hot meals) prepared. We had to supplement meals with our own C rations. I thought this was a crime since everybody else on the division base ate in a regular mess hall with hot meals and no C's. After I talked to the division logistics officer, the situation was squared away, though it took me some time to get through all the bureaucratic hoops.

I took advantage of being in the rear to visit some of our folks in the hospital and to get mail to them. A couple of times

I was able to get out during the day and visit the other two platoons with the armor and cavalry units to see how they were doing. They fit in so well that the company commanders to whom they were attached wanted to keep them. I joshed these guys and told them we had real work to do instead of living the good life in rear areas. (Of course, these units were in areas of imminent danger as well, but we rifle companies had to uphold the mystique that the real action in the Fourth Infantry Division was west of Pleiku.)

I was ready to get back into the field. I was beginning to feel like I had when we were the palace guard around the brigade headquarters in Tuy Hoa. We had scrounged canvas cots on which to sleep but to me they were too confining and restrictive (the sides seemed to ride up around you at night even though the canvas was drawn very tight). In a perverse way, I didn't want to start liking the cot too much, so I slept on the floor with my air mattress and poncho liner as I did in the field. After I held rather informal inspections of the platoons and ensured they were being taken care of and were ready to do their jobs, there wasn't much for me to do during the day, and the noise around the camp was like a big city.

The base worked 24 hours a day to support the Division's 30,000 plus soldiers and there were no restrictions on having lights on at night. If you were outside the camp perimeter there was no difficulty in identifying that a major something was going on inside the wire.

Trucks and jeeps roared around and helicopters constantly came and went. Red dust rose and fell from the dirt roads of the camp and the helicopter airfield. There was always the smell of diesel and aviation fuel being burned in latrine barrels on a daily basis.

I yearned for the clean smell of the forest, its quiet shadows and the absence of pollution. In the division base camp, uniforms were all light green without any reddish dust residue. They were starched and laundered, and the soldiers were clean-shaven with neat haircuts. The black leather portions of their jungle boots shined. The green canvas part of the boots looked like they had just come out of the box. By contrast, it was easy to see who had spent much time in the field. I tried to wash and shine my boots, but they remained reddish green, scarred and definitely different from the boots of staff officers.

I went into the officer's club a couple of times to have a beer and listen to the music of the Philippina bands sing *"Country Road"* and other songs that had been hits in the U.S. a few years past. Even in my cleaned up uniform, still reddish-green and limp, with no starch or "I've been there" badges, and faded camouflaged rank insignia, I was out of place. The staff officers were clean, noisy, and boisterous and they looked at me as if I were a leper. Their conversation revolved around sports scores, Red Cross dollies they had managed to hold hands with, the possibility of meeting nurses, their R&R conquests and what car they were going to buy when they got home. From time to time, when a unit in the field had an action, and the rumors would swirl, they would nod and speak knowingly about what actually happened. They heard it from someone who had listened to the firefight on an FM radio, or they had a friend who worked in the hospital and couldn't join them for a drink because a surge of wounded had inconveniently arrived.

I was reminded of the scene in the film *"Lawrence of Arabia"* when Lawrence comes back to British headquarters in Cairo after fighting in the desert with the Arabs. He is not dressed like the others and is obviously "different" from the vision of a proper British officer. He does not fit in with former comrades, makes others uncomfortable, and finds himself shunned by the regular staff. Human nature sometimes creates strange situations.

In later years I have come to understand that to these men, our actions in the field were similar to football or basketball games. The officer's club residents were removed from the reality of the action, but they wanted to participate in some manner, even if it was just talking about it. The closest most of them ever came to combat were the sporadic mortar attacks on the Base, and hearing about firefights via the rumor grapevine. Somehow it gave them a sense of being a part of it.

I understood these guys had their part to play in the war and without the support of their work, the job of the infantry would be impossible. The seemingly casual shallowness of these "wannabees" angered me, and I felt uncomfortable in their company and they in mine. I was determined that I would try to avoid being assigned out of the battalion when it came time for me to give up the company.

We grunts always commented sarcastically on the "good life" of cold beer, soft bunks and hot food enjoyed by Rear Echelon MFs (REMFs); but division base camp life definitely was not for me.

CHAPTER SEVENTEEN

WE WERE NOTIFIED AT 11:30 PM on 21 February that another unit was going to take over our division rear area duties and that we were to move out the next day. Hooray! I was ready...

The following morning I collected all the troops, marched the two kilometers down to the airfield and finally scrounged a Hook (Chinook helicopter) to pick us up and take us out to the battalion firebase. Unfortunately during the flight, the helicopter received an urgent mission and we were let off at the wrong battalion's firebase (what a surprise for both the strange battalion and ourselves!). However, with the help of the battalion's S3 we finally were able to get another ride to our unit.

My other two platoons were detached from their support jobs and airlifted in on the afternoon of the 22d. We stayed one night and were delighted to leave the next morning. The firebase was in one of those places that had no vegetative ground cover and the dust had been beaten into the finest powder particles. Whenever an aircraft came in, the dirt was blown over and into everything. It was a challenge to keep weapons clean, not to mention ourselves. This was not the only time in Vietnam we had to endure this condition, but at least we riflemen were able to get out into the quiet jungle to breathe clean air most of the time. The poor artillerymen, and those who had to live in battalion firebases, had to put up with the daily dust pollution throughout their combat tours.

As soon as we were out into the field, we got word that the entire battalion would be airlifted the next day to create another firebase. The next morning Company A was attached to the 2-8th Infantry, Company C moved into the field and Company B was airlifted into the new area to secure the new location. We met no resistance. The artillery and battalion CP were brought in as well as a company from the 2-8th. This company relieved us on the perimeter so that we could move into the boonies to establish a blocking position near an identified enemy crossing site on the Se San River.

I spread the platoons over an area of about three kilometers to set up ambushes and static positions. The third platoon sent some people down to the river to get water and they saw an NVA soldier across the river bathing. They called to him to surrender, but he started for the bank; he didn't make it. We fired some battalion mortars and artillery into the trees on the far bank to destabilize any other NVA soldiers that might be there. Apparently not knowing where we were located, our artillery firing encouraged other friendly units to fire into our area of operations. When their artillery rounds fell near our positions, some of our guys were hit by small pieces of spent shrapnel but no one was seriously hurt. The next morning we checked out the area but found only the one individual with uniform, web gear, canteens and entrenching tool. We could not find his weapon, though we knew it was in the brush somewhere.

After this, I put everybody into positions with instructions to make no movements or sounds. I was hoping the NVA would come out of the hills to the river for water and run into our blocking positions, which were in bamboo groves that reached high into the canopy of trees. After we settled in, the jungle/forest came back to life. One bird sounded exactly like a human screaming. The first time you heard the sound it was unsettling, but once you identified the bird itself and watched it make its noise, it didn't bother you except after a long silence. There was also a bird that sounded like a cuckoo and there were millions of ants working, on top of and within the dried bamboo leaf jungle floor. It was hot, with no breeze within the bamboo. Sweat pooled underneath our armpits and

Author writing in journal

backs and ran down our faces and necks to soak our uniforms. The hot sunlight came rippling down through the canopy of trees, into the bamboo, which distorted it into dappled spots on the ground. The warmth of the sun and the lack of movement induced drowsiness in us all. As long as the radios were manned by one of the operators, the other could sleep. The rest of the company headquarters did as well. The quiet period gave me time to think about how we could improve our operations or do something different to better prepare ourselves for the moment when we would at last face organized NVA units.

I wrote in my journal that it was indeed a strange war. It was hard to believe that the previous week another battalion had one platoon with twenty-four men killed in one night's fight just four kilometers south of our location. I had no premonition that we would see that type of action, but I knew it was extremely possible. We were healthy, well trained, well armed, well led (I thought) young immortals. While we respected the enemy's capability, we had little real concern that we could not overcome anything he threw at us.

During one of our hourly checks with battalion, my artillery forward observer, Lieutenant Bill Wilson, was notified that he had been promoted to first lieutenant. Sitting cross-legged on his helmet, he quietly celebrated by eating an extra can of "C" ration pound cake.

We had been warned the NVA were using elephants to transport equipment and goods in the area. The route on which we had positioned ourselves had elephant tracks coming down to the river.

The NVA carried their individual rations (rice) in a long circular sock-like tube, tied and strung around their shoulders. They could carry several days' worth of food in that manner, supplementing whenever they could with chickens, snakes, rats, or other source of protein. I thought their approach was pretty smart. It allowed them to move faster than we did because they were not as tied down with all the comforts we had and the three days of canned food each one of us carried. The additional food was part of my attempt to keep from getting resupplied on a scheduled basis. I reasoned, however, that if we started eating more rice, which was relatively light and filling, individuals could augment their meals with C Ration meat, thereby cutting out several pounds of cans. I started doing this myself and recommended it to the company leadership. I was not going to tell a soldier he could not carry food for himself, but figured it was common sense that the less food you had to carry, the easier the load would be with all of the ammunition, explosives, radios, radio batteries and other high-tech junk we had with us. It began working. I started requesting rice in bags, so that we could distribute it to those who wanted to carry rice instead of extra C's. Some of the guys picked up NVA rice tubes, while others carried it in containers that were easily sealed.

After two days of not finding anything, we moved into the firebase to assume security duties there. We cleared fields of fire and sent patrols out. We found an empty base camp complex with forty-five bunkers about five kilometers north of the firebase, which we destroyed with explosives.

We also took advantage of the break to spend time honing our marksmanship skills. This enabled our new replacements as well as everybody else to improve our shooting.

I received the new M203 rifle that had just come out. This was the over and under weapon I had discussed with the division staff on one of my visits to the division base camp. It was an M16 rifle on top and a 40mm grenade launcher on the bottom and it took the place of my shotgun type M79. I test-fired it and was pleased that the M16 rounds went where I wanted them to go. The grenade launcher was different from my old shotgun-style launcher and more difficult to load. It had a large barrel located underneath the rifle with a breech that had a slide style opening. To insert a round, the operator had to use a sliding motion similar to a trombone being played. After firing, the slide was opened manually, the shell ejected and a new one inserted. With some practice it could be done with one hand, but it was easier and faster with two. This required some concentration that I was not sure I would be able to spare if I were also occupied with other things. I figured, of course, that if I found myself in the position of having to shoot the launcher, as well as the M16, everything else would be going to Hell and I would be in survivor mode. Because the rather ungainly, heavy launcher was underneath the rifle, I learned to adjust the angle of the weapon to make sure the grenades flew to their targets and exploded accurately. I also had to carry M16 rounds for the rifle as well as grenades. However, I was prepared for the tradeoff in weight to gain the additional firepower.

One of the better things to happen while we were in the firebase, was the assignment of another officer to fill the platoon leader vacancy in the first platoon. 1LT Cary Allen was a Regular Army Quartermaster officer who, like all other newly commissioned non-combat arms Regular Army officers, had to spend two years in a combat arms assignment and we were short one officer. He had an interesting first few days... he flew into the Division base camp at Pleiku and checked in with the G1. Learning that his new unit, the 1-8th Infantry, was stationed in Tuy Hoa, he thumbed his way to the coast on an aircraft and checked in...only to find that we had moved to the highlands a few weeks previously. He had to come back up to Pleiku and find the battalion. The morning report picked him up on 23 February, but it was still a few days before he was able to find us and report in. It gave us a chuckle that the personnel guys did not know where the operations folks had sent us. At any rate, he checked in and became the first platoon's leader. Sergeant First Class Johnson had done a great job as acting platoon leader, but he knew that when an officer was assigned he would revert to being the Platoon Sergeant.

After three days of firebase duty, we received word that we had a new assignment and I took the platoon leaders on an aerial reconnaissance over the area in which we would be working. The 28th of February was payday, and Company C came in to relieve us on the perimeter. Major Mercer was a little impatient about having two companies in the firebase, so after we were paid, we moved out.

On payday, each company's executive officer brought a little cash in Military Payment Certificates (MPC) to the field and paid those individuals who always wanted some spending money on them. U.S. dollars were not allowed in Vietnam and MPC was a currency control device to hinder currency manipulation and inflation of the local currency. Many of the troops had most of their money sent to bank accounts with a little bit saved for pocket cash, soft drinks or the beer we were sometimes able to obtain. As part of their enlisted agreement, enlisted men received their food at no cost. Officers were charged for their meals (even C Rations), with the amount automatically deducted from our paychecks. One of the great innovations of the Vietnam War was the Soldier's Deposit program. You could deposit all or a percentage of your monthly pay to an account that accrued 10% while you were in Vietnam. This was an outstanding automatic savings plan which helped many veterans get a new start when they returned to the US.

Assigned to a heavily wooded area, we made only about three kilometers that afternoon, outside the battalion firebase. Since it was division policy to always have a landing zone for your nightly position, we had to blow one in the jungle. It seemed silly since we were less than two miles from the firebase, but if we needed help there was no quick way to obtain it from the firebase without an LZ. Fortunately it did not require much preparation and from a distance our explosives probably sounded like random artillery firing. On the pro side, "Every night an LZ" was a prudent policy in the event of an attack. On the con, it did announce our location loudly to the enemy if there was no open area readily available. After 45 years, I can admit there were times when I let my tactical judgment override the approach since it was a policy, not a regulation. When extenuating circumstances existed, I followed my own common sense.

We recognized early on that we could not rely on having divisional engineers to blow down trees for us to make landing zones. Using my engineer training and a couple of experienced NCOs as instructors, I conducted informal classes in basic demolitions for everyone. I made it company policy for each man to carry a quarter pound of C4 explosive after each resupply while certain individuals (mostly NCOs) carried fuses or blasting caps. In this way we always had sufficient explosives within the company to do whatever blasting we needed without overloading individuals. There was one drawback. I sometimes had a little trouble with a few of my more creative soldiers whenever we ran across a likely stream or pool that might yield a goodly catch of fish with a small amount of explosive set off in the water.

We completed the LZ and set up our perimeter when one of our outposts, a Puerto Rican, came running in, all out of breath. Ordinarily his Hispanic accent was easy to understand, but when he was excited it turned into just jumbled and tumbled noise. We got him settled down enough so we could understand that he was saying, "*Elephant!*". Forewarned that the NVA were using elephants in the area to transport equipment, I immediately saw this as an opportunity for an ambush. We realigned our fire zones and made ourselves ready to do whatever was necessary. Tension was high...

We waited and waited and I had just gotten the idea that the NVA had sensed us and were trying to turn the tables, when The Elephant strolled silently into our ambush site. One minute there was nothing and the next...there he was. Compared to the large Indian elephants I had seen in the zoo, he wasn't particularly huge, but he was still a tremendously large animal and we just stared up at him in awe. He was scruffy looking with a muddy-gray color and had shaggy patches on his body in different places that looked like he was shedding his skin. His tusks were rather short which indicated he might be a young elephant just out on his own. There appeared to be no pack or harness marks on him or other sign that he had been used to haul anything. He seemed to be a wild elephant. Several of us rose to get a better look and when he saw us he moved towards the other side of the boxed-in area. His eyes had a reddish tinge as he tossed his head and looked from one side to the other. He did not look very healthy or friendly. When he saw the other side was blocked as well, he laid his ears flat back and blew a short trumpet call. While not an expert on elephants, I figured he was ready to go and didn't care who he took with him. I told everybody to get away from him. He seemed more startled than angry, so we called it even and permitted him to go wherever he wanted. He decided to leave and made his way through the forest, leaving us staring at his departing backside. The whole encounter did not take more than ten minutes, but they were magic moments that took some of us out of the war for a little bit. It reminded us there were creatures out there uninvolved in the conflict who were just trying to survive.

The next morning, March 1st, we moved slowly up the mountain. It was thick undergrowth and we struggled against the vegetation as well as the slope of the mountain. We couldn't see the sun above the treetops and had only a general idea of our location. We questioned why we were sent up a mountain where it was doubtful there were NVA, but we had to be somewhere. We were good soldiers and did what we were told.

CHAPTER EIGHTEEN

ABOUT MID-DAY, the only thing we could tell about our location was that we were still going up and had not reached the top. If the top suddenly appeared and was defended, we had no pre-planned artillery fire to address the situation except what had been done from a map reconnaissance. Because of the sameness of the slope and vegetation with no identifying terrain features, we did not have a clue as to whether we were 100 meters from the top, or two kilometers.

In times like this, ordinarily we asked for a 'marking' artillery round. The artillery would then fire a smoke round to a specific coordinate we gave them. Then we plotted a general azimuth (direction) to the sound of the explosive "pop" or sight of the smoke to estimate our distance. This gave us at least an idea of our location if we couldn't get it any other way.

Because we could not see or hear a smoke round due to the forest canopy, I stopped the company and requested a high explosive (HE) round that would give us an explosion somewhere distant in the woods to which we could plot our general azimuth. However, the location we wanted the round

135

to hit was just outside of 105mm artillery range. As a substitute, we were able to call on a 175mm support battery, so we requested a round from them. The bad thing about 175s was that while they had a longer range with a larger effective explosive radius, they were a little less accurate than 105 or a 155mm guns. All platoons knew we had asked for a 175 shot and were alerted to take whatever cover they could find until the round hit.

Everyone took cover on the downhill side of something thick like a tree or a rock. The first platoon was our lead element up the mountain. It was reported later that SP4 Joe Grande told his buddies that he had never seen a 175 round go off and he wanted to see the explosion, even though it was unlikely he would see anything given the trees and vegetation.

In this case, for reasons of its own that remain unexplained but probably by mistake, the artillery fired a short round. Three bad things happened as a result. The first was the short round, always dangerous. Second, the trees were so tall the round hit their tops. Third, the resulting explosion sent shrapnel and wood splinters crashing down below, wounding Joe Grande and three others.

I immediately sent out scouts on all sides. We made radio contact with battalion and reported the situation while at the same time requesting a dust-off medical evacuation. We were told to let battalion know when we had an LZ available.

Because of the very tall trees and the slope of the mountain, the helicopter could not land, so we had to blow an LZ out of the forest. The teak and mahogany trees were from 200–250 feet tall with diameters as much as five feet and composed of extremely hard wood. When we blasted them at their base, they toppled over and got entangled in the surrounding trees.

In the meantime, we moved the wounded to a sheltered place where the company medics could treat them with their basic medicines and skills. Grande was the worst, with a pulsing wound in his throat, but the medics kept him alive.

We cut branches out of the way with our machetes and placed additional explosives on tree trunks to blow them into smaller pieces so they fell to the sloping forest floor. Even with all of this work, our LZ ended up being merely a blasted hole in the canopy through which we could see the helicopter hovering about 300 feet above us. We built a small, semi-stable and somewhat level log platform from the blown trees and limbs so we would have a clear site from which to work. The helicopter had to lower a stretcher on a cable into the hole in the trees, all the while having to maneuver against a wind trying to blow it someplace else. The pilot couldn't see what he was

Stretcher evacuation

137

doing, so we had to guide him by radio while the crew chief of the helicopter guided the stretcher down into the darkness of the hole. When the stretcher got down on the platform, we managed to put our wounded soldiers into it for one trip at a time and to tie them down so they couldn't fall out. Grande was the most vulnerable so he was the first one to go up.

Vic Renza was one of the guys that held Grande's stretcher as they started to crank him up.

Renza, second platoon..."*Joe had two I.V. bags in him, one in each arm and they were tied above his head. As the stretcher started to go upward and we steadied it, the downdraft from the chopper ripped the I.V. lines out of his arms. We kept looking up until the basket got into the chopper and then we looked at each other. We were in shock to see we were all covered in blood. Our clothes and faces were red dotted all over and we had to use the water from our canteens to wash it off our faces. It was a very sad day indeed.*"

The real problem was that while there was a paramedic in the helicopter, they still had to wait for the others to be lifted up for treatment and evacuation. This was a slow process as we finally got our wounded out one at a time. On the ground, it was an agonizing sight to watch the stretcher being blown sideways by the wind, sometimes spinning one way, sometimes the other while brushing the limbs of the surrounding trees as it went up. The crew chief had to talk to the pilot to move the aircraft very slowly and slightly one way or the other. The aircrew had to worry both about overcompensating for the wind and the downdraft from the helicopter blades blowing the cable. It was nerve wracking for us on the ground watching. I can't begin to imagine the terror of the wounded men on the stretchers who were in pain, tied tightly to the stretcher with no control over their movements or destiny.

138

By the time the dust-off was completed it was too late to continue up the mountain. As we were beginning to organize ourselves for the rest of the day and night, the helicopter pilot called back to give us sad news. The medical crew had done their best, but Grande died on the way to the hospital.

We infantrymen carried the primary burden of combat in Vietnam; but the angels of mercy helicopter crews who supported us were the best of their breed and it took tremendous skill, courage and dedication to do what they did for us, always at risk and sometimes at the cost of their own lives. We were often jealous of their clean, warm beds, hot food and cold beers back at the base camps. But, when it became necessary for someone to pluck us from the muck and the blood, the chopper pilots were our brothers and suffered as much as we did, often going beyond the call of duty or ignoring safety precautions of their precarious flying machines to save us. We made ill-mannered jokes about their life style, as warriors do with those whom they respect, but we greatly admired and depended upon them.

The hard work involved in the climb and the cutting of the LZ, combined with the emotional stress of losing four of our buddies due to a freak incident, resulted in what I would describe as a group depression. Figuring the troops needed something to take their mind off what had just occurred, I elected for us to get resupplied with water and any mail that had come in since we had left. We spent the rest of the afternoon having water lowered to us on a cable in plastic five-gallon jugs. The resupply pilots also gave us a specific location to mark on our map.

In the monsoon or wet season in the highlands, water was never a problem. We put halazone purification tablets in the water we found in streams and rivers and did quite well. In the dry season, it was a different story. Streams dried up and dehydration was a constant threat. We had to get resupplied with water whenever we could. Most of us carried two or three canteens, but during periods of combat or strenuous activity (like climbing mountains), water was in short supply. We never found a good way to get resupplied while in deep forests...we experimented with putting water in artillery canisters that had held artillery rounds and then dropping them through the canopy, but the canisters were never washed properly and the water tasted strange. Plus, we always ran the danger that a falling canister would hit one of the soldiers on the ground. When they were released into the tops of trees, every branch they hit deflected them, so someone on the ground could not tell where the canister was going to land. After several close calls we decided to forego the artillery canister method since dropping plastic water bottles by free fall merely burst the bottles. We learned that the best way to deliver water through jungle was to drop it at the end of a cable, but without an LZ or cleared space in the overhead, the bottles soon got hung up on branches and the water was lost. It was a major logistical problem that was never solved adequately while I was in Vietnam.

Since the slope of the mountainside did not encourage rapid movement nor were there natural flat places, we formed a perimeter as best we could, though it was highly unlikely we were in any danger from the NVA except through mortar fire. We did not dig holes that night, but we did carve fairly flat shelves upon which we could rest. Some men tied themselves to trees to ensure they did not roll down the slope during the night.

It was not a restful evening. While I could not allow myself to become immersed in grief, I wept quietly in the dark for the soldier who had been killed and the others who had been injured during what previously had been routine actions.

The following day we continued the climb, securing the top of the hill by mid-day. A beautiful sight greeted us, grand mountain ranges with valleys below and everything green in spite of the dry weather. We had a natural two-ship LZ on the top of the mountain, and Company A of the 2-8th was inserted to begin operations in conjunction with us.

We all climbed down the mountain on the other side, sometimes sliding on our rears on the steep slope with only our rucksacks on our backs holding us upright. We tried to keep our feet from tripping over rocks or roots that turned our moves into dangerous tumbles and falls with our weapons. Sometimes our rapid descent was halted as we ran into or grabbed a tree to slow our downward movement or to keep from hitting the soldier below us. It was not a dignified, quiet or stealthily gliding descent. It was more of a semi-controlled crash wave of almost 300 men cursing, muttering or making loud sounds as we stepped, walked, jumped, slid, rolled and fell to the bottom of the mountain. Where it had taken us a day and a half to climb the gentler side of the mountain, we came down in less than two hours. Fortunately, there were no broken bones or sprains.

We moved into the next valley searching the small draws and gullies for any sign of NVA, but found only elephant sign. By this time we realized that not all elephants were working for the other side and some were just roaming around the AO trying to stay out of everybody else's way. We spent the next night on a little knoll, still deep in the woods. The following day we moved only about 400 meters and I set up a CP with the platoons out on patrols around the area. Still nothing out of the ordinary occurred.

The next day we moved downhill through the brush and woods trying to find another LZ. Major Mercer kept flying above us pushing us to make better time. I remember thinking he didn't realize Company B wasn't all mountain goat...yet. It looked pretty simple when you were above the trees, but down on the ground it was a different story. We not only had to put one foot in front of the other to make progress, we had to have some security out to the front, to the rear and on the sides (where possible) to make sure we weren't stepping into an ambush. After all, the enemy had real guns too.

We finally found a reasonably open area we could use for an LZ, just in time to get some supplies and more water before dark (March 4th). Major Mercer landed and told me that my XO, 1LT George Woodford was being permanently reassigned to become his (Major Mercer's) Assistant S3. The Company XO position was a very important job, so I had to make an immediate decision as to his replacement. With Woodford's departure, 1LT George Tupa became my senior lieutenant and was an extremely dependable and reliable officer. As a result, he departed with Major Mercer to become my executive officer in Dragon Mountain. This made me short a platoon leader for the second platoon, but the platoon sergeant, SFC Aljandro Yuson was a quiet but outstanding and effective NCO who could run the platoon well. I always followed the Army policy of ensuring that each person in a leadership position trained his replacement in the event that he became a combat casualty or had to be absent. That way, somebody was always in charge and the next in line was aware of the chain of command. This policy served us well many times.

Since we had just climbed a fair-sized hill, battalion must have felt we were acclimated to the heat and had become experienced mountain troops.

Our next assignment was to climb Mount Cu Grok to see if there were any NVA observer positions in that area. By this time, we had moved back down close to sea level. According to the map, Mount Cu Grok rose 1,482 meters (4,862 feet), almost a mile high. I didn't look forward to the climb, since water would be a primary concern. We could only carry so much for ourselves. In addition, while we had been emphasizing malaria control, too many troops continued to fall out with high fevers when physically stressed.

The first day we only made a little over one kilometer up the mountain. We had three dust offs at three different times during the day for troops with dangerously high fevers. Of course, there were few open areas for LZs, so in two cases we had to blow down trees to create space enough for the medical helicopters to lower their stretchers. We made it to a low lying ridge that night, but had another evacuation. The next day, we kept climbing, but about mid-afternoon one of our sergeants pulled a back muscle and went into spasms that kept him from climbing or walking. In order to get him out we had to chop and blast another hole in the trees. We also got resupplied with water and explosives. With all of the loud explosions and helicopter activity, there could be no doubt in any observer's mind that something was happening on the mountainside.

That night we again had to tie ourselves to trees to keep from falling down the mountainside. It was too rocky to dig out sleep shelves as we had before. The only good thing about it was we knew we would be able to hear any enemy who came near enough to be a security risk. We climbed all the next day without any injuries reaching the top at about 6:00 P.M. with the sun still shining. We were soaked from perspiration and there was a cold wind blowing across the top of the mountain. The way things were going, I figured we would have cases of pneumonia by morning.

There was no sign of mankind having ever been there. As we approached the top, a brief spurt of excitement caused an adrenalin rush when a wild boar crashed suddenly out of the brush and disappeared down the mountainside. What he was doing that high in the clouds was beyond me but then what we were doing up there was beyond me, as well.

The top consisted of a clear rocky ledge about 900 feet long by 20 wide. There was a sheer drop on two sides with a beautiful view of the surrounding mountains and tops of the forests. Of course we could not see down into the trees because of their height, but could see a couple of rivers in the distance that passed between the mountains. We spent the night around the top and had a great LZ, but for once we did not need it for resupply or evacuation.

The next morning, the trip down the other side of the mountain involved the usual semi-controlled falls: arms and legs flailing, grunts and bumps with frequent crashes into trees, feet out from under us and our backsides and rucksacks taking a lot of abuse. Some soldiers discovered that they could use the butt of their weapons as steering oars while the rest of the body was sliding down in a dying cockroach position. As usual, the down went a lot faster than the up.

Once down into the forested valleys, there was much evidence that NVA were in the area: tracks, recent fire pits, and scattered rice where recent spillage had occurred. Since this was a free fire zone, we knew all legal civilians had either left or been moved to other locations. We also saw some cassava (tapioca) fields that had been planted but not recently tended. We burned two empty and old Montagnard villages to deny them to NVA forces, and found a small open area next to a stream that could be used for an LZ for the night. We decided we would take some time for well-deserved baths the next day,

CHAPTER NINETEEN

T HE NEXT MORNING, we patrolled the area fairly well to ensure we were not in the middle of an NVA encampment. We hunkered down next to a stream when Major Mercer did it to us again. I was convinced he didn't do anything except listen to my location reports. Whenever we got close to the blue squiggly marking on the map that meant water, he suspected we were going to try to take a bath, so he found something else for us to do!

This time, after our intensive morning patrolling in the vicinity of the stream, I was sitting on a rock in the middle of the creek with one trouser leg washed when he called and told me to have the entire company ready to be picked up for movement. Twenty minutes later the helicopters arrived and we lifted off. They put us down in the firebase of the 2-35th Infantry Battalion on the evening of 12 March.

All the battalions were operating under General Peers' guidelines. No individual company operated closer than one kilometer from the border. This procedure still allowed a company to be attacked by a superior force launching from the enemy's safe havens in Cambodia. We were trolled up and down the international border trying to entice the bad guys to bite on us. *Whether in fishing or other endeavors, bait never has a good time.*

Once the enemy committed himself to the attack with larger forces than ours, our companies drew themselves into a perimeter and inflicted as much damage as possible while the brigade or division put forces into the area to block his escape into Cambodia or Laos. While this may have been smart tactics on the larger scale, at the company level it was hardly a favorite.

The 2-35th was a battalion of the 3d Brigade of the 25th Infantry Division that was under the operational control of the Fourth Infantry Division. Their companies were in heavy contact, and other infantry units were reinforcing the battalion to try and block the NVA from melting back into Cambodia.

Of course, as soon as the NVA hit a US company as hard as it could, it broke contact and scampered back across the international boundary carrying its dead and wounded with it. We were airlifted the next morning into a well-prepped LZ with the intent of catching the NVA before they disappeared. In addition to Company B, Companies A and C of our battalion were also lifted in and we all moved into the contact area. In addition to our battalion, the 3-8th Infantry Battalion of our brigade was moved into the region with two rifle companies. This made a total of eight infantry companies within a small area, all trying to contact the NVA who had been hammering the 2-35th the day before. This made our tactical situation almost as dangerous as an attack by the NVA, since each company fired their evening artillery defensive fires. Because the companies were in close proximity, there was always the chance of a stray round hitting another unit.

During the days to follow, none of the companies found anything, but one evening when we stopped, an enemy mortar slipped between the cracks of the U.S. units and serenaded us all night. Some of the rounds landed within Company B's perimeter but because we were protected in holes, the shrapnel caused damage only to ponchos and equipment. Of course, my air mattress was one of the ones that suffered, which made it a *"hard ground's night"* for me. Ah, well...it certainly wasn't the first one and it would hardly be the last...

CHAPTER TWENTY

WE WEREN'T THE ONLY ONES receiving mortar fire that night. The newly established 1st Brigade supply base, 3 Tango, was a lucrative target for the NVA which sought to disrupt our logistics support. On 13 March the troops at the base received a warm welcome from the NVA.

The base at 3 Tango provided a location where helicopters could land, refuel and rearm. There was a mobile hospital that accepted casualties from the field prior to shipping them to the rear for more sophisticated treatment. The company had supply representatives who bundled up the unit's needs for resupply and coordinated the movement of personnel in and out of the field. There were 105mm and self-propelled 155mm artillery batteries with mountains of ammunition that could cover the brigade's maneuver elements as they moved through their areas of operations. Overall, 3 Tango was an important link in the chain of support facilities that ran between the division's battalion firebases and its headquarters at Camp Enari.

3 Tango Forward Supply Base

SP5 John Rose, one of the Company B cooks was located at 3 Tango with other portions of the unit supply and support elements. He remembers the 13th of March, 1967 very well...

"I had spotted activity on the mountain located behind the shower area several days before the mortar attack. I didn't realize that this activity was relevant to the enemy being in the area.

I went to my cot that evening and was laying there thinking about home when I heard shelling going on outside my tent. This was not unusual to hear during nighttime, but it was different that night in that all the usual sounds were in reverse. I laid there thinking how odd it was sounding, so I got up and went to the door flap of the tent and looked out to see small orange atomic bombs rising from the ground about a block away from our location. There were trucks lined up and they were the main target because they were loaded with ammo and supplies. I turned around and started back to get my rifle-helmet-pants at my cot. I woke George Power in the first cot by the door and told him we were under attack. He really didn't understand the danger we were in that night since it was our first time under fire. He thought it was our artillery being fired at the time. I put on my pants and helmet and ran for the bunker on the other side of the tent. When I got outside I was about 7–10 feet behind Gene Sousa who was running for the bunker also. We got inside the bunker, which was already filling, with cooks and GIs. When the medic stopped by later, we were asked if anybody had been hit and Sousa and another cook from Headquarters Company said they had been hit in the back. I figure that some of the mortars must have hit the trees along the road next to our camp and rained down on Sousa while we were running to the bunker. While we were in the bunker the shelling was fierce for some time and then it stopped. The flyboys arrived with napalm, but they didn't hit the mountain that really was the main mortar area. The jets hit another mountain on the other side of the base. All was quiet after that and we went back to our cots to turn in. We were very well shaken by the attack but we settled in for the night.

I got up the morning after and got the star burners lit and got the coffee on and started to put the bacon on the grill. Just as it got light, I heard the shelling start again and I ran from the cook tent to the bunker and dived into the bunker again. I thought I would be first hitting the opening, but there were 3 people ahead of me into the hole. We stayed inside the bunker for some time until the flyboys got there. We watched the jets come and lay down napalm, which started above our bunker and was like a flamethrower into the mountain *behind the shower area. The enemy had us bracketed with the way the road system and tree lines were at our base area. They sure caught us flat footed that night. After the jets went away we looked at the damage all around us...the trucks were demolished, tents leveled. Our sleeping tent had holes in it like if you were sitting in a planetarium looking at the star system. My mosquito net had a hole about the size of a half dollar burned in it where my head would have been if I had stayed in my cot that night. The cooks of Company B were as follows on the roster that day: Sp5 Taylor, George Power, Gene Sousa, John Wamsley and John Rose. We heard that other GIs were wounded during the night."*

In the field we heard that 3 Tango had suffered eleven casualties during the attack. No place was completely safe in Vietnam and everyone went through their own version of combat, even if it didn't involve the moving and shooting life of an infantryman .

We moved out into the area in a search mode looking for leftover NVA, but found nothing. There were no good LZs, so we had to drop C rations and mail from about 100 feet up through holes between the trees along with the mail. Someone had sent one of the soldiers a bottle of gin, but it broke upon impact. People were squeezing the mailbag to the last drop.

We moved on. We walked for 12 hours and still only made five kilometers. The terrain was rugged with heavy vegetation, and we were wary of moving too quickly for fear of running into an ambush after the recent activity.

It is difficult to describe the different types of vegetation we scrambled through. In addition to the high canopy, through which little sunlight came, there was often secondary growth, brush and thorny wait-a-minute vines. There was a particularly evil tree that had four to eight-inch spikes jutting from its trunk. If you put your hand out to catch your balance, you might end up with your hand speared or scratched by the thorns. Of course, there was toxin on the spines, and unless treated immediately, the scratch or puncture became infected and the individual became a walking wounded, totally miserable and thinking about how bad he hurt, rather than being an alert soldier looking for the enemy.

We hated bamboo as much as we disliked the enemy. It grew together in large stalks and canes and a single cane was sometimes 8 inches in diameter. It was tough and resilient. It was difficult to have enough room to swing a machete with any cutting force when you were in the middle of it, and its fibrous nature sometimes made a less than razor-sharp machete bounce off the stalk. With a sharp edge the blade would bite into the stalk and bind, forcing the lead individual to have to pry the blade loose to release the machete for another swing. This was tiring work and slow going.

Even when the bamboo was not close together, it was always difficult to move through it with a large rucksack. If you tried to duck under fallen canes, the rucksack caught on them. If you turned sideways to move between the stalks, the rucksack caught on them. If you tried to back your way through the thicket, the rucksack caught on the stalks you couldn't see. In addition, the bamboo floor was seldom even. Over years, the base of the bamboo thicket added to itself and you might step on a root that gave way and your foot would end up in a hole. There was the danger of spraining it, but just trying to extract it with everything you were carrying and still maintaining your balance was physically exhausting.

The root nodes were always uneven and while you were looking down trying to find firm footing, the rucksack would catch on one of the stalks keeping you from moving forward. All of this while trying to maintain walking silence. Fortunately, in a really deep thicket, the sounds of bamboo chopping were muted or often swallowed by the surrounding vegetation. However, we were always at a distinct disadvantage when moving through bamboo. If you were outside the thicket, you could see the tops of the thicket moving. If you were at a higher elevation, you could even see individuals as they chopped or moved through the stalks. On the other hand, from the bamboo floor, you couldn't see up or out. There was always the threat that the enemy for whom we were looking was outside the thicket and could set up an ambush, catching us where we had little mobility or reaction options. One of my greatest fears as a company commander was getting caught by a mortar attack while we were in a bamboo thicket. As a matter of course, if I could identify the vague outlines of the thicket on a map, or just before we entered it, I always had artillery concentrations planned ahead and to the sides of us, just in case.

Out of the bamboo, in the thickest and darkest part of the forest or jungle, it was easier to go single file, rotating point men with machetes in order to be able to just move from one step to another. Even following an individual, you had to be careful and not let too much space get between you and the person in front of you. It was easy to lose someone if they got too far from the column, just because of the difficulty of seeing another person. There is no telling how many NVA we bypassed if they kept quiet and let us go our way because of the ease of camouflaging people and positions in heavy brush and vegetation.

As we moved, there was no water and it was extremely dry. We had three soldiers with high fevers of unknown origin (FUO) and they had to be extracted. We located an open area big enough for a helicopter to evacuate them and a tracker team with dogs was dropped in to work with us. We found nothing of interest for them. The next day was more of the

154

same but we did find an LZ that was acceptable for bringing in a hot meal and water as well as some beer and soda. We walked into the firebase the next day and took over perimeter duties. The firebase was on the bank of a beautiful river in the forest that allowed us to get clean again and even do some light fishing. There were some avid fishermen already in the firebase who thought it was great sport to fish with hand grenades. Of course when we had the results for supper, we purists overlooked exactly how they came to the meal. I had a chance to visit our forward supply area at 3 Tango where I saw the results of the mortar attack the previous week.

Second Lieutenant Larry Rodabaugh (he was promoted to 1LT a few days later), who had been on TDY for three months helping to build a training center and train replacements in Pleiku, returned to the company. The second platoon was short a platoon leader because of Tupa's departure, so Larry got the job.

After a few days in this location, the entire battalion moved by truck back down to the site of the old battalion firebase, west of Duc Co in the Ia Drang Valley, and we stayed as perimeter guard. We had eleven cases of malaria in the company even though everyone had mosquito nets. Even with constant use and reminders for protection, everyone was still vulnerable.

Though it does not reflect well on whomever the individuals were, I was told years later there were some GI's who resented being out in the bush in Vietnam with the chance of being maimed or killed in a war they didn't invent and who preferred being in the rear or even back in the U.S. Imagine that! Some of these individuals, I am told, deliberately courted malaria by not taking their tablets or using their nets in the hopes of contracting malaria so they would be evacuated out of the field to safer places. I don't know if the ploy worked…but if it did, that individual faced the danger of continuing relapses of malaria for the rest of his life. Malaria is not cured, just sup-pressed for periods of time. Of course in these people's minds the possibility of being killed versus the possibility of having malaria for the rest of their lives was not much of a decision. We had a rash of fevers of unknown origin, but they slacked off after weather changes.

There were also some cases of high fevers from individuals who were recently returned from R&R and who, upon diag-nosis, had contracted a social disease during their recreational activities. The company's R&R instructions covered protective measures prior to departure, so if an individual determined not to follow the appropriate procedures, I did not consider these incidents to be combat-related.

Once an individual had been diagnosed with something like that and returned to the field and started having high fever for the second time, I was hard pressed to stop the company and order a medical evacuation. One individual had returned from R&R with the problem and subsequently had to be evacuated three times for high fever. After this had happened to several persons, I finally refused to let individuals in that category be evacuated unless their temperature reached 104 degrees and they began to slow down the company. If the medic told me the individual was in danger of dying or becoming comatose, I reluctantly permitted a dust-off to be called. I have had it argued that these were young virile soldiers, away from home for the first time, placed in temptation's way and who may have had the attitude that they were in danger of being killed when they returned, so why not live life to its fullest whenever possible? What did they have to lose, so why blame them? I completely understood that argument, but by not taking appro-priate preventive measures during his R&R, the individual involved deliberately put his fellow soldiers at risk by reducing the amount of firepower available to the company whenever he was evacuated. In addition, the unit lost any tactical advantage of surprise it may have had when a helicopter landed unnecessarily. I don't know whether my evacuation policy for FUOs caused by non-malarial reasons sent the appropriate message or not to others going on R&R, but fortunately in the end it affected only a few individuals. The policy I suppose, was cold and ruthless, but I felt more responsibility to the majority of my men than sympathy to a few.

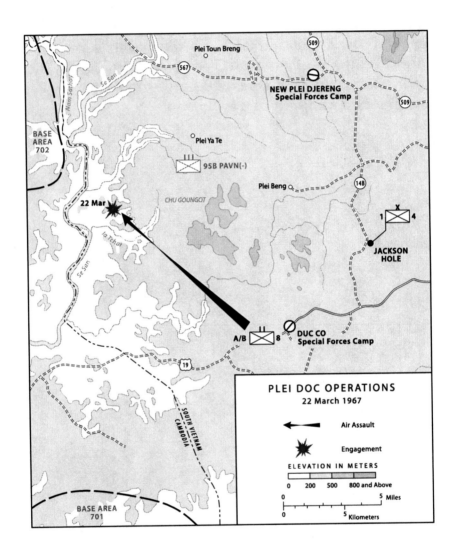

Plei Toun Breng

NEW PLEI DJERENG
Special Forces Camp

BASE
AREA
702

Plei Ya Te

95B PAVN(-)

CHU GOUNGOT

Plei Beng

22 Mar

1   4

JACKSON
HOLE

A/B   8   DUC CO
Special Forces Camp

PLEI DOC OPERATIONS
22 March 1967

Air Assault

Engagement

ELEVATION IN METERS

0   200   500   800 and Above

0   5 Miles

0   5 Kilometers

SOUTH VIETNAM
CAMBODIA

BASE AREA
701

CHAPTER TWENTY ONE

IT WAS LATE AFTERNOON and the helicopter hovered just above the still burning and smoldering short grass of our landing zone northwest of Duc Co, not far from the Cambodian border. The LZ had been "prepped" by artillery fire and gunships. We jumped the last two or three feet from the skids into a clearing that had been previously used as an LZ. It was difficult not to land on stumps of trees that had been cut when making the LZ.

The roaring noise of the "slicks" (our troop helicopters) with the gunships covering them made even shouting impossible to hear. When Hunter, Surface and I—with radios and heavily filled rucksacks—spilled off the helicopter, we overbalanced and stumbled with our loads on the sooty, still hot grass stubs. Bent over, we shambled towards the edge of the burning area. The windblast from the helicopter covered us with soot, smoke, and a few sparks as the aircraft powered forward and upward, on its way to pick up another load. Our eyes squinted against the smoky wind as we moved off the burning ground into the scrub, while the rest of Company B was delivered and moved on past us to their allocated positions.

I stopped just off the landing zone and shrugged out of my rucksack. The two radio operators did the same. Hunter put up the long antenna on his radio so we could call battalion headquarters to establish communications. We reported the airlift was proceeding smoothly and we had landed with no opposition. As the platoons landed, the platoon leaders checked in with me to make sure nothing had changed in their initial deployment orders. They continued to move their men into the scrub and into an interlocking defensive perimeter until the entire company had landed.

Company A had just finished its insertion, when we began ours, Because I was on one of the lead aircraft, Captain Bidd Sands, the Company A commander, jogged over to finalize our coordination on this joint operation. When the helicopters were gone, it was eerily silent and the only sounds that could be heard were men's movements as they adjusted into position.

It was always a relief to hear the last helicopter after an unopposed landing. Even at the best of times, the racket of multiple helicopters and the zooming of gunships got into your brain and muddled any clarity of thought. As the last helicopter whop-whopped out of sight and sound, the jungle or forest waited in silence to see if anything else was going to disrupt normality. No birds sang and no insects buzzed. Everything was dazed from the cacophony and crush of noise. I always enjoyed this little period of silence after the overwhelming rush and roar of machines, then the almost instantaneous quiet that swept over us like a fresh breeze with a lifting of physical tension. The adrenalin and worry that had been running through our bodies in anticipation of enemy contact slowed down once we were on the ground and realized no one was shooting at us. We were back in a ground environment where we thought we had more control over our immediate universe instead of being relatively helpless and dependent upon others while hanging in the wind waiting to land.

Unless there were multiple deception landings taking place to draw the NVA's attention elsewhere, there was seldom any question about when or where an airmobile landing occurred, particularly if there was a pre-landing preparation. In this case there had not been time to coordinate or plan multiple landings so if there were NVA in our vicinity, they knew U.S. forces had just landed and generally where we were. All they had to do was watch from a safe distance and wait to see in which direction we moved.

Bidd and I watched the last of Company B land and move off the LZ. Company A's 1SG Dave McNerney waved to Bidd to indicate that the unit was ready to move whenever he was.

We took a little extra time before we started moving the companies because we had not had much time to discuss the operation. This was our last opportunity to do so face to face.

On a side note, Bidd had received his return orders to the U.S., but had extended for five days so he could go on this mission with his company. It was to be a tragic decision on his part, though completely understandable by anyone who ever led a rifle company and who had bonded with and cared for the men in it. In our opinions, we were the only ones who knew our companies and we were the only ones who could take care of our own. Our men were often closer to us than our blood families because we were all responsible for each other on a daily basis. We experienced the intense trauma and emotion of life threatening situations together. We saved each other's lives and sometimes were the last person to try and comfort someone who was dying. It has always been so for those who participate in combat, but it is one thing to know about it and a completely different thing to live it. Bidd was caught in the moral dilemma of returning to his stateside family, and leaving his company to someone less experienced, or carrying out one more mission to make sure "his" troops had the best leadership he could provide.

On this particular day, all we knew for sure was that a long range recon patrol (LRRP) had not reported within the last 24 hours and communications with them had been lost. The 1st Brigade ordered the 1-8th to insert two companies into the area to try and find the unit.

Colonel Lee always insisted that our companies should be ready to react on short notice. We company commanders naturally had honed our SOPs and trained our NCOs and soldiers to accommodate anything that might be thrown at us, so Bidd and I were able to respond quickly. Company B was the battalion perimeter guard. As part of the normal alternating routine, we had already prepared to move into the bush once we were replaced. However, the decision was made by battalion that Company A would join us in the conduct of this operation. Company A moved into the firebase for pickup while Company C moved in to take the perimeter.

Since no one knew where the LRRP team might be by this time, we had adjacent areas of operation in which to conduct our searches. We still had to be careful in planning friendly artillery fires as part of our defensive postures while moving into unknown territory. We needed to know each other's plans, and where the other company was at all times, in order to preclude any friendly fire incidents.

Our brief coordination meeting resulted in Bidd taking Company A and heading west into his assigned AO, while I took Company B and headed in a more southwesterly direction. Doing this, we put some distance between our two units before we had to stop for the night. In the meeting we also agreed that if we heard firing from each other's location we would immediately start for the other's position to provide reinforcement and support.

I was not comfortable however, with our situation with regard to the NVA. If they had been watching our landing, they knew that a relatively large force was on the ground. I did not want them to know exactly where we were, so I instructed my officers to operate a silent bivouac that night. No digging, no smoking, no talking, no blowing up of air mattresses (they rustled and squeaked) and no tents. I told them I didn't want to hear anything but mosquitoes.

As we settled into our evening defensive position, we could hear Company A digging in about 300 hundred meters away. It was the first time we could hear how noises carried when a company prepared a defensive position. I resolved that we would do better in the future. In the meantime I was glad I had decided to keep our presence as low key as possible.

The weather was clear and warm, no rain in sight and lots of stars. I lay on my poncho liner admiring the constellations until I fell asleep. It could have been a delightful campout under different circumstances.

None of us knew the following day would be a bloody one, filled with tragedy and misery for over 200 men.

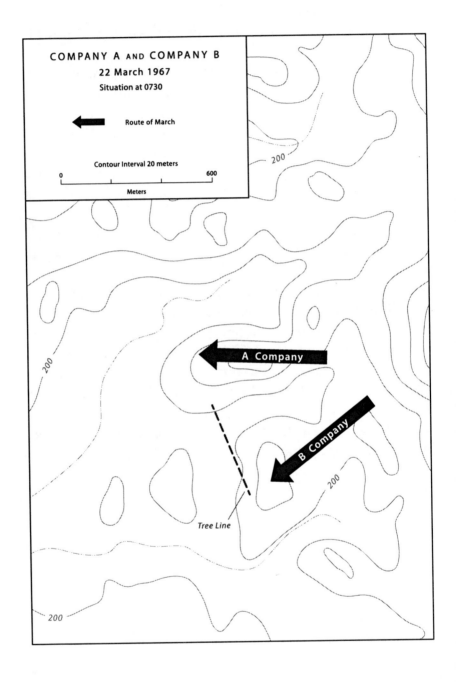

CHAPTER TWENTY TWO

THE NEXT MORNING, 22 MARCH, both companies continued in the direction they had traveled the previous day. We were moving along on ridgelines with trees that were close together and brush blocking the way between them. We pushed through, but we could not see much beyond the next tree or section of brush. Long-range visibility was limited in all directions. Although we stayed on the higher ground, we crossed small wooded ravines that slowed us down because we had to secure and clear the far sides. I couldn't see it, but the map showed an open area to our right between our route of march and Company A's. As we had discussed, I knew Bidd was traveling in a westerly direction on the ridgeline to our north.

Company B was in a column led by the fourth platoon, while the 3d, 2d and first platoons followed. The headquarters group was just behind the third platoon. My initial plan was a movement to contact formation that gave some flexibility in the event we found the enemy. In effect, if the lead platoon came in contact, another platoon could move up in support, or I could keep a platoon in reserve and send another platoon out to either side to come at the enemy from another direction.

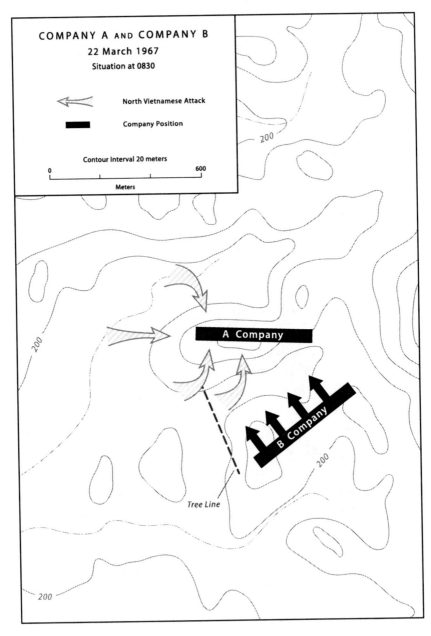

Company A also moved out the next morning. Its initial formation was also a column of platoons with the second platoon in the lead, followed by first, fourth and third platoons.

Not long after starting, Bidd brought his first platoon up on the left flank to act as a flank guard for the rest of the company. This gave him two platoons in the lead followed by his command group and then the other two platoons still in column.

Around 0730, Company A's first platoon with its 3d Squad leading, was surprised by concealed automatic fire from the front. PFC Jacob Horn, the point man, was killed immediately and another man wounded in the initial burst. SGT George Olsen, the 3d Squad leader tried to get to Horn and the wounded man but was also shot. Automatic weapons and rifle fire slashed into the platoon columns from the front and the left side.

The NVA had positioned themselves on the ridgeline in front of Company A and down on the southern side of the ridge which was Company A's left flank. Beyond the NVA on the left side of the company was a large open area between Companies A and B. This area was bordered to the front by a large tree line.

The attack was well planned. As in all successful ambushes, it took the lead elements of the company by surprise. The initial moments were confusing and it was uncertain from where much of the fire was coming. The shouting and screaming of men, booms of rocket propelled grenades (RPGs), the racket of machine guns, the hard chatter of the enemy's AK47s, along with the subsonic cracking of hundreds of rounds zipping through the trees and the thunks of bullets hitting their trunks: all led to confusion and uncertainty of where, precisely, to shoot. Olson reacting by instinct, tried to get to his wounded men, but he, too, went down...

George Olsen, Company A: "*I had a sharp pain in my right thigh and there was the chatter of automatic weapons. I could see rounds striking all around. I looked behind me and could see Cook had been hit. Medeiros was OK, but I didn't know about Weakly or Gordon. When I was hit I lost my M16. It was about ten feet to my front and every time I tried to move, an automatic weapon opened up, pinning me down. I couldn't get to my weapon or Horn....I rolled to the side to get the hand grenades that were on my ammo pouches and noticed that one round had stuck in one just below the fuse. I got rid of it in a heartbeat. It saved my life. Our platoon medic checked my wound and put a field dressing on my leg. The medic then headed for Horn. He only got a few feet, when he was shot in the upper left arm. This knocked him to the ground, but he continued moving toward Horn...Horn had already died of his wounds. What was amazing, I saw this same medic at the 25th Evac Hospital in Pleiku with a dressing on his arm treating our wounded as they came into the hospital.*

The first sergeant crawled up to me and checked my wound, patted me on the back and told me I would be alright. He then crawled to the front, passed Horn and disappeared into the jungle. I'll never understand how he got past the NVA soldier who shot up the 3d squad, but he did. I didn't see "Top" again until much later. Second Lieutenant Shannon (FO) started calling in artillery to our front. He was getting very close, so close the NVA soldier, who shot Horn, Cook and me, jumped and turned to run. Part of his web gear swung out and the movement caught my eye. I grabbed Medeiros's M16, came up on my knees putting the weapon on full automatic and fired. It fired one round and jammed. But I got him with the one shot. To this day I don't know why someone didn't shoot me. My squad is basically wiped out and there's no one between us and the NVA. Prentice and Sedies, with their machine guns were the first to arrive to support us. Prentice laid the barrel of his M60 over my legs and began firing toward the front from where we had received fire...

Sgt Murphy, the 2d Squad leader must have been directly behind the platoon leader, because it didn't take him long to get to me. He moved his squad through the area where mine lay, using hand and arm signals. He was only a few feet in front of me directing his squad, when a sniper's bullet got him in the head and he died instantly. Sgt Murphy was the only KIA in his squad.

The 3d Squad owes him a lot, because his actions prevented the NVA from overrunning us. Prentice and Sedies moved their gun a few meters to our left. Prentice was killed while manning his gun. Sedies was wounded, while retrieving the machine gun, after LT Pryor ordered him to get it. Sedies died of his wound later that morning.

Medeiros and I were monitoring the radio to keep abreast of the situation. I was at a ninety degree angle to Medeiros' left shoulder, when automatic fire came through the perimeter hitting him in the left forearm. Later we discovered he had also been hit in the back of the right leg.

Something had happened, because the artillery had stopped for a while. It finally started up again and the 1SG showed up again. Gunships came into our area and the 1SG wanted to mark the left flank, so we popped smoke. I remember "Top" rolled a grenade into the smoke and yelled "Damn it, it hit a tree! Take cover!" The NVA started pulling back and I heard a lot of firing to the rear of first platoon and I thought the NVA had gotten caught between the two platoons (1st and 2d). What I learned later was the third platoon had surprised the NVA and attacked. The third platoon was coming to re-enforce the first platoon. The third platoon saved our butts that day. The NVA had no choice but to pull back. That was the last thing I remember of the fighting.

The next thing I remember is that choppers were flying overhead and kicking out explosives, chainsaws and gas so an LZ could be constructed."

1LT Richard Sauer was the platoon leader for the third platoon and though wounded, was the only real officer who survived the fight. He remembers the day well:

"My platoon was in the rear that day as we had been the lead platoon the day prior. We always rotated platoons as the lead platoon usually got in the action first. Some of the day I cannot recall, however I can remember a lot of the action.

The first platoon took immediate fire and casualties as they were leading the company. It was apparent this was more than a small firefight. The enemy forces almost had us cut in half from the start. The 1st Sgt was with me and my platoon and he left to go up to the front. My radio operator got a call that we were going to be cut in half and they were in danger of being overrun. I took the radio and talked with the endangered squad and determined that we had to take my platoon forward to link up to form an effective perimeter. I grabbed one of my squad leaders, Sgt Ross Rembert, and told him that he and I were going forward to link up [with the forward squad, and then bring the rest of the platoon forward.

We were engaged in a pretty good fight at that time, but we had to link up. He and I went forward taking pretty good fire from the enemy. We linked up and I told him to go back and get his squad and I went back also to bring up the rest of the platoon. I made it back to my platoon when I got shot the first couple of times.

The gunshots broke my leg, however another of my squad leaders, Sgt James Woods was there first to bandage me up. Sgt Woods was later awarded the Distinguished Service Cross

(DSC), the Army's second highest award for valor, for the self-less acts of bravery he performed that day. Rembert got back to his squad and they were involved in some heavy fighting that included snipers in the trees. Despite being wounded, Rembert continued to lead his squad.

We were able to work our way up fighting and crawling to a position to link up and form a somewhat lopsided perimeter that afforded us some fields of fire and cover for each other. I don't actually remember when I got wounded again with shrapnel from an exploding mortar round that broke my right foot. That left me pretty much immobile. I used the Forward Observer's RTO radio to call in artillery. I don't recall who brought me his radio after he was killed. An Air Force Forward Air Controller came up on the artillery frequency and he and I began to coordinate airstrikes in on the enemy positions. The battle continued to rage all day.

I went in and out of consciousness several times, but I know that my squad leaders and men did everything they were trained to do and more. When things got particularly bad at one time, someone in my platoon helped to prop me up against a tree in the upright position so I could continue to shoot."

PFC Kermit Coleman was point man for the second platoon, on the right side of the company, when he, SGT Ron Snyder, and SGT Roy Pacheco encountered enemy machine guns. Pacheco was hit in the chest. When SP5 John Bockover, senior Company A medic, got to Pacheco, he said that Snyder and Coleman were laying down a field of fire. Pacheco was treated for a sucking chest wound while the other two were firing at the swarming NVA who were on the ground and in the trees.

Ron Snyder tells it this way: *I was near the front with Kermit when first platoon got hit, when they ran into that outpost, that machine gun nest, ... we were in two files, I looked up past Kermit, Roy (Pacheco) was behind us, and saw a gook looking at us, but he didn't see us. I said "Kermit, look in front of you." and he said something like "Well shoot the SOB, because my gun isn't working." So I shot him and then everybody started shooting at us, and we started taking lots of automatic weapons fire... that was when Roy got hit. Someone came around and started asking us for smoke grenades to mark our position and you know, we ran out of smoke grenades in no time. Then they started calling in artillery, I suppose they threw the smoke grenades for gunships...I think they lost track of where we were...Rawlinson, the chopper pilot who did come in for us, told us later that he couldn't tell from the smoke where we were anyway...you know it was triple canopy jungle and they couldn't tell if we were up here or if it was right underneath the smoke...anyway we started getting explosions all over and there was a big explosion to my left, throwing dirt and everything all over me and when that happened, I don't know if I got shot at again, but I started shooting and my automatic weapon got one shot and stopped. I looked and a piece of shrapnel stuck in the bolt action...so I crawled back to where Roy was wounded. He was laying back on his rucksack because he had been too wounded to even shoot his weapon and said "Roy, can I borrow your M16? I don't have a gun here." I don't remember if Kermit had already been shot, you know he had been shot in the legs and he went back and he was holding up a plasma bottle for one of the guys and he got shot through the hand. I got Roy's weapons and started shooting. I was laying on the ground and Top came up and he was standing up and said "We're going to have to move the perimeter out." I said "There is no perimeter. I'm the only one here. The first platoon is over there somewhere and I don't even know where the next guy behind me is." He just kind of looked at me and walked*

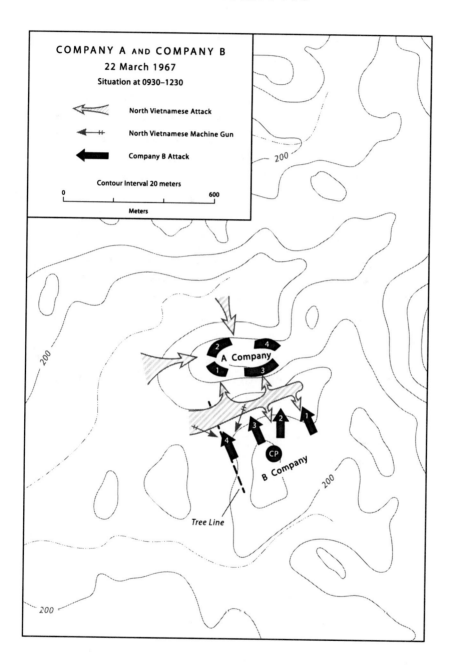

CHAPTER TWENTY TWO

COMPANY A AND COMPANY B
22 March 1967
Situation at 0930–1230

North Vietnamese Attack

North Vietnamese Machine Gun

Company B Attack

Contour Interval 20 meters

0   600

Meters

*away...I just stayed there...I mean, where am I going to go?
I had been shooting at these people all day. Anyway, I know
it was pretty nasty stuff...it didn't get any better, some of the
gun ships were shooting through our perimeter because they
didn't know where our perimeter was and Rawlinson did
come in...he was the only helicopter we had for support and
he wasn't able to land until he had dropped some chain saws
and we got an LZ cut..."*

The first platoon was left and abreast of the second platoon in
the lead and was able to link up with them as the initial shock of
the ambush wore off. Some men in the first and second platoons
were able to pull back a bit to link up with men on their left and
right. In so doing they left some rucksacks outside the line they
were establishing. When he wanted to start blowing an LZ, at
great risk to himself, 1SG McNerney was able to retrieve these
rucksacks and obtain additional C4 explosives.

Initially, as the NVA started identifying Company A's lines,
they began moving down the first platoon's flanks on the left
(south) and the second platoon's flanks on the right (north).
As the fight continued, the CP group, still behind the two
lead platoons, was killed by a mortar or B40 rocket. The two
platoons managed to form an imperfect horseshoe-shaped
perimeter, while the fourth and third platoons, further to the
rear, formed separate defensive lines facing outwards. For some
time this was the configuration in which the company fought,
but as the day continued, the third platoon moved forward
and to the left to support the first platoon. The two linked up
to form a defensive position on the south side of the ridgeline.

While the other platoons were receiving fire from the ground
and from snipers in the trees, the fourth platoon received most
of its fire from snipers. Even so, it became obvious that the
company was being surrounded while getting hit with machine
guns, AK-47's, hand grenades, mortars and B40 rockets. The

NVA's heavier AK47 rounds penetrated the vegetation indiscriminately to find their targets. The smaller rounds fired by Company A's M16s were often deflected by the brush and were not as effective as the enemy's.

Everyone had hit the ground when firing started, but ISG McNerney came up from his position in the rear and started telling everyone *"We have to get a perimeter! Start pushing out!"* Some of the men in later years, found this humorous because in many cases they were the only ones on the line, in thick brush and trees, not being able to see but a few feet ahead of their rifle because of the vegetation. The tall trees put the ground and everything else in shadow, but the falling leaves and wood dust from the shooting and explosions made it clear that there was nothing but death waiting for anyone who stood up to look around.

When the men hit the ground, behind trees or in thick brush facing away from the center, many had lost visual contact with those on their right and left. This left them unsure if and where any line had been established. In addition, it was unclear where the enemy was, though to each individual it appeared as if the entire NVA force was focused on him. Scrambling backward into the center of what had been the route of march did not seem to be a good idea. On the other hand, going forward directly into what was becoming the enemy's fire zone did not seem to be prudent either. So in response to the 1SG's order to *"Start pushing out,"* there didn't appear to be many options.

Finally, something like a three-quarter perimeter came into being when the third platoon attacked towards the first platoon on the left and linked up with it. After about four hours of fighting the enemy on the north side, the fourth platoon linked in with the rear portion of the second and the rear portion of the third to enclose a small but full perimeter from which to fight.

Shortly after the attack began, Sergeant James Woods started taking care of business as well. The citation of his Distinguished Service Cross tells part of his story:

"...Sergeant Woods distinguished himself by exceptionally valorous actions on 22 March 1967 while serving with an infantry company during an attack by a numerically superior Viet Cong force near the Cambodian border. (Author's Note: the citation is in error, it was a main line and well trained North Vietnamese Army battalion, not a VC unit.) *Heedless of hostile fire which was raking positions of his unit, Sergeant Woods ran from man to man in the defensive line to offer encouragement and direct their fire and movement. When medics ran out of first aid supplies, he unhesitatingly moved beyond the defense perimeter to gather first aid packets from discarded equipment in the field. He was pinned down by outbursts of hostile fire many times, but dauntlessly continued until he had gathered all of the extra supplies available. At one point, Sergeant Woods spotted a small group of insurgents moving toward a small rise from which they would have a firing advantage on the friendly force. He again left the perimeter to cut them off and placed himself between the enemy and his men. As they appeared out of the undergrowth, he killed all of them before they could inflict any casualties on his platoon. When he discovered that his platoon had been separated from the rest of the company, Sergeant Woods once again left the safety of his unit's perimeter to cut a path through the thick vegetation to the company's position. He then returned to his men and used the trail to move the wounded to a helicopter landing zone for evacuation. His courageous leadership throughout the firefight enabled his men to repulse the overwhelmingly larger hostile force and inflict numerous casualties on the insurgents...."*

The description of the fight by medic John Bockover, is very graphic as he describes what he saw and experienced.

"*We were being overrun and the trees were full of them. It was said we were outnumbered about 20-1. I would say within the first four or five minutes, we had twenty seven killed and forty five wounded. I heard "Medic!" and started running like hell to the front. I'll never forget running over a dry creek bed. There was a tree hanging over it and I ran right into it, about knocking myself out......Top made his way from the rear up to us and started running around telling us to get a perimeter formed. When they first hit us, everyone just fell where they were. The firepower coming in was so heavy you couldn't move. I dove in next to Blair Dennis on my way to get a wounded man. We were laying down a field of fire, when I saw his head drop and he was dead.*

...Top took command of the company. I was working on a man, when I saw a chink throw a hand grenade. I didn't want him to get hit anymore, so I covered his body with mine. I was hit in the shoulder with shrapnel. Top took out a machine gun that had five men pinned down outside the perimeter. He threw one hand grenade and it came back on him cracking some ribs. I had to wrap him up. By now we were running out of ammo and water and choppers were flying over at tree top level kicking them out for us. Top ran into a clearing waving his arms at spotter planes to mark our position and then he grabbed an orange banner and hung it in a tree for a marker. Bob Gillespie of the fourth platoon was hit in the chest real bad and I had to give him an IV....Jimmy Peirce brought John Mott up to me with half his face blown away. I cut a hole in his throat and inserted the end piece of a pen in his throat, so he could breathe. He looked at Jimmy and said "Sgt Peirce, did I earn my CIB?" and then he died. That has affected Jimmy to this day."

SP4 Bob Gillespie, Company A, found a little grim humor in the day "... *machine gunner Jay Macaulay was running* low on ammo, so I volunteered to get it from the other side of the perimeter. While moving, I was shot in the chest and received a sucking chest wound. When I was first hit, I thought the bullet went through my heart. I did not see a lot of blood, so after a few minutes I realized the projectile had missed my heart....The bullet entered from the left front and exited from the center near my heart....Then two of my friends came to my aid, Sgt James Peirce and Richard Gorman. Gorman gave me a cigarette and said, "I hate to tell you Bob, but smoke is coming out of your chest! Sgt Peirce said in a stern voice, "Gorman, don't say something like that!" We all started smiling and it kind of lightened things up a little. To this day I still love Gorman for saying it."

Murphy's Laws:
"A sucking chest wound is nature's way of telling you to slow down!"

Tom Carty, the radio operator for Company A's fourth platoon remembers the action: "... sounds of gunfire erupted from up front. In a split second, everybody hit the ground. Taking cover anywhere they could, behind small trees, rocks and even brush. The intensity of the gunfire kept growing and growing at an alarming rate.

...Straight ahead, off to my left a little was fourth platoon's only machine gun spitting lead. Coming from the rear, walking toward the front of our company, came Top. He came shouting encouragement to the men as he walked by our positions. When Top reached the LT's position, he told us, "I'm going up front to where the action is." Then like a ghost he was gone.

Next the third platoon came up our column, breaking off to the left to join up with first platoon in a desperate effort to form a perimeter. I got a call on the radio from the CO requesting another radio. My platoon SGT, Sgt Minor, sent

Luis Flores with a radio to the CO's position. Luis came up the column with the radio to my position. We had a short exchange of words and Luis headed off toward the CO.

Then 1st or second platoon called 62 Charlie requesting us to stop firing our 60mm mortars, because mortars were exploding all around them. I informed them, we were not firing a mortar. A call comes over the radio from either 1st or second platoon's RTO "They got me" a voice says. Then I could hear the gunfire coming through his handset. Then gook voices were on the radio. We lost contact with the rest of the company. That was the last radio contact we had with them for at least four hours.

An enormous amount of gunfire erupted from the area the third platoon had headed towards. There were shouts, "They're in the trees! Shoot the trees!" Everyone fired into the trees. The machine gunners from third platoon fired their guns from the hip. Vegetation was falling like rain. We fired out to our front. The NVA were all around us, everywhere. Then it rained artillery. I mean it rained artillery! I can't begin to tell you how many rounds landed around and on us. The artillery came screaming in, and then exploded with a deafening roar. Shrapnel was hitting everyone and cutting vegetation like a weed eater. It didn't seem like the artillery would ever stop. Round after round after round of artillery came screaming in, exploding and sending hot deadly metal in all directions killing NVA and US soldiers without discrimination. All we could do was lie on the ground and pray. You could not move. Next came the planes dropping bombs. Bombs and more bombs and bombs, bombs, bombs...some bombs were so close you were literally lifted off the ground from the concussion. Shooting, grenades going off, men screaming, artillery exploding, you had to yell for anyone to hear you.

My LT took a piece of shrapnel in his neck. I can still see his hand on his neck, with blood running through his fingers. He said he was OK...

At this point in time I realized everyone between the front of our perimeter and the back of the perimeter was wounded or dead. After the bombings, the intensity of the battle diminished greatly. The Huey gunships came next. They made a couple of passes over the fourth platoon's position, firing their rockets and shooting their Gatling guns.

The choppers' first pass was kind of close to us, the fourth platoon. The second pass was very close. It became apparent the gunships had mistaken the fourth platoon for NVA. The fourth platoon Leader looked up the battalion radio frequency and I changed the frequency of my radio and talked directly to the Battalion Commander, telling him to call off the gun ships. He did and finally the shooting stopped. There were about fifteen of us, who had not been wounded or killed at the back of the perimeter. We worked our way forwards to the front of the perimeter. For the next couple hundred feet, there were bodies and wounded everywhere. Most of the wounded had been moved to a central location. We tended our wounded, assuring our buddies they had the million dollar wound, meaning they were OK and were not going to die. They were going home. I remember making sure every wounded soldier, who could still use a weapon, had one loaded and ready to go."

CPT Sands' headquarters group was following his first and second platoons as they moved along the ridgeline. As part of the headquarters group, SGT Ted Schultz was one of CPT Sand's RTOs and he describes his experience that morning:

"Junior Wilkerson and I would alternate days as the RTO and carried the radio for CPT Sands on the Company net. I was the RTO on the 21st of March, so Wilkerson carried it on the 22d. The radio added about 12 pounds plus a spare

battery to your rucksack plus the normal load of ammo, smoke and fragmentation grenades. When carrying this heavier load through thick jungle and hilly terrain, having the radio was not a pleasure and, of course, you were a prime sniper target. Thus, becoming an infantry rifleman for a day was not a bad situation...however, I did carry an extra radio battery to support the RTO with the radio. The CP also included the artillery forward observer officer, LT Thomas Shannon and his RTO Jerry Pickworth. Thus, there were five of us in the headquarters command post of the company, which moved along with the platoons when on patrol.

When we broke camp on the 22d, it seemed like any other day, but the jungle was very quiet with no birds or other jungle noises that you normally hear. This seemed very unusual, so it made us cautious. As I remember it, we were pretty much in a single column until CPT Sands flanked one of the platoons to the left. The CP group was toward the front right behind the flanked platoon and I was at the end of the CP group.

I remember being on a ridge line and it was impossible to see the company formation or any more than the man in front of you because the jungle was so dense. In fact, we approached the crest of a small hill, which put CPT Sands, Wilkerson LT Shannon and Pickworth ahead of me and to the left about five to ten meters and on the downward slope of the hill, while I was still on the upward slope...

At about 7:30 AM, the battle began with heavy mortar and small arms fire. It seemed like no longer than a half hour from the time we broke camp. The first platoon took on a lot of fire and the NVA were swarming us with machine gun fire and sniper fire from what seemed like all directions, but mostly from the left and a lot from the trees. We started to call in artillery very close to our positions. I believe CPT Sands called in this artillery fire and the coordinates were on our own positions. I saw glimpses of NVA movement to my left. There was a lot of heavy small arms fire from all directions making it difficult to pin point where to engage the NVA. At that time, the first of two NVA rockets or mortar rounds hit near the front of the CP. It appeared that the second of the two was a direct hit on the CP. I am not sure if those rounds killed CPT Sands and LT Shannon because I don't know their exact location in the CP or when both of them were killed. They were only about five to ten meters in front of me at that time. I couldn't hear any movement from their location. I could not see them and we were also engaged in heavy small arms fire. I received severe shrapnel wounds in my neck, shoulder and back from the blast of the second mortar round. The shrapnel came within ¼ inch of my spine but my rucksack took most of the hit and the little crest on the hill protected me from the full blast. The concussion from the explosion also ruptured both ear drums and I had loud ringing in my ears and could not hear. I didn't see Wilkerson and Pickworth until what appeared to be about an hour into the battle and they were badly wounded but still alive.

I tried to bandage my wounds to stop the bleeding and continued to fire my M16. I know I hit at least one NVA at close range, but unsure if I hit any others because of the thick vegetation. Napalm was called in, I believe by Company B that was trying to come to our aid. The napalm was very close in front of our position and I could see it. I saw an ant hill to my forward left only about three meters away, so I crawled to it for added protection while continuing to fire my M16. I seemed to be taking on more close small arms fire on that side of the ant hill, so I decided to move to the other side. Since this was only a few meters from CPT Sands, this is where I found both RTO's. However, I did not see CPT Sands.

Wilkerson was badly wounded. Wilkerson was yelling for a medic and wanted water while Pickworth was within a foot of him, alive but quiet and motionless. I tried to attend and comfort them and keep both conscious the best that I could while covering our position. Since neither of them had a radio with them, I decided that I needed to find one to make contact with the rest of the Company. I could hear the heavy fighting going on but I could not see any of my comrades. I figured the radios had to be close by over the crest of the hill. I left the protection of the ant hill and the two wounded RTOs and crawled out about five meters further forward and to the left where I thought the radios might be located. I found one of the radios but it was not operable. I did not see the other radio. I also never came in contact with CPT Sands or LT Shannon or their bodies. I then crawled back to the ant hill where I left Wilkerson and Pickworth. When I returned they were not moving or making sounds. I didn't have time to check on them again since the small arms fire was much heavier. Thus, I am not sure that they were still alive. The reports I saw years later indicated that they were killed by small arms fire; however, I know that my wounds were from the mortar attack.

...I continued to fire at the NVA movements mostly on the ground. I could not see them in the trees or at least didn't focus on the trees since my neck wounds were making it difficult for me to move my head to look up. I am not sure if I killed any more NVA since I was very groggy and semi-conscious. A short time later I lost consciousness from loss of blood. It seemed like from the time of the initial NVA contact 7:30 AM to the time that I lost consciousness was no more than two hours, however, I found out later the battle lasted all day and we were not evacuated out until very late in the day."

During periods of stress like combat, it should be noted, the perception of time can slow down or speed up dependent upon the activity and the individual. Almost all of Company A's survivors are under the impression that CPT Sands was killed early in the morning, not long after the initial contact. However he and I were talking to each other just before mid-morning, giving updates on our respective situations. After mid-morning I was no longer able to contact him on the radio. From that point on we had no contact with Company A until about mid-afternoon when we were finally able to get closer to their lines.

Even in a confusing and chaotic firefight, Company A's training and experience, combined with the procedures established by CPT Sands and his NCOs, enabled them to hold off a superior force. Once 1SG McNerney realized there were no officers capable of taking charge, his immediate assumption of command provided a central focus enabling the platoons to pull together an effective defense until help could arrive.

CHAPTER TWENTY THREE

ON THE 22D, two aircraft were assigned to the 1-8th as Command and Control (C&C) helicopters. The primary bird arrived at the firebase early and Colonel Lee took it up for his usual morning reconnaissance of the company areas of operation. As Companies A and B continued the search for the LRRP team, he could not see us because of the tree cover and vegetation on top of our respective ridgelines. Based upon our radio reports however, he had a good idea of our locations.

When Company A reported its location and that it was in heavy contact, Colonel Lee was not far away and immediately flew to the site of the heavy firing. Artillery had been called by 1LT Thomas Shannon, the Company A FO, and the C&C helicopter was careful not to get in the line of fire.

As Company A was trying to respond to the NVA ambush with artillery and a request for gunships, Colonel Lee's helicopter flew too low over the area of contact. Narrowly missing crew and passengers, the helicopter was hit by NVA ground fire.

Meanwhile, the morning's backup C&C helicopter, piloted by 2LT Sid Richardson and Warrant Officer (WO) Don

Rawlinson, arrived at the battalion firebase. It was shutting down when the radio crackled to life.

Don Rawlinson, helicopter pilot: *"There was shouting* (on the radio) *about being hit and on fire. There was confusion and a broken message about a ground unit being overrun. As the returning* (Colonel Lee's Command and Control) *aircraft broke over the trees we could see smoke bellowing out of the aircraft. It looked to be on fire, there was a lot of smoke coming from the hellhole* (main cabin) *and the tail compartment.*

They shot a high-speed approach, landed and shutdown. They jumped out and moved away from the aircraft very quickly. I believe that it was the crew chief that grabbed the fire extinguisher and put the fire out. We talked to the crew for a few minutes to find out what was happening and where the 1-8th was and how to get to them.

We were told that they were in the jungle not far from the border and that we should be able to see smoke coming up from the jungle floor. They said that fighting was intense and that the last they heard they were being overrun."

Ordinarily Colonel Lee would have moved to the backup helicopter and returned to the action. In this case, he went to the battalion Tactical Operations Center (TOC) to request additional helicopters and to ensure that coordination had been started for additional fire support. Radio contact with battalion from both A and B companies was difficult because of the terrain. Our short radio antenna was used for internal company communications and short distances. Since the battalion firebase was several kilometers from us, the radio operator had to stop, take off the short antenna, unlink the long antenna and screw it into the radio base in order to talk longer distances. The longer antenna made it difficult for the RTO to move because it got caught in brush and lower tree branches while at the same time advertising the location of a command node to the enemy. In this case, because of the type of terrain and vegetation we were in, even long antenna communications were garbled and broken.

With Colonel Lee's approval, the S3 gave immediate permission for Rawlinson's backup helicopter to fly to the site of the firefight and act as an airborne communications relay. This enabled the commander to determine what companies A and B needed that could not be heard by the battalion TOC. Because companies could only carry a certain number of things, a firefight created requirements for additional "stuff". Ammunition, grenades and water went fast, even with conscious fire conservation. To create LZs, nothing could beat additional explosives, axes, gas and chain saws. Medical supplies were often critical necessities as well. Not long after Rawlinson's helicopter took off for our location, Colonel Lee's request for additional aircraft was answered and he was soon flying over our action again.

Rawlinson continues: *"One thing about being backup is that as long as you are not needed, you know everything is fine. However, once you receive a call you have no idea what you are about to get into. In this case we knew it was all bad.*

As we flew to their location, I was impressed with the beauty of the morning. I can still see vividly the bright sunny landscape and a clear crisp blue sky. As we made our way into a small valley we barely could see what appeared to be smoke off in the distance. It was very faint but the closer we got the more apparent it was smoke and not haze.

One of us radioed the 1-8th (Company A) *in an attempt to make contact. We then began trying to pinpoint their location. As we neared the smoke I came to a near hover over the jungle. I let the aircraft settle and stuck the chin bubble into the treetops in an attempt to try and see to the ground. We continued to call them on the radio. Finally they answered;*

we wanted them to tell us when we were directly over their heads. Once they called out that we were hovering over their heads I made a mental note based on geographical reference points. You know the typical thing like a tall tree, a mountain peak, discoloration of the leaves and the roll of the tree line...

I wanted to know what they perceived as their immediate needs. We asked how we could help them. Their response was our worst fear; they had dead and wounded. The automatic weapons fire could be heard over the radio. We could hear the same automatic weapons fire simultaneously and could only hope it wasn't being directed towards the aircraft. We knew that we needed to get into the area to get the wounded out. We discussed what supplies were needed first. It was decided they needed chainsaws first.

One of the hardest things to do was to leave them alone. I pointed the aircraft back towards Plei Djerang. We radioed ahead and told them we needed a little bit of everything. Chainsaws, water, grenades, gas, ropes and ammunition were among our first trip. We hot refueled and began loading supplies."

One of the items most platoons carried was a fluorescent orange canvas panel used to mark ground positions to be seen from the air. Once the helicopter had received Company A's shopping list and was on its way back to the rear, 1SG McNerney climbed a tree and tied one of these marking panels in the branches. He hoped this would help the helicopter crew find their location again.

Rawlinson: *"On our first return we pushed a case of grenades out the door over their location. They told us the case of grenades broke open in the fall. It was raining grenades on them. That meant that we had to lower the chainsaw by rope. While I hovered the Huey, my crew chief and gunner began lowering the supplies. Every once in a while you could hear*

188

the gunfire directed toward the aircraft. Once the supplies had been lowered, we pulled back and flew in a holding pattern while they worked on getting a hole big enough for us to slip into. This was our time to discuss what was going on and who was going to be on the controls. It was decided I would fly and the aircraft commander (AC) would back me up in case I was hit. We sustained numerous hits to the aircraft. Some were too close for comfort.

We could hear the endless gunfire. It sounded horrible from the air. All we could do was sit by helpless... Well it dawned on us we didn't have to just sit by. We began calling for air strikes. We radioed out for gunship support. Then we called for heavier hardware."

Down on the ground, SP4 Bob Feagin started a small LZ at 1SG McNerney's direction. He was the best man on a chainsaw and volunteered for the job. As he put it...*"What I didn't know was that while I was cutting down trees, there were snipers trying to cut me down."* Ron Snyder said *"Bob Feagin cut a better LZ as we tried to keep him from getting shot by sniper fire. It is dangerous work using a chain saw in a firefight, but we had the right man for the job."*

Rawlinson: *"We could see the progress the troops were making cutting the hole. We could see the trees either falling from the chainsaws or explosives. It was slow going at times due to the fighting. We wanted to be able to help them, but there was no way. We wondered what it was costing in lives just to cut the LZ. Again we felt helpless."*

As the trees fell and the bottom brush was cleared away, the LZ took shape as a hole in the jungle. In spite of Feagin and his crew's hard work the hole was still too small for a helicopter to get into. Fortunately it was large enough to hover just above and throw or lower ammunition, water, C4 explosives and gasoline.

Finally, the hole was expanded enough for the helicopter to make a try at landing.

Rawlinson: *"Our first trip was the most dangerous. You didn't have points of reference yet for hovering and touch-down...It was readily apparent that I was not going to be able to set the aircraft on the ground... I lined up for an approach. As I got closer, I noticed that someone had climbed a tree and placed a cloth panel up in the branches. Now that took guts. As I approached the hole and came to a low hover, it did not look like I could get into the LZ. It's funny what one remembers when under pressure. I remember hovering forward as far as I could. I put the rotor blade on a tree, told either the crew chief or the gunner to lean out and clear the tail rotor on the way into the hole. I peeled the bark off the tree as we lowered ourselves into the LZ. The crew chief hung suspended by a "monkey strap" out of the aircraft while we descended into the LZ and gave me directions as to which way to move. He guided our tail rotor around the trees and limbs until we finally got to the ground for a low hover."*

Even though the helicopter was at a low hover inside the LZ hole, it was still too high for ground personnel to lift any wounded to it for evacuation. Medical evacuation helicopters with cable baskets were not available until later and by then the LZ was expanded sufficiently for one ship to land carefully.

While Rawlinson made additional supply runs with water, ammunition and explosives, enemy fire was directed at the aircraft numerous times. Rounds hit the fuselage, rotor blades and the first aid kit behind the pilot's head. Miraculously they did not hit any of the crew.

The support the helicopter provided was tremendous, and the pilots risked their lives every moment they were in the area. They not only had to worry about the enemy, they had to be concerned about friendly fire.

Rawlinson: "*We were trained to call for fire support, so we knew the location of the artillery batteries and the direction of fire. It was pretty easy to avoid, as long as none of the rounds were errantly long, we would be OK. "Faith."*

To avoid the jets and other fast movers we had to stay parallel and within bounds of their runs. Trying to time our getting in and out was based on their actual firing or bombing runs. Sometime with the napalm it would be very hot and it would pull the air out of your lungs.

There were six gunships in all, three on each side making gun runs. They carried 5,000 rounds and would fire short bursts multiple times on each successive gun run. We could easily see them and maneuver in and around them. I actually contacted Delta Troop and asked them to continue their runs dry while we made one run in under fire. I was hoping that the enemy would keep their heads down just for a moment while we landed.

It truly was a crowded sky with artillery, bombs, napalm, machine gun fire, sounds, smells…it was so noisy at times I could not hear what was being transmitted on the radio.

We made one trip into Company B and took some wounded out, but we pretty much were dealing with Company A all day.

We supported and flew for the units for 11 hours and 30 minutes."

CHAPTER TWENTY FOUR

IN SPITE OF THE HELICOPTER ASSISTANCE, Company A was still fighting for its life. Company B was on the way, but it had its own problems.

At the beginning of the fight, we were moving along our ridgeline, trying to see through brush and trees, we heard AK47 and M16 firing from the west accompanied by B40 rocket and mortar explosions. I immediately tried to contact Bidd but got no response. From the frequency of the firing and intensity of the battle sounds I knew he was in trouble and that we needed to get there as fast as we could. The moment is still clear to me. As Rawlinson said, the weather was warm and at helicopter level it was probably bright and clear. Underneath the jungle canopy, however, it was a world of shadows, broken only by those streaks of sunlight that managed to evade the trees and branches and make it to the floor of the forest.

Thoughts were tumbling through my mind like dice. I reacted out of instinct, halting the company and ordering its platoons to face right towards the ongoing battle. I reminded them to watch their rear in the event there were more NVA somewhere around us.

Because we did not know the tactical situation of either the enemy or Company A, I wanted my men in a formation that would provide flexibility yet give us maximum firepower when making contact. If the enemy was between us, we could reduce the pressure on Captain Sands by forcing the NVA to fight in two directions. If the enemy unit was on the northern (opposite) or western side of Bidd, we would be able to come up from the south or east and reinforce in place. Depending upon Bidd's status, we could maneuver to either side and attack from those directions.

Making a right face, we moved towards the sounds of the guns. All four of my platoons were on line left to right (4, 3, 2, 1). Some were in column, while others were more spread out. My CP group was behind the second platoon.

The fact that we had not been fired upon suggested that the NVA had no idea we were in the area. I was hoping that our attack would be a complete surprise, and throw the NVA into disarray and confusion long enough to stop any encirclement of Company A.

All birds were silent and the only sounds we could hear were our own heavy breathing, the swish of our clothing against the brush and the tremendous exchange of firing and explosions ahead of us. Company A had artillery support and we were prepared to call in a barrage in front of us as well. I told Bill Wilson to make sure the two unit's fires were coordinated so we didn't hit each other. We started moving downhill off our ridgeline and I began to see more open area to my front and the tops of trees in a tree line to my left front. We were moving into a large bamboo thicket, which I did not like at all.

Colonel Lee, flying above in his primary C&C helicopter, called me on the radio...

"82...this is Pineapple. 81 has contact. I want you to move to support, over."

"Pineapple, this is 82. Roger...we are already moving and enroute. Will keep you posted, over."

"Roger, out."

Shortly after that I was able to contact Bidd.

"81 this is 82...we are on the way. What is your situation? Over..."

"82...81...We were hit hard from the west and the south and they are surrounding us. It is a large force and we have taken serious casualties. How soon can you get here? Over."

"81...82...We are about 300 meters from you and will be there as soon as possible...over."

"82...81. We need help...hurry. Over."

"81...82...Roger, out."

I had never heard Bidd's voice so emotional, so I knew the situation was extremely serious. I told the platoons to speed up but to move with care because I wanted us to see the enemy first. It would not do anybody any good if we were to run blindly into the bad guys and lose whatever advantage of surprise we had.

Cliff Rountree of the fourth platoon had something of an epiphany during our movement to contact. *"We were moving towards the shooting and I remember thinking about my father and that I was connected to all the generations of soldiers that had ever done this same sort of thing. Moving to contact the enemy. No particular hate towards them as individuals, but their job was to kill us and ours was to kill them. It was a clear mission and we needed to do it well in order to survive. I remember thinking that the best advice I ever got was "Do your job...and if you do that, things will take care of themselves."*

Rountree and the rest of the fourth platoon approached a small ditch, just before entering the tree line on the west. As they did, they started receiving fire from an NVA machine gunner hidden just within the tree line. The green tracers used by the NVA ripped into men and the ground raising dust and ricocheting off brush and trees, sending their burnt out rounds spiraling into the air.

Another machine gun opened up from the fourth platoon's right flank. The automatic fire of this gun cut the platoon in half and halted it. The platoon leader assessed the situation. The two machine gun positions, one from the tree line on the left and the other on the right, hidden in the brush, dominated the large open area. The platoon had to cross this space to get to Company A's ridgeline.

One of the initial bursts from the machine gun to the right hit two soldiers, dropping them immediately. The fourth platoon medic, PFC Robert Jenkins, dashed across open ground but was shot as he reached the two men.

His posthumous Silver Star citation reads:

"While the platoon was attempting to cross an open field, two of Private First Class Jenkins' comrades were struck by enemy fire and fell wounded. Without regard for his safety, Private First Class Jenkins unhesitatingly began to crawl toward them. While crossing an open area with little cover, he received several wounds, but continued to expose himself to the barrage of hostile rounds. Before reaching his wounded comrades, Private First Class Jenkins was mortally wounded. His aggressiveness, determination and personal bravery are in keeping with the highest traditions of the United State Army. Losing his own life while attempting to aid his comrades marks Private First Class Jenkins as a soldier of unparalleled dedication to duty, and his intrepid actions reflect great credit upon himself, his unit and his country."

Bosch, the platoon leader, called me...

"6, this is 62, over."

196

"This is 6, go ahead, over."

"6, 62...we have a machine gun on our left and right and they have cut my element in half. I have at least two men wounded or killed and my medic just tried to get to them and I think he was killed. I am trying to move my rear elements around to flank them but the tree line on the left is filled with NVA and snipers in the trees and the open area is covered by the right machine gun between us and 61, over."

"62, 6...don't let anyone else try to reach the wounded it is just a set up for more killing. Give me some locations for the redlegs (artillery) *and keep trying to knock out the guns. Get your elements consolidated and keep focused on moving forward. Maybe 61 can do something about the gun on your right, out."*

It was a hard decision for me to tell Bosch not to try and reach the wounded soldiers, when they may have been alive and medical attention may have made a difference. While we were uncertain about their status, I was sure the machine gun would kill anyone else trying to reach them. It was later in the day when we determined the first two soldiers had been killed by the initial enemy machine gun fire, and then killed Jenkins as he tried to reach them and treat them.

One of the great attributes of the American soldier is his willingness to help someone who is hurt, regardless of the consequences. It is something a commander has to be concerned about, because the person who is helping another is not firing his rifle and is not assisting in or influencing the action. He has been taken out of the fight as effectively as if he had been killed or wounded himself.

Jenkins was doing his job, but another few moments of consideration might have revealed there was little he could do because of the machine gun. If he had stopped to think, he might have been available later to treat many more wounded.

However, it was an extremely brave act, and he is completely deserving of his award.

Because of the ferocity of the rifle, machine gun and B40 rocket fire, fourth platoon began taking more casualties and its machine gun team went down. That left the platoon without the heavy automatic fire a machine gun brings to the fight. Pounded by the enemy's heavy firepower, the fourth platoon got bogged down and could not move forward. LT Aronhalt's third platoon was to the right of the fourth platoon and was affected as well.

"61, this is 6, can you see the gun between you and 62, over?"

"6, this is 61...affirmative, it has pinned down my left element and the open area doesn't have much cover or concealment. We are trying to do something about it right now, over."

"61, 6...Roger that...be aware I am sending 59 and 60 around your right flank to take some of the pressure off and maybe break you loose, over."

Our surprise attack was no longer a surprise. We had hit the NVA rear guard. The two NVA machine guns had delayed us long enough for the NVA main force to establish a defensive position against us while still attacking Company A.

I directed the first and second platoons on our right, to conduct a sweeping hook to the left around the third platoon. I felt this would relieve the pressure on that unit. In order to do this, the two moving units still had to keep the enemy in the front occupied so their movement would not end up leaving their right flank vulnerable.

The NVA attacking Company A were alerted by the western machine guns and the battle with third and fourth platoons. Understanding that another US force had come up behind them, the enemy sent units to stop us. Meanwhile, we had come down off our ridgeline and into the open ground between A and Company B. This put us at a disadvantage for we were on lower ground than the enemy.

As the first and second platoons crawled forward, they hit a series of small cross gullies, which slowed their progress and made them visible to the enemy. As soon as the enemy detected them crawling around in their rear, they started focusing sniper, automatic and grenade fire on them as well as on the third and fourth platoons. Heavy fire from the front and reports from the platoon leaders told me we were now engaged all along the line by the rear elements of the NVA units that were trying to surround Company A.

While the platoons returned fire, they could not match the NVA maelstrom of fire. The forward movement of all platoons halted. Even so, we had succeeded in surprising the NVA and had forced them fight in two directions. They were still attacking Company A, yet had to defend against Company B. This put them in a poor tactical position, for as long as Company A could hold out time would be on our side. We had the NVA in a classic hammer and anvil situation. Good job!

Given Bidd's last message, I nevertheless was unsure how Company A was faring. It was obvious from the amount of fire directed at our left, center, and right that there were more than enough NVA to address both Companies A and B and still have firepower to spare. I started thinking about other options.

Back on the left flank, the NVA machine gun between the fourth and third platoons was still active and causing damage to anyone trying to move forward across the open areas. Aronhalt sent SSG Frankie Molnar's squad to try and do something about it. Working forward across some of the dangerous open area, Molnar's squad finally silenced the machine gun. Molnar's citation for his Bronze Star for Valor tells the story:

"While moving his squad to silence the enemy emplacement, Staff Sergeant Molnar had to take his men across an open area

of approximately 50 meters. He took upon himself the task of establishing a one-man base of fire, drawing the enemy's attention and allowing his squad to silence the enemy positions. While returning to his company's perimeter, his squad again came under heavy enemy fire. At this time he put his squad on line, pointing out the more effective enemy positions. With disregard for his personal safety, Staff Sergeant Molnar exposed himself many times to the enemy's bursting rounds, distributing ammunition and giving words of encouragement to his men. He returned his men to friendly positions without a single casualty. Staff Sergeant Molnar's aggressiveness, devotion to duty and personal bravery are in keeping with the highest traditions of the military service and reflect great credit upon himself, his unit and the United States Army."

Even though the third platoon finally knocked out one of the NVA machine guns, the western NVA machine gun in the tree line was still the primary threat to our left flank. It threatened, in particular, the fourth platoon whose squads were isolated in the open area towards Company A with the tree line on their left. Snipers in the trees could see down into the brush and were taking a toll anytime anyone made a move.

By this time we were working with the artillery which was firing concentrations on those areas where I was pretty sure Company A was not. I wasn't exactly sure how far we were from them, so I was trying to be very careful with the artillery fire.

I started crawling towards the fourth platoon with my two radio operators to see for myself what was happening so I could determine my best options. I left the FO and his assistant behind on a little rise of ground so he could have better communications with the artillery. We scooted forward on our bellies cradling our weapons in our arms. Trying to keep low and behind any cover we could find. Our route took us behind and to the left of the third platoon into a no-man's land that was not completely cleared of enemy.

The battle still raged to our left. The booming crash of the artillery, cracks of rifle fire, and chatter of automatic weapons were the only sounds we could hear. Our M60 machine guns made a rapid *"Chunkitta, Chunkitta, Chunkitta!"* sound at 200 rounds per minute fired in short bursts while their Soviet-made RPD machine guns had a *Budabudatbudabudat! Budabudatbudabudat! Budabudatbudabudat!* as they spit their 150 rounds per minute. Position was everything for a machine gun, and right now they had the advantage.

As I was crawling toward a small tree stump for cover, it disintegrated from a burst of fire intended for me. We started receiving heavy fire from in front of us. Several rounds went through my backpack, destroying my air mattress one more time. Small spurts of earth and leaves jumped up all around us. The booming of mortar rounds and artillery shook the air while the *humms, thuds* and *snaps!* of rifle and automatic fire zipped around us. Hunter and Surface, the two radio operators crawled right behind me. Neither thought this was even remotely a bright idea.

The terrain was against us. In the fourth platoon area it was relatively open with the long tree line on their left from which the enemy machine gun fire was coming. In the third platoon area the terrain and vegetation was about half open shrub and small brush, while the other half was forest. The other platoons and the CP group were in bamboo and tall forest. The ground was lightly rolling with several deep gullies and in the CP area vegetation was extremely thick bamboo. Large trees grew out of it, and 100 meters away from us there were NVA snipers in them. They could see down into the foliage but our ground troops couldn't see up out of it. We were at a distinct disadvantage, but I had a personal problem I had to overcome before I could figure out our next move.

Even though we were in an extremely dangerous situation, my attention was drawn to the myriad patterns of sunlight that dappled the bamboo and forest floor. My mind also took note of the vegetation that drifted down through the bamboo as it was cut by the tremendous volume of fire directed at us. It was like a heavy snow storm of bits of leaves, bark, and vegetable matter caused by a strong wind. The sun shining through all this created a golden haze of movement that was spectacular. I mention this side note because I found that when I was in a critical life threatening situation, my mind initially became more sensitive to the immediate environment.

I noted things I ordinarily would not. This phenomenon first manifested itself back in Tuy Hoa during the Christmas attack. I came to the conclusion that my rational mind was trying to disassociate itself and escape from the horror and violence that was going on around me by taking refuge in my sense of nature.

Colors and odors became more sharply defined, sounds were amplified and movement of all things moved into slow motion. My mind wanted nothing to do with what was going on around us and threatened to become dangerously dreamy and lethargic. To put it in the vernacular, I was in danger of drifting off into *La La Land*. The first time it happened to me I said to myself, *"Man, I can't operate like this!"*

As a protective device, I devised a mental check list to break the spell and focus on what needed to be done and what options I had available to me. After the first few times I learned to recognize what was happening earlier in the cycle and how to jerk myself quickly back into reality and the needs of the moment. These lapses only lasted a few seconds, but the loss of even that much time was dangerous.

In this particular instance I instantly snapped out of my reverie and recognized we couldn't move much farther forward without setting ourselves up to be killed by sniper or automatic rifle fire. I pointed out to Hunter and Surface what remained of the jagged stump, shrugged and smiled as if it had all been part of the plan. Trying to crawl around a bit to see if there was another way to avoid the snipers just attracted more RAT A TAT TAT! TAT TAT TAT TAT! ZIP! ZIP! SNAP! SNAP! THUNK! bullet sounds. The little gouts of dirt in front of me and to the sides, quickly convinced me that there was no safe way forward. About that time Bidd Sands called on Surface's radio and wanted to talk to me. Looking back at Hunter and Surface I motioned them to move back the way we had come so I could talk to Company A without being distracted by the killing fire.

Taking the radio handset from Surface, I keyed the talk switch. *"This is 82...what's your status?...over"*

"This is 81...we are still split and they are all around us! I have artillery falling to my south flank, is that you?..."

"82...affirmative...we have good fire support but are trying to keep it away from you...is your Redleg adjusting fire for you?...over?

This is 81...affirmative, but we're receiving mortar and rocket fire and the bad guys are too close for effective artillery...we need you to take some of the heat off...over"

I closed the radio call promising to get there as fast as we could, suspecting already that it was going to take longer than any of us wanted. I aimed a quick little prayer upwards that things would work out well.

Seeing that we couldn't go forward the way I wanted, we crawled back to the position where we had left the FO. He was talking to the artillery and getting good responses. I wanted to put artillery along the tree line to fourth platoon's left where the machine gun was dominating the open area with the snipers, but wasn't sure how far Company A's positions extended. In addition, I didn't want to chance any short rounds that might end up in fourth platoon's area.

Dick Surface: *"I remember that we were trying to get to Company A as quick as we could...we got pinned down and started fighting...fourth platoon started taking casualties...and I remember Sholly saying "We have to go down there to see what they are doing." And I am thinking "We have a job to do here and he wants to go down there to the fourth platoon?" So he took off and me and Don Hunter followed him. We came through the trees and sort of up over a little knoll and all of a sudden it just opened up...automatic weapons fire... and Sholly went sliding down and there was a little tree about 12 inches and all of a sudden the bark started shattering and Sholly was down a little bit and we were just sort of waiting...he looked back and made a gesture like "Look at that!" So we headed on and they were in the trees and they started shooting between Sholly and us and I went backwards faster than I could have gone forward and by that time he was still interested in going down there to see what was happening... then CPT Sands called me and I was talking to him and he said he had been hit bad and wanted to talk to Sholly...so I hollered out that CPT Sands wanted to talk to him and he had to come back to talk on the radio...then we went back to where we had set up and I remember we were still taking fire and Sholly took some smoke out to throw and an A1E Sky Raider came out and sort of circled around...it was a South Vietnamese pilot flying that thing. He came in where the smoke had been thrown and released a bomb just behind us and the bomb started tumbling about 50 feet above our heads and you could hear it "Whup, Whup, Whup..." We all just lay down and kissed the ground...the bomb hit right where Sholly threw the smoke...then the aircraft fired his machine guns and took off, then the jets came in...and there were these big orange explosions...then the gunships were coming in, and you could feel the heat from those bullets coming right and by us...and I was thinking "This is not real good".*

In another area of the battlefield, one of the second platoon machine gunners, Victor Renza, had an exciting day as well...

Renza, second platoon: *"Well, we were only about 1,000 yards from the shooting and Sholly got us on line and we started walking through the jungle. We could hear the intensive firing and we were walking toward them. We all got on line, then the NVA knew we were coming and opened up on us... we were stopped. The fourth platoon got a little ahead of the rest of us and started taking a lot of fire from the NVA and that platoon took most of our casualties...I was in the second platoon at the time...every time we tried to move forward we took heavy fire...there was a trench and I was a machine gunner and I had my bipod legs on the top of the trench and I bent down to do something and when I came back up, this NVA had been waiting for me to do that...you know when someone is targeting you, because a lot of the weapons are set on automatic, but this guy took a single shot at my head and it just went by my ear and it was a single shot...I went down and just a little ways down from me a kid (we were all kids at 19) stuck his head up and got a bullet right between his eyes, and he was dead instantly...at that point CPT Sholly said pull back because we weren't able to go forward...*

You know, sometimes there were things that were funny... the word was to go East...do you have any idea where East is...when you are in a trench and the NVA are shooting at you, machine gun fire is going over your head and there are explosions and shooting all around you? Go East? Which way is East? I remember now that East was the way we had come, but I wouldn't have known that in that trench...Go East!! Finally someone figured out which way East was and we started out... someone, Parker maybe, put Piambino, the guy who was killed, over their shoulder and took off. I came right behind him...the bullets were cracking over our heads... we got to a point where we started a small perimeter..."

The first and second platoons had set up a base of fire out of the forward edge of the bamboo thicket and trees and hammered the enemy. In addition, they continually tried to maneuver towards Company A, but they were still unable to break through.

Recognizing that we were not getting anywhere, I had the first and second platoons withdraw a short distance while leaving a screening element to maintain contact with the NVA. I got a detail from the second platoon to construct a small clearing in the bamboo.

I had a plan to break the stalemate, but I had to get the wounded out first because we couldn't take them with us. I planned to spread the fourth and third platoons laterally along the front line to keep the NVA focused. The first and second platoons would then break contact and do a deep right hook east and north to outflank the NVA positions. They would then drive west and link up with Company A from the east.

My initial reaction to the stalemate had been to do a blitz-krieg by forming everybody into a strong spear attack with a good base of fire and slash and dash the last few hundred meters to Company A. I discarded this plan because even though it might be faster, I thought it would create more casualties along the way than the flank attack. At this point I had no real idea of Company A's casualty situation or I might have reconsidered this option.

Because we were off the ridgeline and out from under the real forest canopy, our LZ was in the bamboo thicket. The

NVA who were in the tree line and overlooking the open area between B and Company A had good visibility and clear shots at anything flying near us. Their rounds slapped into trees and snapped and cracked through the bamboo.

We started bringing the wounded to the CP and the LZ so we could get them out as soon as we could get an aircraft into the opening. I didn't want to start a major maneuver until we had gotten the wounded out and their numbers were increasing. A small hole in the bamboo was key to getting them out, but enemy fire was too intense to do much cutting or even to hover a helicopter.

All we had were machetes to cut the LZ, which just bounced off the bamboo or caused it to split. Trying to handle split bamboo without gloves was something like trying to handle broken glass but worse. We had explosives, but bamboo cane splits and shatters under explosives leaving splintered canes still to be cut. I didn't ask for chain saws because I knew they would leave the canes fragmented and split just as the machetes did. As a result, cutting the LZ was slow going and I couldn't execute my right hook until it was large enough to enable us to evacuate our wounded. Complicating matters further, tempo of the action was increasing and creating shortages of grenades and ammunition.

A medevac helicopter made a quick run over our position to see about picking up our wounded by basket, but received so much enemy fire it couldn't get close. Crewmembers aboard this aircraft were wounded by the intense fire directed at them.

In one of my radio reports to battalion, I asked for ammunition anyway we could get it. Looking at our little hole in the bamboo as guys hacked at the canes trying to widen it, a helicopter suddenly appeared like a dragonfly darting through the air. There was an increased roar of firing from the enemy as they saw the fat bumblebee target hovering over our small opening. It was Colonel Lee in his C&C helicopter tossing cases of ammunition into our small LZ like Santa Claus. Just as suddenly as he came, he was gone. A while later, the battalion executive officer, Major Bill Tausch, suddenly appeared and did the same thing. On that run the helicopter was hit several times and barely made it back to the firebase.

We had artillery available to us in the form of 175 millimeter (mm) and 8-inch guns from Duc Co; 155mm from another firebase, and 105mm howitzers from our own Ia Drang firebase. As I have said before, I had a close relationship with my Forward Observer, LT Bill Wilson. He knew from previous experience where I always wanted to put artillery and as usual, he did an outstanding job under a great deal of pressure. He put it on the enemy with whom we were engaged, but also in areas the enemy might use to reinforce or withdraw.

We used the 175's in a general support role outside of the close-in fight area because their explosions were large, but they did not have pin-point accuracy like the other artillery pieces. The 155's were great but were limited in our area. They were self-propelled on tracks, meaning they had to fire from a semblance of a road or a support base. The 6th battalion, 29th Artillery's 105's were our work horse artillery and those upon whom we depended the most. On this particular day we were using it all. We fired it into the tree line just beyond our bamboo field trying to avoid Company A. We also fired it into the general area around us to discourage any NVA trying to come from the rear.

There were also helicopter gunships, sorties of Air Force F-100 jet aircraft, and several flights of AIE Skyraiders with loads of napalm and guns. There was a small fixed wing Air Force Forward Air Controller (FAC) plane above us who controlled the "fast movers", the Army's term for Air Force jet aircraft, and on one of our radio nets. It became too confusing to relay messages about air support, so he and I coordinated directly about where I wanted the Air Force to put their bombs and where to strafe enemy positions.

At one point I popped smoke to identify our central location to the fast moving aircraft and they came winging in from the sky with guns blazing. Because the aircraft moved so fast, they couldn't see our specific locations and started firing into our positions. After a soldier was wounded by their fire and more were threatened, I frantically called them off. I redirected them to the possible enemy reinforcement and withdrawal routes outside of our immediate firefight area. It was just too difficult for the F100 pilots to tell exactly where we were located in the canopied forest and bamboo.

Our fire support structure from division to battalion was superb, and everything a company commander could want in a battle, we had available. On the ground, we had a great deal of firepower with all four kinds of artillery shooting for us. Above, screaming F100s circling high with guns and bombs, hungry A1Es with both 20mm guns and bombs, and predatory helicopter gunships with machine guns and rockets. All of these guys wanted a piece of the action. It was a team effort and I was energized and impressed at how well the different machines, men and systems meshed into the intricate puzzle of combat in my little corner of the world. All I had to do was tell them where to go.

As the fight progressed, I turned hyperactive. My adrenalin rush was at its peak when I was on two radios alternately talking to the FAC about his F100s and A1Es and what types of loads they had and where their targets were located. Then I was talking to the gunship lead pilots as to where they could best be used. Bill Wilson gave me updates on the artillery as we continued to coordinate targets for air and artillery. Changing frequencies shifted me back to the platoons to tell them what to expect next. Then I reported my situation to battalion before shifting back to the air support guys.

I relied heavily on the expertise and professionalism of my radio operators, Hunter, my communications sergeant and Surface, my driver and official RTO. They memorized frequencies so they could switch channels quickly. If I needed to communicate information to someone, without actually doing the talking myself, they passed the message almost verbatim. They were always on top of the situation and were part of an overall team that made things happen. I could be at my best because of the quality of these men. While none of us were indispensable, these guys were invaluable.

As in all immediate danger situations, my training kicked in and I entered a mental zone quite unlike my normal awareness. It was as though another person took charge of my brain and my voice. I operated "on automatic" with no distracted thinking. When a situation developed, my mind immediately assessed the options, selected an appropriate response, and started issuing orders. At one point, as if swept up in a limited out of body experience, I observed myself crouched against a small tree on our little elevation, watching the LZ detail chop at bamboo. With a radio handset in each hand, I alternated talking on the radios, telling Hunter or Surface which channels to change on their respective sets. I was pumped, I was excited, I was talking fast and could see what I thought was happening on the battlefield as if it were in slow motion.

We couldn't use 250 or 500 pound bombs as part of our close air support, but they could be put on possible egress or reinforcement routes in hopes of hitting any NVA moving on those routes. We could use guns in close air support, but we had to be sure the aircraft knew our location before they started their strafing runs. The platoons popped smoke for their locations in combination with map grid coordinates.

Even so, we had wounded from friendly rounds that hit our positions.

As I write these words, I have to laugh at myself for being impressed with my ability to multi-task in handling our support. All competent company commanders, of which the 4th ID had many, did the same thing under similar circumstances.

Our problem was not the support available or its employment. The three main players in this party, were Company A, the NVA and Company B. The difficulty was that we were all so close together. Our main challenge became finding targets that did not include Company A as well.

I sought to maintain a running conversation with Bidd to keep him apprised of our situation. Around 0930, at the height of a particularly vicious storm of explosions and automatic weapons firing, Bidd called me, but his transmission was extremely weak though we were only a short distance away. He sounded tired and weak as if he had lost blood.

"82 this is 81, over..."

"81...82...go..."

"This is 81...my element is split and they are all around us...I don't know how much longer I can hold...we really need help...over..."

"81...have you been hit personally?..over..."

"82...Negative, but we need you now...over..."

"81...82...I understand buddy...but they have us blocked all along the front and they're between us...we're doing our best, but we're taking casualties too and there's too many of them to get through as fast as we want...over..."

"82.....81...Roger...just...hurry...over..."

81...82...Wilco...we're coming...hang in there... out..."

That was the last conversation I had with him.

My guts churned because we couldn't do more than we were doing while my friend and his guys were literally dying

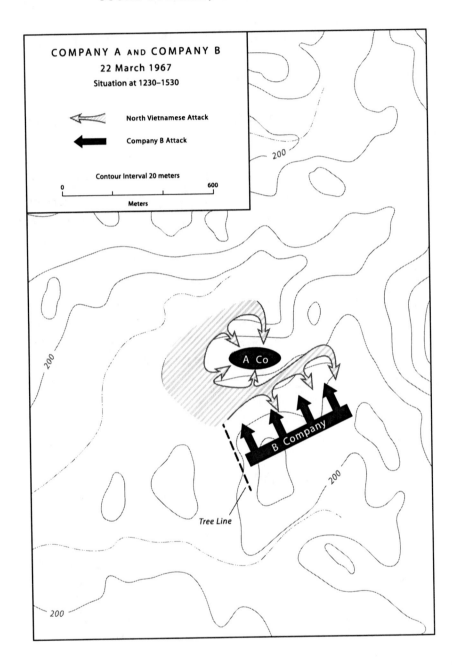

a few hundred meters away and I could hear their guns and grenades answering the NVA's attack. My comments to him sounded like lame excuses, but I didn't know what else to say. I was afraid we were going to be too late and I hated myself for even thinking it.

Based upon a timeline I put together later, Captain Sands and his command group were probably killed shortly after our last radio conversation, somewhere between 9:30 and 10 o'clock.

Fighting continued through the day as we maneuvered forward, back and around the flanks trying to break through the enemy lines to Company A. My plan to make a right hook sweep fell apart when my reconnaissance couldn't find the enemy's open flank.

I was afraid if I moved two platoons too far to the east I would split my forces too far apart, leaving both groups of platoons insufficient combat power to do their jobs. I also had the thought that if we were running low on ammunition even with limited helicopter resupply, the enemy should be having the same problem. They had to carry all their supplies and they had failed in their initial hope of quickly overrunning Company A. Their supply routes were being interdicted by our air and artillery, and time was not on their side as we built up sufficient strength to overcome them.

While most of our guys spent much of the day locating snipers and other NVA soldiers, shooting and moving to better positions, and trying to stay alive, there were odd moments.

There were small gullies all over the place where men could take cover. One Company B soldier was sneaking down one of the gullies and reached a corner. As he came around the corner, he surprised two NVA soldiers coming toward him in the same gully. They all saw each other at the same time and froze...then without a shot being fired, all parties reversed course and ran back the way they had come. Humorous in the after-telling, but that was not the way I wanted our soldiers to react.

Dick Surface: "*One of my friends, Jim Foreman,*(fourth platoon) *said he got kind of hungry, because we had been fighting all day...and there was this little trench where he was and he was watching it and he grabbed a can of C rations and started eating...then a gook threw a hand grenade at him, but it hit a tree and bounced back and killed the gook when it went off...he said it was kind of funny that he was eating while he was pinned down and people were throwing grenades at him. It was like it was just another day at the office.*"

Finally, the artillery, aircraft, and individual efforts enabled the 4th and third platoons to pull back and consolidate their positions, leaving their dead in front of them near the tree line.

Saying the platoons were able to consolidate their positions is a cold and distant description of what really went on. Each man was looking for targets, moving and shooting, throwing grenades, trying to look out for his buddies, calling for more ammunition, and hearing that hated call for "medic!"

SFC Grandstaff, the fourth platoon sergeant was furious and frustrated. He told me, "*I couldn't do anything about the two machine guns that had split our column and the medic and the guys kept trying to help the wounded, but were getting shot as they showed themselves. I kept trying to get everybody back together to form a front so we could direct our fire better, but we were just too vulnerable. Finally I realized that I had to do something to get us motivated again.*"

Grandstaff's citation for the Silver Star describes his form of "motivation'"

"*...When his platoon became separated from the rest of the unit and pinned down by enemy machine-gun fire, Sergeant First Class Grandstaff moved through the rain of hostile fire to rally his men and position them in a defensive formation.*

214

He delivered an extremely telling volume of fire into the enemy positions, neutralizing a number of them. Then, ordering his men to rejoin the main unit, Sergeant First Class Grandstaff remained behind and used his weapon to lay down a deadly sheet of covering fire. Seeing one of his men wounded and lying in the open, he ran to the man's aid, all the while maintaining his devastating fire and began carrying him to safety. Several times Sergeant First Class Grandstaff was temporarily pinned down by heavy fire as the enemy tried to thwart his rescue attempt, but he doggedly moved onward until he finally reached the relative security of the perimeter. His unmitigated courage and spirit of absolute determination heartened his men, eliciting their best effort throughout the battle. Sergeant First Class Grandstaff's extraordinary heroism in close combat against a numerically superior force is in keeping with the highest traditions of the military service and reflects great credit upon himself, his unit and the United States Army."

Renza, second platoon: *"the fourth platoon was still out ahead of us...they took about 6 killed, but we couldn't recover the bodies, because every time someone had gone out to see about them they got shot too...Sholly called in gunships, they came in, opened up and were right over us...we started screaming "Call them off! Call them off!!" Because they didn't know exactly where we were and their machine gun fire was hitting about a foot in front of us...the next thing I remember is that CPT Sholly called in the Air Force, the helicopters go away and F100s come in and their screaming engines hurt our ears..."*

As our little LZ was expanded in the bamboo field, helicopter pilot Rawlinson was able to work his helicopter in on a one-time shot to toss out some more ammunition and take out some wounded. He was able to hover low enough without landing and we were able to boost some of our wounded up to the crew chief who pulled them further inside the helicopter.

However, because of the heavy fire the helicopter attracted I made a decision not to endanger the helicopter again.

As I mentioned briefly, one of our air force assets was the A1E Skyraider, a propeller driven aircraft. Compared to the jets it was much slower, but because the pilot had more time to see the target, its close air support was more effective. The slower speed allowed the pilot to drop a bomb or strafe an area with greater accuracy.

As our clearing was widened, from the CP's little elevation, I could see across the tops of the bamboo and make out the larger tree line. This was the area from where a great deal of enemy fire was still coming. The Air Force spotter asked me if I had a target for napalm. This was the first time they indicated they had such a load and I had a perfect place for it. I directed him to drop it on the edges of the tree line. I figured that would account for snipers in the trees, as well as any ground positions that were opposing the fourth and third platoons.

There were two A1Es and they knew exactly what they were doing. They flew in from east to west with guns chattering. Then just over the open area and before the tree line they released their loads. It was gratifying to hear the *"Whump! Whump!"* *Whump!* of the silver canisters. They tumbled through the air and exploded among the tree tops close enough to hear the crackling fires and see rising smoke. The jellied fire hit the trees and fell down into the underbrush and the enemy below. It stuck to and burned anything it touched, creating a horrific firestorm as far as we could see into the forest.

Several runs of the napalm seemed to do the trick. Most of the intense shooting coming our way dropped to an occasional burst from the enemy away from the tree line. The firing coming from Company A had dropped as well. I didn't know if they had been overrun or if the enemy had started withdrawing as a result of our combined actions.

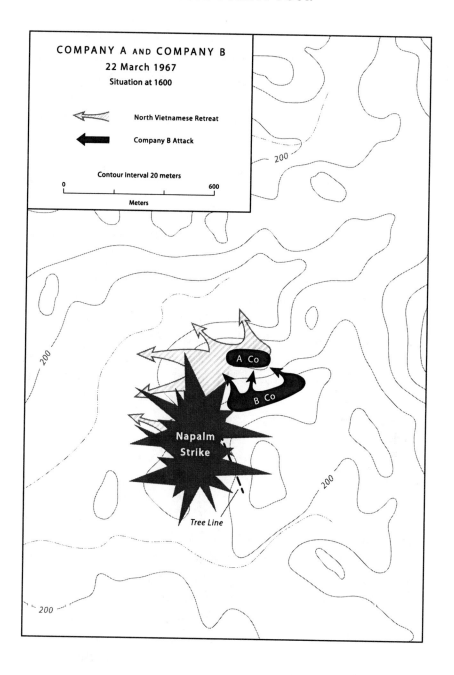

COMPANY A AND COMPANY B
22 March 1967
Situation at 1600

North Vietnamese Retreat

Company B Attack

Contour Interval 20 meters

0   600

Meters

A Co

B Co

Napalm Strike

Tree Line

McNerney told me later the enemy had been assembling in the tree line in preparation for a major attack on his southern flank. He said if they had done that, Company A would have been unable to hold. He was completely surprised but satisfied, when the napalm came out of the sky and down on top of the NVA. He was convinced it was the napalm attack that broke the back of the main enemy effort.

As enemy opposition weakened, we found his fire lessening and we were able to maneuver platoons again. Because the fourth platoon no longer had a machine gun team, I replaced them with one of the second platoon's guns and the gunner.

Renza, second platoon: *"I was in the second platoon, but the machine gun team from fourth platoon had been killed along with medics and other riflemen...so my friend, Bob Sanzone, who was in the fourth platoon, said "I want Renza." They called me up to the CP group and I remember going up to the CP group, which was in the middle of the perimeter circle, and Sholly said to me, "You are now in the fourth platoon." So that was how I got in the fourth platoon...we left the other gun in the 2d..."*

I told the battalion commander we were moving again and taking our dead and walking wounded with us. This was a tough decision because we were still not sure of Company A's status. There was no radio contact with them. Because of the terrain and roving units of NVA, it would have been extremely difficult, if not impossible, to find our KIA bodies later. This was before the day of the GPS and I subscribed to the philosophy of not leaving anyone behind, dead or alive. Colonel Lee told me years later there had always been a question in his mind. Had the bringing of our dead and wounded with us slowed us too long in getting to Company A? I had the same question at the time. I could not raise the unit on the radio but the firing had slackened to the occasional burst of automatic fire and rifle shots. It was obvious that at least temporarily, most of the intensity had gone out of the action.

Our arrival even two hours earlier would not have made any difference. CPT Sands and his CP group had been killed much earlier in the day.

Five of the bodies of our soldiers, who had already been killed, were in the napalm target area and had been burned badly. There was never any question of identification for we knew exactly where they had fallen, and marked them as we retrieved them to take with us. I knew their families had to have their remains for any closure to such a tragic event. While bringing them out was the correct decision, their physical condition later created a great deal of confusion, sorrow and misunderstanding within the soldier's families.

A commander's most hated thing to do is to write the family of every fallen soldier telling them a little about their soldier and how he died. While it was on a case by case basis, in an attempt to soften the blow on the family, I always described the circumstances of the battle, and something personal about the man himself. Dependent upon the facts of the case, I some-times did not get into specifics as to an individual's injuries if they were involved in a particularly violent death, but might relay more general, though still true, details.

In this instance, in my letters I had not mentioned the fact the bodies had been burned hours after the soldiers had lost their lives. As a result, months later I had to answer several separate Congressional inquiries initiated by families wanting to know why their relatives' bodies showed evidence of hav-ing been burned to death. My letters to them said their loved ones had died as a result of wounds received in combat, which was all true, but with nothing further to explain the condi-tion of the bodies. In these formal Congressional demands for information, I had to explain in greater detail exactly how each soldier died and how they had become burned. Via the inquiring Congressmen I had to assure the families their service members had not been killed by napalm released in error over a US position, or by an unfeeling or incompetent commander.

Renza, now in the fourth platoon, continues: "So *now we still had to get to Company A, but we had to go out and retrieve the dead bodies. Grandstaff said to me "We are going to go here and set up the MG on this little knoll." It was amazing, the napalm had burned all the underbrush away and now we could see into the tree line. Grandstaff said "Set up the MG on the knoll and we are going to go down in front of you and pick up all the bodies, if we start taking fire, we are going to get down and you start firing over our heads." That just about scared the life out of me...because now I had the responsibility...I set up the MG and they went down and started bringing the bodies back and started laying them down next to me...they were not only shot but they were burned... after they got them all back, the Company Commander said "Put the bodies in ponchos." So we put the bodies in ponchos, with a guy on each corner. We also had to carry our own rucksacks, our weapons, 100 degree heat, some NVA firing, but not bad, because the ones near us had either been killed by the napalm or were running for their lives after the strike. It was only 400–500 yards to Company A. When we finally got there, their perimeter might have been only one guy in a position...that's how thin it was. Cliff Rountree and I were on the front of one of the ponchos. When we got into the Company A perimeter, there were bodies everywhere, US and NVA, because Company A hadn't been able to get to their bodies yet. Then Sholly took over the two companies because he was the senior officer on the ground...and put us all together...then we started policing up the bodies."*

When we got to Company A's perimeter we walked by men in their prone positions, some behind trees, some behind ant hills and others just laying in the brush with rifles ready to fire. Even though they were glad to see us, they maintained an eye out for NVA even though I had a rear guard platoon doing the same.

I was met by 1SG McNerney, who gave me a quick briefing on the unit's tactical status and positions. He confirmed my fears. Bidd had been killed along with his radio operator and forward observer team. It wasn't machine gun or rifle fire that killed them, but we couldn't tell if it had been a rocket propelled grenade or a mortar round.

1SG McNerney and I just clasped hands and looked at each other, both of us too weary and too professional to cry. That didn't mean we didn't want or need to do so, but we still had jobs to do and men to take care of. Our feelings and grief were shoved into our personal emotional cubbyholes to be taken out and examined at a later date. Maybe.

As McNerney and I tried to identify the cause of Bidd's death, we realized at the same time that it really didn't make any difference. A lot of good men and two fine officers were simply gone.

CHAPTER TWENTY FIVE

McNERNEY HAD TAKEN CHARGE after Bidd was killed and he and his NCOs had been successful in holding off the NVA all day, though with heavy losses. Over the radio, Colonel Lee told McNerney and myself that, since I was the senior officer on the ground, I was to assume command of both companies for the time being, with McNerney still being the senior man for Company A.

Since McNerney had lost more men, we established a Company B perimeter and moved all of his men inside. By this time it was late afternoon. We had been fighting all day and were still receiving sporadic fire from the NVA, but nothing that presaged an immediate attack. Even so, we did not rule out another onslaught in the evening or the next day and prepared for that possibility.

Our position was on a ridgeline similar to the one we had traveled that morning. There were hardwood trees with brush interspersed among them. The ground was rocky and covered with fallen branches and vegetation from all the automatic fire, mortar rounds, and rockets that had landed within our perimeter. It was not good soil for digging holes. Our fighting positions consisted of what little earth we could scrape out, supplemented by rocks and a few sand bags. The perimeter positions used trees, ant hills, and other shallow depressions we could improve upon in the event of a ground attack. While we had some logs to lay over our scraped holes, we were still very vulnerable to mortar or rocket fire.

As a priority, we moved all of our wounded near the center of the perimeter where they would be better protected and cared for. We could easily evacuate them from there as soon as we got the LZ improved. We also wrapped the twenty-eight killed, in their ponchos and placed them near the center of the perimeter for evacuation after the wounded.

Rick Sauer, Company A, third platoon Leader: "*When the battle was over, we started to reorganize and bring the wounded to a central location to be evacuated. My men made a make shift litter with poles and a poncho and carried me up to the 1st Sgt's location. He and I had a conversation about me being evacuated and I lost the disagreement. The next thing I knew I woke up on a helicopter being flown out.*

Everybody performed in a heroic and valorous manner. Like the 1st Sgt said many times, A Co received the Medal of Honor that day. He just had the privilege of wearing it. If he could have, he would have had it cut into 108 pieces and given one to each of the men.

In reference to Company B, 1st Sgt McNerney and I talked about it many years later... We owe our lives to B Co, for without them fighting all day to get to us, we would not have survived. It was their presence that deterred another attack."

The LZ was still not large enough to accommodate a helicopter easily. With Company B taking over the perimeter, Company A was able to put enough people to work on it to expand it enough to accommodate one ship at a time. Because it was only a one-ship LZ, it was still a hairy job. The helicopter blades hit tree branches on the way down and back up threatening to crash the helicopter, killing anyone on board or nearby. It took a great deal of skill and nerve to get in and out of such makeshift holes in the jungle.

On the first attempt to land a helicopter, Rawlinson brought the aircraft down with the crew chief and door gunner guiding him, but it was still too small to accommodate the helicopter all the way to the ground. Finally it was wide enough to get almost all the way to the bottom. Several news reporters had bummed a ride with their equipment and were trying to get into the battle zone. When it appeared that the helicopter couldn't land yet, it tried to climb back out. However, there was too much weight for the direct pull upward and the aircraft was in danger of stalling and crashing. To reduce the weight problem, the door gunner, SP5 Albert Ekstrom, started pitching the reporter's equipment out the door. When the reporters began to complain, he helped them out the door for the remaining few feet to join their equipment. After that, the helicopter was able to climb back out of the hole.

Work continued on the LZ and not long after the aborted attempt to land, the LZ diameter was increased to the point where the helicopter could hover down without scraping the bark and branches off too many trees. We started evacuating the wounded that evening. Many lives were saved by the pilots and air crew who were able to get the helicopters into the LZ.

Rawlinson described the evacuation of the wounded: *"Because of the multiple* [bullets and shrapnel] *holes in the aircraft, the crew chief had to flatten them out or have something thrown over them so the wounded were not injured worse on the jagged parts of the floor. We took all the wounded to 3 Tango* [the nearest support base with medical facilities] *and refueled and got supplies there.*

"3 Tango, 3 Tango, Blackjack 895 requesting straight in approach to the aid station with wounded on board..over."

"3 Tango...requesting movement to refueling area...over."

We also re-armed ourselves and refueled at the fuel bladders. We peed and vomited there. As the day wore on into evening the blood, feces and body fluids began to smell horribly, which was typical due to the heat. The crew chief and gunner washed the blood off the floor while we were refueling."

By the time we got all the wounded out, it was nightfall. The reporters who had been pitched out of the helicopter began making a nuisance of themselves. They started taking pictures and asking questions of men who had just been through hell. It reminded me of hyenas circling a kill and darting in to grab a bite from the body. It was a disgusting situation. I finally made it clear they were not welcome and needed to leave. I was not very polite to them and made them leave as soon as room on helicopters became available. I am not sure what anyone wrote about the action, but the only thing I was clear on was that we as leaders needed to protect our soldiers from thoughtless and insensitive reporters, who only wanted newsworthy sound bites for their media. These people seldom thought about how callous and insensitive they were when asking soldiers how they felt when their best buddy had just been killed next to them, or what they thought when they saw blood, guts and gore on the ground where the wounded and dead lay until they were evacuated.

Once we had started evacuating the wounded, Colonel Lee and a good friend of mine, CPT Wally Williamson, the Battalion Logistics Officer, arrived on one of the evacuation helicopters. Colonel Lee had appointed Wally to take over Company A to replace Bidd Sands. Rather than risk any more helicopters in the small LZ at night, we decided to wait until daylight to evacuate the bodies of the dead.

Although the heaviest fighting had ended, danger remained. We were still in an area where the enemy had set up an ambush for a heavily armed infantry company, and we were close to his base camps across the border. Under the circumstances there was no reason to think he would not try again. We were on a ridgeline that sloped off gently on the left into the open area we had been fighting over all day. To the front, and on the right, it sloped down into heavy forest. The rear was relatively level with a combination of tall trees and brush similar to that of the adjoining ridgeline. The air was calm, but there were no bird or forest sounds. The roar of gunfire and explosions of the day sent most forest dwellers out of the area. Any that remained had not seen fit to resurface. The sickening sweet stench of death mixed with the sharp odor of gunpowder and explosives drifted through the bullet torn brush. It permeated the entire area and became worse as human flesh began to decompose. It wasn't just our own dead. It was made worse by the surrounding NVA bodies that had not been dragged off.

I sent out a perimeter sweep that evening to ensure the enemy forces were gone and were not assembling in secret. The platoon found several wounded NVA soldiers. When it found them, the NVA still resisted with grenades or rifles and had to be killed in place. There were individual snipers in the area, but when we found them, we killed them.

We prepared a night defensive position with scraped holes for our soldiers, moving what overhead cover we could as protection against mortars. We cleared firing lanes and positioned claymore (fragmentation) mines and trip flares. For the evening, we placed listening posts away from the perimeter to provide us early warning in the event the enemy decided to come back.

Dick Surface: "When we finally settled in with Company A, the smell of death, smoke and other smells were really bad... then they got the platform LZ built and got the wounded out.

227

The next day we got the KIAs out...but that night I rolled up in my poncho next to all the bodies...I remember thinking that if we got over run, I might be mistaken for being dead if I were next to the bodies. But I had to go on radio watch in the night...We got an occasional round into the perimeter that night, but it was mostly quiet...just a few small firefights in the night..."

The next morning I sent 1LT Bennie Bosch and his fourth platoon on another perimeter sweep to clear the area and ensure there were no attacks being readied against us. While they were doing this, Lieutenant Colonel Lee, along with Colonel Adamson, the 2d Brigade Commander to whom the battalion was temporarily attached, flew in. When the brigade commander found we had a perimeter sweep ongoing, he told me he wanted a prisoner. In between the helicopter noise, the dead being evacuated, and supplies being brought in, we had been hearing single shots or a flurry of them, then silence. When I radioed Bosch and asked what was going on, he said the NVA wounded were resisting with grenades and rifle fire as they had the night before. He said they had to be shot to keep them from killing our soldiers who were spread out and checking the brush.

Bosch, originally from Cuba, had been at the Bay of Pigs and been taken prisoner. He hated Communists with a passion most of us could not comprehend. He was still pretty emotional about all the good men the companies and his platoon had lost the previous day. Suspecting what was going on with the emotions and tensions from the day before, I told him I didn't want to hear anymore firing and needed a live prisoner. It was reported to me years later that when he heard this order, he ignored the prisoner part and turned to the platoon and said, *"The old man doesn't want to hear any more shooting. Get out your machetes!"* This may have been exaggerated hyperbole,

I wasn't there, but the story does provide a sense of how angry and bitter we were about losing so many good men. Later in the day we did find a wounded NVA soldier further out from the perimeter, and were able to send him back to the rear for treatment and interrogation.

The final casualty totals were: Company A, 22 KIA and 43 wounded. Company B had 6 KIA and 4 wounded. Years later, when I was working in the US Army's Center of Military History, I looked up the records and discovered we had fought the NVA's 6th Battalion, 95B Regiment that was disbanded temporarily as a result of the losses it took during our battle.

The story of First Sergeant McNerney's actions during this event were pieced together and resulted in his being awarded the Medal of Honor. The wording of his citation is formal and somewhat stilted, but reflects what he was doing when his men saw him in various roles at different times of the action.

MCNERNEY, DAVID HERBERT

"First Sergeant McNerney distinguished himself when his unit was attacked by a North Vietnamese battalion near Polei Doc. Running through the hail of enemy fire to the area of heaviest contact, he was assisting in the development of a defensive perimeter when he encountered several enemy at close range. He killed the enemy but was painfully injured when blown from his feet by a grenade. In spite of this injury, he assaulted and destroyed an enemy machine gun position that had pinned down 5 of his comrades beyond the defensive line. Upon learning his commander and artillery forward observer had been killed, he assumed command of the company. He adjusted artillery fire to within 20 meters of

the position in a daring measure to repulse enemy assaults. When the smoke grenades used to mark the position were gone, he moved into a nearby clearing to designate the location to friendly aircraft. In spite of enemy fire he remained exposed until he was certain the position was spotted and then climbed into a tree and tied the identification panel to its highest branches. Then he moved among his men readjusting their position, encouraging the defenders and checking the wounded. As the hostile assaults slackened, he began clearing a helicopter landing site to evacuate the wounded. When explosives were needed to remove large trees, he crawled outside the relative safety of his perimeter to collect demolition material from abandoned rucksacks. Moving through a fusillade of fire he returned with the explosives that were vital to the clearing of the landing zone. Disregarding the pain of his injury and refusing medical evacuation, First Sergeant McNerney remained with his unit until the next day when the new commander arrived. First Sergeant McNerney's outstanding heroism and leadership were inspirational to his comrades. His actions were in keeping with the highest traditions of the U.S. Army and reflect great credit upon himself and the Armed Forces of his country."

First Sergeant McNerney's award of the Medal of Honor was representative of the actions of the rest of the Company A soldiers fighting for their lives and those of Company B who were trying to come to their aid.

Although he projected, of necessity, a first sergeant attitude on the job, David McNerney was a kind, gracious, and gentle man. I was proud to call him friend. We kept in contact long

after both of us left the service until he died in 2011 in Crosby, Texas. In recognition of his sacrifices, American Legion Post 658 and the U.S. Post Office in Crosby now bear his name.

CHAPTER TWENTY SIX

WALLY WILLIAMSON OBVIOUSLY would have preferred to get a company under less stressful conditions, rather than in the manner he did. We both thought the world of Bidd Sands and mourned his passing. Wally was concerned that he might not be able to live up to Bidd's confident and professional style of leadership. I passed to him the same advice I had received early in my career, that he knew more than he thought he did and to just let the training take over. I made some notes for Wally, based on my own hard earned experience, and passed them on to him during our short time together.

Of course Wally already knew most of it. He was a good professional soldier and had been paying attention to what was going on in the field, hoping he would get his own company some day. However, I felt that if I reminded him of one thing that he could use to save a soldier's life, it was well worth passing on some of my thoughts. Like most of us, he was willing to listen to anyone who might offer something he could use, and he was gracious about listening to me at a very scary time for us all.

We spent most of the 23d evacuating our dead and making sure we had found all the personal gear and weapons of the wounded and killed. We continued to send out platoon-sized patrols to sweep the area, to count enemy bodies and to search for weapons, documents and any other intelligence material that might give us information about the enemy and his plans.

The next day (24 March) we moved southwest with what was left of Company A. Rodabaugh had rejoined us the day before, so now I had all platoon leaders present.

Evening planning meeting. L–R: Rodabaugh, Hunter, Sholly, Bosch.

Shortly after we started, we came across several bodies of an NVA command group with weapons and field telephones. They were in the area we had identified as a possible avenue of approach and had been killed by artillery. We continued south and linked up with Company B, 1-12th to augment our force. We put the three companies into one perimeter, but still had enemy prowlers all night. B/1-12 killed an NVA soldier when he tried to ambush one of the outposts, but we were still too strong a force to attack in strength, so the night passed without a major incident.

The next day we were resupplied with water and "C" rations. All three companies split up and moved into their own search areas. Every once in a while we would find dry ground disturbed and grass broken with footprints in the dust...signs of people walking and dragging heavy objects. These were trails made by dragging multiple dead bodies, but other than these indications, we found no enemy units. From the direction of their movement they had headed back across the border into Cambodia.

Following the trails, we moved towards the border as closely as we were allowed before stopping. We linked up with Company A again about midday, in a small valley LZ that was barely open enough for two ships and formed a perimeter for security. Captain Al Treado and his Company C came in and Company A was lifted out and back to the firebase to undergo outfitting and receive replacements. Company C moved out into the bush.

We were moving out ourselves, when a gunship that was strafing along the border a few kilometers away had an engine malfunction and auto rotated into our recent LZ. We were told to return to the LZ and provide security for the helicopter and its crew until an engine part could be flown in.

When we made contact with the pilots, they were extremely nervous. They had just been shooting up the border and they thought the NVA had seen them go down and would soon be knocking on the door wanting the helicopter and whoever had been throwing lead their way. These pilots were very young Warrant Officers who slept on nice cots and blankets in wooden floored tents every night. They were fed cafeteria-style hot meals when they came in from flying and hit the officer's club for their cold evening beers, movies and USO shows. It is doubtful either one of them had ever spent the night under the stars in Vietnam.

We fired some preplanned artillery concentrations outside our perimeter to keep "Charlie" honest and the pilots thought the rounds were incoming. They started saying, *"But they don't leave gunships on the ground 1500 meters from the border!"* As part of our perimeter defense, I had the pilots aim the helicopter's machine guns on a section of the perimeter. If we were attacked from that direction their firepower would be most welcome, even if it was from a fixed platform.

The warrant officers kept asking when another helicopter was going to come in and I kept getting the answer that the part had to come from Saigon, so it was going to be a while for it to be flown up. We told the pilots they were going to have to forego their hot showers for one night to see how the real war was fought. *"But they don't leave...etc. etc."* It was all very humorous for us and we milked it as far as we could, but of course they were right. The gunship had multiple rockets left, two miniguns and two M60 machineguns. It would have been quite a catch for the NVA. Another bird finally came in about 6:00 PM as the light was starting to fade. They had a couple of mechanics who repaired the gunship. After they got in the air, the fixed helicopter made several passes above us, waving and wagging from side to side, thanking us and reminding me of a happy puppy. They had a good story for the club that night.

The next day was Easter, which came and went with little difference from other days except we had enough water to

236

shave in. We headed east away from the border and linked up with Company C.

The two companies continued east. After about eight kilometers we reached the Se San River and established an LZ and night defensive positions. The following day, 28 March, Colonel Lee came in, bringing Colonel Tim Gannon, (call sign Mustang), who was to be our new battalion commander. Gannon was introduced and had an opportunity to see how his companies set up when deep in Indian country.

The next day we moved out to assess a B-52 Arc Light strike near the border.

Arc Light was the code name for high altitude bombing strikes by B-52s with 500, 750 and 1000-pound bombs. Because these were general area bombs (before "smart" bombs) and were released from very high altitudes, there was no guarantee of their accuracy. The only thing sure was that the bombs would hit the ground somewhere.

When one of these strikes was scheduled, battalion would move us at least five kilometers away from the general strike area. Even though we couldn't see it, the attack was an awesome event, a manmade earthquake. Even from five or more kilometers away, the earth shook, rolled and vibrated. The continuous roar of the exploding bombs put the loudest thunder in the world to shame and vibrated your nerves, muscles and eyeballs. The trees swayed, birds fled, and you could feel the pain of the earth through the soles of your boots. The tremendous explosive power of the strike gouged great craters.

The next day we would usually follow up to do a battle damage assessment (BDA). In heavily wooded areas, it was difficult to move because of all the downed trees. Three hundred foot giants would be blown crossways into other trees and snapped like matchsticks. Branches and smaller growth would fill in the gaps under the logs laying across each other. It was like trying to move through a giant Pickup Sticks game. Depending on the type of earth into which the bombs exploded, the craters were ten to twenty feet deep and fifty to a hundred feet across.

Other units in Vietnam reported underground tunnels and assembly areas hit and destroyed in Arc Light operations. We found a lot of dirt and jungle moved, but never any indication that enemy installations or troops were hit. My theory was that the NVA had safe haven installations in Cambodia, a few kilometers away, so why make the effort to dig major tunnels or underground facilities just across the border in Vietnam? I don't know if my guess was correct, but further south and inside Vietnam where a convenient border was nowhere near, the NVA had multiple underground command posts and hospitals.

Cleaning clothes in B and C Company

During our move eastward, Company C hit five or six NVA on the south flank, killing one and wounding a couple of more. There was one friendly casualty with a leg wound. We secured an LZ and got a dust off. We searched the area but found nothing else. From his size and facial structure, the dead NVA looked Chinese to me, which would have been interesting information, proving a direct indication that Chinese advisers were accompanying the enemy. We passed back our suspicions, but of course never received feedback.

We took a day off on the 29th of March next to a shallow and clean, swift moving stream. Both companies had an opportunity to wash clothes and bathe under close security. We alternated platoons on line, thus permitting everyone to get their turn in the water. This didn't happen very often but when it did it was always a special treat for us because it allowed everyone a little mental and physical stand down time. We stripped and sat down in the stream with our bar of soap, lathered up our clothes and ourselves and just enjoyed the feel of the cold moving water. We put our wet clothes on and allowed them to dry on us while we went about our business. We moved both companies to another secure area and established a linked perimeter.

We had been permitted to take the day off, so to speak, because the official battalion change of command from Colonel Lee to Colonel Gannon was going to be held at the battalion fire base. A helicopter took Al Treado and I to the firebase.

In addition to the bath, the trip was a nice change for us. There was a military formation with people representing each element of the battalion and there was even a detachment from the Division band that played real music. The ceremony was short as these things go since we did not have a review or long speeches. The fact the ceremony was held in a fighting man's location, surrounded by artillery, bunkers, sandbags, radios and guns was a symbolic way to exchange the responsibilities of a working rifle battalion in the middle of a war.

Battalion change of command

Colonel Lee was being reassigned to Nha Trang to work as a Liaison Officer for the Korean Divisions. A good commander, as well as a friend and mentor to we junior officers, he had permitted us to do our jobs without a lot of micro management. As far as I was concerned, there was no higher compliment than when your commander respected your judgment and permitted you to do your job.

One of my favorite recurring mission statements from him was, *"Sholly, go out and find something!"* To me that was the equivalent of General Eisenhower's mission in World War II to "... *enter the continent of Europe and, in conjunction with the other United Nations, undertake operations aimed at the heart of Germany and the destruction of her armed forces... .*"

We would miss Colonel Lee, but we were now focused on showing our new boss that he could trust us, as well.

CHAPTER TWENTY SEVEN

WE DIDN'T KNOW MUCH about Colonel Gannon, our new battalion commander...he didn't talk much about himself...it turned out he had spent time in the Special Forces, but this was his first tour in Vietnam. He took the call sign "Mustang" because he had moved up through the enlisted and officer ranks without having attended a military service academy. Originally used in WWII for someone who received a direct battlefield commission, the term morphed into a description of an officer who had prior enlisted experience before becoming a commissioned officer. So...Mustang he became...a fitting call sign to someone who had his own ideas of how to run a successful combat battalion. After Vietnam he had other assignments, but ultimately was reassigned to the Special Forces and commanded the 7th Special Forces Group at Fort Bragg, NC. With only three such Groups in the entire Army, someone clearly thought Gannon was a pretty good officer. After all was said and done, so did those of us who served under him.

After Treado and I returned from the change of command, we moved the two companies out through some of the roughest vegetation we had encountered. After eleven hours of slogging, cutting, and pushing through cane, saw brush, dark forest, thorny vines and just plain thick shrubbery, we finally broke through to more open terrain where we could move less hindered. We found another creek and decided to get resupplied at this point since it was payday. During this break, Al received notice that his command time was up and he was to take Wally Williamson's former position as the S4. He left the field when Captain "Pete" Peterson, the former S2, flew out to take over Company C.

We took advantage of the break to get a helicopter to do an aerial reconnaissance over the Ia Drang Valley, which was going to be our next area of operations.

While Company C stayed in the general area, we were directed to move back towards Duc Co. We got about two kilometers from the camp, envisioning a hot meal and cold drinks, when we were told to change directions and begin a move thirteen kilometers south into the Ia Drang Valley to secure a site for a firebase the next day.

I knew it was going to be a good hike with perhaps a fight at the end of it or even along the route, so I chose to move for a couple of hours that evening in order to close the gap as much as possible before stopping. This excited the operations officer, Major Mercer, of course, and we had another of our famous discussions, but he wasn't the one that might have to attack an area with tired troops after a bone-jarring run or forced march. The next morning we got an early start and stopped about two kilometers from the proposed firebase area to allow air strikes to clear the area. We were primed and ready for a ground attack. I had promised the troops beer and soda when we were settled.

All the stir was anticlimactic. We moved into the area with no opposition and got busy building bunkers and setting up a perimeter defense. The battalion headquarters started moving in with the arrival of the roaring, dust-blasting Chinook helicopters, carrying command trailers, generators, artillery pieces, ammunition and large slings of supplies. Orchestrated by the S3, the firebase moved sometimes as often as every three days to stay in range of the various units in the field. The battalion headquarters was vulnerable during these moves because there were times when only two or three artillery pieces were available for fire support to the companies in the field, while the other tubes were in transit.

Adding to the general hubbub, Companies A and C were airlifted into the firebase and immediately pushed out into their new areas of operations. I extended the perimeter and escaped from the mayhem and noise into a little gully, where I was shielded somewhat from the blowing dust and loud noise until things settled down. After the quiet of the jungle and forest, where you relied on sound for survival, loud noises and helicopter-dust storms made me extremely uncomfortable.

It was during this period I had to shave off my mustache. I had been growing one for a while, but it never achieved the magnificence of LT Chuck Aronhalt's handlebar. Mine was always sort of sandy colored but it blended with my continually dirty face. I thought it was doing fine texturally until I scrubbed it truly clean one day and found I looked like Felix the Cat with each hair going its own way. I hadn't realized that dirt was holding it together so well. At any rate, Colonel Gannon decided I didn't clean up too well and the mustache was outside regulations, no matter where we were or what we were doing. In response to subtle command pressure (like a direct order), I held a little ceremony and shaved it off while

Surface took pictures at critical points. It's amazing to what ends one will resort for a little entertainment!

We stayed eight days in the firebase, the longest period of time we had spent in one place since we had come to Vietnam. During this time I went back to Dragon Mountain to check on the company rear and tend to administrative matters that was impossible to do if you were constantly dodging gunfire.

Company A had enemy contact on 9 and 10 April. Colonel Gannon, the FSO and I overflew them during their pursuit of the NVA unit and assisted them with fire support and in positioning troops to block possible withdrawal routes across the border.

The company pulled out of the firebase on 12 April and moved into the Ia Drang, with its Agent Orange defoliated trees. The terrain was zombie-land—wide open, with leafless, dead trees whose branches looked like fleshless hands and fingers reaching for the sky. Dust clung to everything as we walked. It was a bizarre landscape.

There were so many ants, I had become convinced that all the mountains in Vietnam were built by ant colonies. I had learned to respect the ant's ability to chew anything that got in their way. Ant beds were all over the place. Some built anthills that turned into the mountains we were climbing, but others were underground and were not visible during the day. We often laid our air mattresses on a clear space of ground, void of sticks or rocks that could puncture them. Then, in the middle of the night, with your ear against the rubber fabric, you could hear a tiny *scrunching* noise. The sounds were ants chewing through the rubber and if you weren't quick, you were soon trying to sleep on a deflated rubberized ground sheet. We discovered that if you squirted some of your insect repellent on the ground before you put down your mattress, you were less likely to have it destroyed by ants. Of course, it took a few air mattresses to learn this little trick.

Being the experienced mountain goats we were, we climbed parts of the Chu Pong Mountain massif overlooking the Ia Drang Valley and spent two days looking for NVA outposts and tunnels. After two days on the mountain, we found nothing. We dropped into the Valley, further east than anyone had been in a while, hoping we might surprise some NVA in an assembly area. We crossed through LZ XRAY where the 1st Cavalry had their big fight in November 1965 the subject of Hal Moore and Joe Galloway's book and movie...*We Were Soldiers Once...And Young,* but still no signs. We were resupplied and received two dog teams and pathfinder trackers, but even with the augmentation we found nothing.

Even with my emphasis on maintaining field strength up, it was difficult to keep large numbers of personnel humping at any one time with R&R's, illnesses, wounds, reassignments, appointments and so forth. While there was a definite difference from peacetime training duties, there was always still one thing or another that kept a large percentage of soldiers away from fighting the war on a daily basis. When I had assumed command of the company in December 1966, there were 77 soldiers in the field out of 156 assigned, a 50% split between the rear and the forward area. I found that unacceptable and worked to reduce the numbers in the base camp or on other non-combat duties. Using various techniques, I had finally increased the field numbers on 19 April 1967 to 130 out of an assigned 156. This gave me 83% of my soldiers in the field, the highest number in the battalion, and I was extremely pleased at the overall increase in combat power available to me.

We spent a night on the Ia Drang River, had great baths and plenty of water to drink. After our baths, we had a rain that compared to the Biblical flood, but when it ended we got some mail and hot soup that perked up our morale.

During our stop on 19 April we had one of our knife throwing competitions. As a child I threw anything that had a sharp blade, so I was fascinated when I was issued a real bayonet. Throughout my Vietnam tour, I used bayonet throwing as a stress reduction activity as things got a little slow and no one was shooting at us. The platoons put together some throwing teams to compete, so when things were calm we had company competitions. Of course, with a lot of people just learning to throw bayonets, a lot of blades and handles got bent or broken and had to be replaced. Our supply folks became upset at all the property paperwork they had to go through to justify our losses, but I felt the contests were good for stress reduction, team building and bonding, not to mention combat training.

It may sound a bit exaggerated, but it was, and is, my opinion that the more a soldier handles a bayonet, sharpens it, throws it and uses it for practical things; the more he becomes familiar with and confident in all of his equipment. There is an intangible but real sense of becoming a better warrior if you are able to master all the tools of your trade. It also helps to develop in the soldier what is known as the *"Spirit of the Bayonet"*—that deep surety of confidence, aggressiveness and knowledge—which further results in the certainty that he can overcome anything nature or the enemy can throw at him.

One of the few major disagreements I ever had with Top Lopez was about his concern with damaging government property. I finally had to remind him that I was the one who signed for all company property and that I took full responsibility. I made sure the supply system knew I thought it was important to be outfitted with enough bayonets. I am convinced it developed a kind of unique spirit we would not have had otherwise. I don't know whether it was because individuals developed some skill in throwing or because they took some perverse pride in having a unique commander with a strange skill set. I do know we left a lot of trees with strange markings as we moved through the jungle. It was the knife throwing that got me the radio call sign "Blade". Surface used to joke that if the bad guys ever got to the headquarters element they would all just give me their bayonets to take care of business. I am not sure that would have been very successful, but on the plus side, I could hit non-aggressive, non-moving and non-shooting trees pretty well.

We moved on, but we had to find a hasty LZ where LT Aronhalt and SFC Grandstaff could be picked up to go in for award ceremonies. I put both of them in for Silver Stars based on their actions in the March 22 firefight. Grandstaff received his award, but LT Aronhalt's paperwork was screwed up somehow and he was unable to receive the award that day. As I have previously mentioned, he had a superb handlebar mustache that was the envy of the entire company. It was properly waxed and cared for and he looked like a fierce Turk. Unfortunately, while back in Dragon Mountain he had been required to shave the mustache so he could look like a "real" American soldier when he received his award. He was not in a great mood when he returned a few days later, minus his award as well as his mustache.

CHAPTER TWENTY EIGHT

O N 21 APRIL we moved east to take up blocking positions. I set platoon-sized ambushes in several likely places in our area of operations but netted nothing. I accompanied the third platoon with SFC Morales as the acting platoon leader. As we were moving we received the word to reverse our direction. Apparently the day before, an RVN ranger battalion had been in the area we just left and had gotten hit pretty hard. It had lost quite a few men as well as a tank. For this reason we were reoriented back into the area to see what sort of action we could stir up.

It was obvious the NVA were in the area, but it was puzzling that we had not been able to find them. Company C, for example, was mortared the night before with one man wounded. As we worked the area, we were learning more about trails, water and sheltered places, but the NVA's VC guides were more at home than we were. As a result, they were either extremely good at staying out of our way and choosing when they wanted to fight, or our commanders relied too much on our military intelligence to tell us where they were. Our intelligence sources were very good about telling us where the NVA had been, but not very accurate about where they might be now...

We kept moving and needed water, so we drifted southeast to the headwaters of the Ia Drang River and then headed west again. In the process, we ran across an NVA weapons cache consisting of 81mm and 60 mm mortars, ammunition boxes with .30 caliber ammunition, Browning automatic rifle magazines with ammunition, and a .45 Caliber submachine gun. We searched the area but found nothing except a spot where the enemy had harvested bananas in the last two to three days. There were no friendlies in the area. We called in a helicopter to evacuate the arms cache and moved on.

We spent the night about 400 meters from an NVA mortar that kept firing rounds at us, hitting all around our perimeter. We could easily hear the *Ka-thunk!* and *Cough!* as the rounds were dropped into the mortar, ignited and left the tube on their trajectory. It was a fearsome and anxious feeling, waiting for the life-ending explosion that might happen in the next minute. I timed the flight from the cough to the blast; 27 seconds is a long time to think about where it might hit. However, somehow knowing when the round was scheduled to hit gave me something to think about other than the consequences of a lucky shot. Since the rounds were not hitting inside our perimeter, I knew they had no observer adjusting their fires. In effect, the gunners were aware we were out there and were just taking pot shots.

Being able to hear the rounds fired, plus the fact we had an azimuth to shoot along, meant that we should have been able to get pretty close to their position with our artillery. In the event, we weren't any more successful than they were, but we kept trying to make them shut up so we could get some sleep. They finally quit about 0500. I called it a draw.

The next morning, on 24 April (my birthday), we moved in the direction from where we had heard the mortars and found the firing location. The NVA squad was long gone, leaving no trace in which direction they had gone.

During the course of the day, we found three battered and worn bicycles that could have been used to transport ammunition or food and destroyed them. We then found an old Montagnard with what looked to be leprosy. We got him airlifted out since he might have had some information on the bad guys. Of course, my leprosy comment unsettled imaginative people in our unit who thought that we were all going to catch leprosy. It took some doing to explain that leprosy was not contagious, but some were still not sure.

It rained extremely hard the next day and it was pretty miserable. Since we were shifting back and forth, always just missing the NVA, with someone coming in behind us making contact and, it seemed to me that we might have a watcher who was following us. In that way, the enemy could avoid a fight with the unit that was obviously seeking him, to concentrate on those that might be less prepared.

Hoping to use the rain to throw anyone off our trail, I continued to move after dark, despite the Division policy of stopping early in the day. The ground was very chopped up so I had to set up my wet poncho lean-to a few feet away from the snapped together ponchos of the radio operators and the 1SG. It was close enough that Hunter or Surface could hand me the radio handset if I needed to talk, though because of the shortness of the cord, one or both of us would get soaked trying to stretch it out between the shelters in the pouring rain.

Sure enough, after we settled into our new position, Major Mercer called to discuss my violation of policy. Our heart to heart discussion left me chilled and soaked while stretching the handset cord as far as it would go, while he sat warm and cozy in the waterproof TOC, in my mind's eye, probably sipping a hot cup of coffee. He fussed at me about following movement policies of stopping before sundown and establishing a strong perimeter before settling down for the night. I was cold, dripping wet, tired and cranky, so I allowed as to how I was big enough to run my own company, figured I knew what I was doing, and I was really aggravated and hoped someone would pick on us besides him! This began to generate heat on both sides and Colonel Gannon finally took over the radio and told us to knock it off.

I felt pretty bad about the whole thing after I settled down because I knew the enemy could listen to our conversations and this would have given him a good chuckle. Once the Major and I had these little venting incidents where I growled at anything from higher headquarters that I thought was interfering with my command prerogative, things calmed down and we always were able to conduct business as usual.

Since 22 March, because they were in short supply, we had not had enough medics assigned to us. We finally received on temporary assignment, a guy who was overweight and who apparently did not know how to get along in the field. On top of all that, he was lazy, liked to sleep late, and was slow getting anything done. I was not sure why I was burdened with him, but he was better than nothing. For three or four days in a row he kept the company from moving out early in the morning because he couldn't get his gear together early enough to make the departure time. I liked to leave our night defensive position as close as possible to sunrise in order to move during the cool of the morning, to keep the bad guys off balance, and to be prepared for any surprise attack that might come near dawn. Because everyone had to take care of his own preparations, I decided it was not fair to assign anyone to help this fellow, except for giving him advice in how best to prepare himself the night before for the next morning.

Everybody in the command group talked to him, but he was consistently still rolling his poncho hooch or eating breakfast when we were ready to go. Finally, I told him the next time he was not ready, we were going to leave him for the NVA who usually checked our positions after we were gone to see if we had left anything. I suspected he did not believe me, but I was serious and told him so.

The next morning the platoons were ready, as was the headquarters section. I asked Top if the medic was ready and he said no, that he was still eating breakfast. I shrugged my shoulders and gave the order to move out. About five minutes later, the medic came running up behind us, poncho dragging the ground, his pistol belt undone, his rucksack open, his bootlaces not tied and his face contorted in anxiety. He was sweating heavily. I didn't stop the column, but talked to him while we were moving. I reminded him that he was of no use to me if he couldn't stay up with the unit and he had had his last chance; he could move with us or find his way back to friendly lines alone through NVA country. His choice was of no importance to me. It is amazing what the proper incentive will do for a man. We had no more trouble with him, he got his gear ready to go at night, and if he didn't eat breakfast before we left, he ate it on the move. All the books on leadership mention motivation as an important element of command. This was an example!

As we kept moving through the Valley, I thought to myself with great pride that I really had a great group of trained troopers. I noted they were moving along carefully and continually looking up in the trees for snipers. I realized I was doing it as well, but then I stopped to think. What was going on was that we were not looking for snipers; we were looking for the large red ants whose nests hung from trees like hornet's nests.

In the areas that had not been sprayed with the Agent Orange herbicide, the nests were almost impossible to see in the leafy branches. In the denuded Valley, they hung like gourds from the dry branches, warning us to not put a hand on that specific tree. This particular ant species was very aggressive and territorial. It had a very painful and toxic bite and would leap out one or two inches from a tree onto a passing warm body. The acid in the bite would eat a little flesh around the site of the puncture which could then become infected if not treated. As with a swarm of bees, if a person was attacked by a sufficient number of these insects, the effect could easily be fatal. Since we were the intruders, nature was not always our friend. The enemy was not the only thing we had to worry about.

In late February 1967, the 1st Brigade and the remainder of its units had been reassigned from the Tuy Hoa area to the area west of Pleiku. Our battalion was released from the control of the 2d Brigade and rejoined the 1st Brigade. Colonel Charles A. Jackson had replaced Colonel Austin as the 1st Brigade commander and the brigade established its headquarters in a cleared area. Humorously, the location became Jackson Hole as a play on Colonel Jackson's name as well as the famous town in Wyoming.

We moved into the battalion firebase to be airlifted into Jackson Hole as the area security company. I operated the company on perimeter defense as well as two daily patrols and four to six ambushes every night. I also put ten men on an outpost on the small mountain to the west. Occasionally, the outpost on the mountain encountered single NVA soldiers moving through the area, but they either got away or refused to be taken prisoner, and were killed in the subsequent firefight. Again we received word that the area we had just left in the Ia Drang was active again. Long Range Reconnaissance

Patrols (LRRP) saw an estimated two NVA rocket companies moving across the border.

On the morning of 26 April we air assaulted back into the Ia Drang Valley to secure another firebase for the battalion. We came in so close on the heels to the gunships and artillery preparation that I got some shell fragments in my rucksack and ruined my air mattress again. As usual, Surface and Hunter were with me as we got off the helicopter and I could tell they still didn't care for my desire to be on one of the first helicopters.

About mid-day, while the rest of the company were busy building bunkers for the perimeter defense, I sent a couple of squads of the first platoon to set up an ambush on a set of knolls a couple of hundred meters to the west of the firebase that overlooked what appeared to be a well-used trail running southwest towards the border. The trail paralleled a major creek flowing into the Ia Drang River. We had stopped on the knolls a few weeks earlier. I had thought then that the trail was a perfect NVA route, and the rise would be a perfect observation post for an ambush by artillery.

The trail was about a thousand meters east of the knoll, which was at 207 meters in height elevation. It was wooded enough to provide good observation down onto the flats where the trail ran, and was a good defensive position if that became necessary. Someone traveling the trail would not be able to see anyone set up in the trees, but the reverse was not true. A good artillery and mortar plan aimed at the trail would provide great indirect fires without giving away the position of the small unit that was directing the attack. A sneak and peek squad of six or seven men was a good size for the job and it was a good plan. When the patrol reached the knolls, one squad dropped off to set up the ambush site while the other began its return to the firebase.

Shortly after arriving at the ambush site, two men went out to set up some trip flares and claymores for close-in defense. They were spotted by a passing NVA patrol, (not on the trail) that opened up on them with automatic and small arms fire. PFC David A Ferreira was wounded in the initial burst. *"... In spite of his wounds,"* his Army Commendation for Valor reports, *"he continued to cover the movement of the other man allowing him to reach the outpost position where he could better place effective fire upon the enemy. PFC Ferreira continued to support the outpost in spite of his painful wounds until his comrades could rescue him..."*

So began another quiet evening in the Valley.

Our individual training on how to adjust indirect fire paid off. The men on the outpost started moving both artillery and mortar fire onto the enemy, delaying the NVA attack. The other squad heard the firing and immediately returned to the site, managed to link with the outpost and set up a larger perimeter. Shortly thereafter, it became clear that the patrol was surrounded by an estimated NVA company and were in a fight for its life. The two squad leaders, SGT Dennis Burk and SGT James Bloom did an outstanding job of coordinating the defense, calling in fires and taking care of their men against superior numbers. They managed to hold their positions until help arrived. For their bravery and coolness under fire, they were both awarded the Bronze Star with a V device for Valor.

Company A—reinforced by the Reconnaissance Platoon, received orders to move to the site of the firefight, but it was a good distance away, so it took some time to reach the beleaguered outpost. Since no other forces were available in the area, I geared up and was going to take the rest of 1LT Cary Allen's first platoon, and the fourth platoon, out myself to reinforce the patrol and outpost. When I told Colonel Gannon what I wanted to do, he reminded me that my primary responsibility was the protection of the battalion perimeter and refused to let me go. I was sorely disappointed...the ambush and location had been my idea and I felt responsible for my guys being under fire and attack, but he was absolutely correct. If the battalion firebase was attacked, it was my responsibility to coordinate the defense with the forces that were left. Still, it tore at me since I could hear the firing and explosions from the firefight on the knoll as the responders got ready.

I spread the second and third platoons around the perimeter into the vacated platoon positions. Putting Allen in charge of the reinforcements, the two platoons left at a serious quick march and made it just before dark in record time.

PFC Cliff Rountree of the fourth platoon remembers what happened to him as the platoons moved out: *"As I was getting ready to go, I chambered a round into my M16 and it jammed on me. I couldn't get it cleared. So here I was, the platoon was moving out and I had a bum weapon to fight with. Finally I shouted that my M16 was jammed and needed another rifle. One of our artillery guys loaned me his and I finally moved out with the rest of the platoon."*

Coming up on the NVA from the rear, the platoons surprised the enemy with a pincer movement. Maneuvering his platoon, along with coordinating his moves with the fourth platoon, Allen took a squad and threw hand grenades among the enemy killing several. The rest of his platoon and the fourth platoon did the same elsewhere. Then the first and fourth platoons shot the NVA from the rear and sides and charged through them to reinforce the outpost's defensive perimeter.

Back at the firebase, I was fidgety, anxious, and nervous... This was the first major company firefight in which I was not a participant since I had assumed command. It was an empty feeling, knowing we had taken casualties, but not how many, and not knowing how many more were going to occur.

Damn it...it was my company and half of them were in a fight without me! Allen and Bosch were good soldiers and platoon leaders, but....

The sounds of the hard chattering fire of the AK47s, and the smaller *Tk! Tk! Tk!* of the M16s, booms of the grenade launchers and grenades came to us muted because of the distance. It was obvious that people were fighting, killing, and dying.

By this time I had gunships on station and they started providing close-in support. Because of the darkness, the helicopters had difficulty identifying exactly where our two platoons were located. Two soldiers were wounded when the aircraft fired their initial bursts from their machine guns.

Rountree: *"As we got near where the firing was, I saw an NVA on the hill and was going to shoot him, but Bosch went berserk and shouted "Cease Fire!" I don't know what he was thinking. The first platoon assaulted up the hill and secured the top. We did some shooting as well and pretty soon the NVA were either dead or had withdrawn.*

We started taking fire from our own gunships and Grasso was wounded. I took care of him until the medics could get to him."

Rountree's citation for the Bronze Star for Valor describes his actions a little more dramatically than he does himself... *"As the battle progressed, the hostile fire became extremely intense and many men were wounded. Although not a medic, Private First Class Rountree began administering first aid to the injured men in his unit. Moving swiftly from man to man while under heavy fire, he did an amazing job treating the casualties. He gave morphine, made litters, and applied other medical techniques to the wounded. On several occasions he became pinned down, but disregarding the intense enemy fire, he fought onward and continued to care for the wounded. Due to his astounding display of aggressiveness and bravery in the face of the enemy, he was personally responsible for saving the lives of many of his comrades..."*

Like other men who did heroic things under great stress, Rountree commented to me years later that during these moments, you took bravery for granted.

As the helicopter continued firing, the platoons were finally able to get their positions identified with strobe lights but that was of little comfort to our wounded. Even so, the gunships were a major factor in building a wall of tracer steel around the outpost perimeter. The men were glad to have them.

Allen was normally a calm, controlled voice on the radio, but the adrenalin was flowing when he reported back to me that the enemy had been routed and he and Bosch were consolidating the position. As an educated man, his precise opening words would have embarrassed his old English teachers but the importance of talking is the act of communicating an idea to someone else. His report did that quite well when he shouted, *"We annihilated them sons of bitches!"* Not quite true, but close enough to soothe my potential ulcer.

The element of surprise made Allen and Bosch's attack successful. They were able to hit hard, fast and accurately because they knew anyone moving in front of them were bad guys and had to be taken out with no compunction, whether by grenade or bullet. While we estimated we had faced at least an NVA company, we knew that the force wasn't traveling alone and that once it regrouped it might be back with more.

Our casualty count revealed that we had taken two killed and eight wounded. Sobering numbers. We continued to fire artillery, mortars and flares in support of the two platoons but given the diminished strength of our company back on the perimeter, we were still at high alert with everyone manning their positions in the event of a firebase attack. A misty rain had started to fall.

Company A got to the ambush site about 0030 in the morning. It was decided to bring the two dead (SP4 Emmanuel Fenech and SP4 Jerry B. Formey) and the wounded back to the firebase rather than try to cut an LZ in the dark with bad guys still around.

Company A stayed on the site, dispatching one of their rifle platoons, and the battalion reconnaissance platoon, to escort my two platoons with their dead and wounded in poncho litters. Two to four men carried each litter, depending upon the size and casualty status of the soldiers they were lifting. It was slow going for them...

We fired constant artillery and mortar flares to illuminate the night for the returning platoons. The firebase was on high alert, and assisted by the flares, prepared to defend against any attackers.

The command did not want to land helicopters in a place where they might become targets, so we had to wait until the wounded arrived before they came in. We kept a running dialog on when the platoons thought they would get to the firebase. It was not an easy thing to calculate, because in addition to carrying the wounded and dead, they still had to move with security out, prepared to fight.

As we had discovered on 22 March, carrying dead and non-ambulatory wounded was not an easy task. Besides the casualty, the bearers had to heft his weapon and gear along with their own baggage.

The four platoons finally made it to the firebase. The low overcast, the rain, and the jiggling flares swaying to and fro in the light wind reflecting on the wet bodies of our dead and wounded lying in the mud, made for a nightmarish scene.

We held ponchos over the wounded to keep the rain off them as much as possible, while they were treated by the medics. The helicopters came as soon as we gave them a green light and they conducted a difficult night evacuation. It was altogether a miserable night with no sleep for anyone.

The next morning it dawned clear. Company A made a sweep of the ambush area, which we had not been able to do the night before. Fifteen NVA were found dead, as well as a wounded NVA soldier who killed himself while trying to throw a grenade at our troops rather than surrender. A dog tracker team was attached to Company A. It moved out on the trail, which led southwest toward Cambodia.

Meanwhile, I took the third platoon for another patrol through the area of the firefight. In addition to the fifteen NVA bodies and their weapons, we found 17 rucksacks filled with about 600 pounds of rice. The group had obviously been carrying supplies for a large unit.

Intelligence reported the NVA were going to attack a U.S. firebase in the next few days, so after losing the trail to the west, Company A returned to the firebase to augment the battalion perimeter in the event ours was the one targeted.

When I returned to the firebase from our patrol, Wally Williamson, Company A commander, and I made an aerial recon over the Ia Drang area trying to spot any NVA, but with no success.

With two companies on the perimeter, I sent Bosch and Allen with some of their men, back into Dragon Mountain to take a short break. As they left, we received some substantial weapons upgrades for our firebase perimeter. In addition to our six 105mm guns, we received five 155mm Self Propelled Guns (artillery), three M60 tanks and two Dusters (twin 40mm guns, originally used for antiaircraft weapons, but found to be extremely useful against ground attacks and for cave busting).

Company C, operating in the AO, hit an unknown-sized force late in the evening of the 28th. It killed six enemy and captured one, incurring one friendly killed and one wounded.

Colonel Gannon, Captain Harton, the artillery liaison officer, and I flew over the area of contact. We didn't see much, but did adjust artillery fires and blocking fires, while recommending targets for the gunships that were supporting Company C.

On 29 April, 1LT Chuck Aronhalt and Dick Surface went with me to Dragon Mountain to check the rear area and visit some of our wounded from the outpost fight a couple of days before. Only one man from the company (SGT Larry Malding) was still there. The remainder had been evacuated to Qui Nhon that morning. The Company C FO who had been wounded, was there as well, so we were able to chat with him.

I did some administrative work, signing papers and so forth. Since it was the day before payday, I got a little cash from the XO, 1LT George Tupa, and he and I went to the officer's club. We had a couple of beers and watched a re-run of Bob Hope's December RVN tour.

After visiting the Club, I returned to the company rear area. SSG Pitts, the supply sergeant, set me up in the back of the supply room tent with an empty cot and some blankets. Not being used to two beers, I went to sleep immediately. Sometime later, Pitts turned on an electric light to get something from the supply room. Not remembering where I was, and thinking I was in a bunker in the field where someone was using a flashlight (a definite no-no), I roared, *"Turn out that damned light!"* Surprised, SSG Pitts immediately answered, *"Yessir!"* I lay there collecting my thoughts and slowly remembered where I was. I began to feel pretty foolish; Dragon Mountain was a big military city, with lights all over the place. There were no more lights in Company B's supply room that night, but I did apologize the next morning.

The next day, the 30th, I felt extremely uncomfortable and nervous. There were too many people, too much noise and too many walls you couldn't see beyond. Who knew if there weren't NVA lurking in an ambush around the next tent? I thought I really would be a basket case if, when I got back to the states I got caught in a traffic jam. It was time to get back to the quiet of the forest and the familiar anxiety the NVA's mortars caused.

CHAPTER TWENTY NINE

SURFACE WAS ABLE TO FIND A JEEP. We drove out to the brigade trains area at the Oasis and caught a helicopter back to the firebase. When we landed, we discovered we had missed out on a little excitement.

Because the small knoll where we had set up the ambush on the 26th was so useful for tracking activity going east and west on the trail, our command wanted us to put another observer post out there. Friendly Harassing and Interdicting (H & I) fires had hit on and near the knoll every night since the fight, and daily patrols had been checking the area every day as well. Nothing had been seen or heard. It was decided to field another squad-sized OP. A unit of six or seven men would be quiet enough to avoid notice yet strong enough to defend itself, if necessary, until reinforcements arrived. We already had the reinforcement run down pat.

As luck would have it, the first platoon drew the duty with SGT Burk in charge again. The platoon escorted the squad out to the knoll in the afternoon, left it to get set up, and returned to the firebase.

PFC John Barclay, a member of the squad, had joined the company on 27 April, the day after the ambush firefight, and was assigned to the first platoon as one of its replacements. At the Oasis, on his way out to the battalion, he had a conversation with a member of the ambush squad who was going back into Dragon Mountain. The man was still hyped up about the action, and retold the gory details to include the fact about dead bodies still being out there.

After being informed he would be a part of the OP squad, Barclay heard conversation among some of the old timers about this being a "suicide" outpost. In some soldier's thoughts, it was too soon to be sending someone out to a place where a firefight had just taken place. This talk further unsettled him, but he knew his duty and kept his mouth shut.

The mission was only to observe and report, not to become involved in another firefight unless it was absolutely necessary in self-defense.

Unlike a few days earlier, the weather was hot and dry. As the platoon moved towards the knolls, Barclay started showing signs of heat exhaustion. As he said in a later discussion"...*My legs shook after a bit. I'm sure* [our objective] *wasn't much more than a kilometer away, but fear was now playing games in my head. Would I be able to make it to the hill? If I did, would I be able to find a way to turn back with the others? We were getting close and I could smell the bodies of the dead. I was getting sick and dizzy. Was it the heat, or was I being chicken shit? My knees buckled as we moved up the small ridge where we were to set up. I fell backward and my helmet made a hollow thump as it struck the ground. A medic had me lay down and I was forced to drink saline solution. I was told it was the heat and that I would get used to it. Whoever was in command said that I could return to the firebase. I found a way to survive. Ken Brosseau* (Barclay's buddy and another new replacement) *looked at me with some concern and asked me if I was going to be alright? I could leave and go back and always wonder about whether I had the balls to be a soldier. I finished the fluid and stated I felt fine. I was on a mission with a squad of men that never flinched when told to stay on the rocky ridge in the middle of the Ia Drang. I wasn't any better or any more afraid than they were."*

The squad got set up with their claymore mines and trip flares with a dead NVA body still on the knoll and the place stunk. It got dark and there was no sound. Then...

"Two NVA with AK-47's hit a trip wire on a flare ... but a claymore malfunctioned and didn't fire. Our men were stellar in their composure during the exposure of the two NVA. Not one man fired our weapon. Complete discipline was maintained to the point where I'm sure the enemy didn't know if the trip flare was new or old. I'm sure they didn't know we were there. Possibly killing them with small arms or grenades may have started an assault that could have included mortars and we didn't have cover."

At this point the squad leader called for flares to illuminate the area, but the squad could see no enemy.

"Brosseau was positive we were being probed as he saw movement near my left side. My entire body shook and wouldn't stop. We managed to work out a method of staying alert ... by leaning on each other, back to back ... I wondered if we were within range of an approaching enemy ... Brosseau was positive he saw movement so I let a grenade fly ... I threw a second one within minutes. The shaking didn't stop."

The 4.2 mortars from the firebase were now firing on either side of the knoll to discourage any NVA that might want to attack the hilltop. The outpost still had not seen any enemy other than the original two. No shots were fired from either side. However, at this point, our firebase came under enemy mortar fire and some 15 rounds of the 30–40 rounds the enemy fired landed within the perimeter. This attack lasted from 9:55 PM to 10:40 PM. One trooper was wounded.

Barclay continues his experience…"*Then I got terrified. Our mortars stopped. The NVA's 82's* [Russian-made mortars used by the NVA]*were now landing inside the firebase. My mind was running at a pace greater than it needed to be. It bounced from logic to logical extreme and what-ifs. What if they didn't know we were there and after the 4.2's landed and grenades were thrown, they decided that we should be taken out? Is that why they tried to shut down our tubes? Would grunts come out to help in time if we needed them, or would they not come due to a chance of an ambush set up for them? The tubes were close enough to hear them leave and I knew we were within their range too. Would they switch them to land on us and follow with a ground assault? Would we be better off slipping away and establishing a new perimeter? How many were there? Did they have a lot of security for their tubes? Would it be possible to take out the mortar crew with a counter attack? It was surreal.*

Morning came and we did find Chicom grenades that were not exploded. We didn't take long to roll up our stuff and slip away…. . I felt older … I felt confident and damn happy to be alive. I remember a rousing applause and some whistles and cheers from soldiers as we walked into the wire… .

Few people ever knew the terror we endured. I attribute the discipline of not firing our weapons, as a major factor in surviving. Our job that night was really taken for granted, as just another day and night at work."

While the observation post did not monitor any large scale movement that night, it did identify at least two NVA soldiers who were probably just as startled as anyone when they tripped the flare and a world of artillery and mortars started falling on them. Given human nature, they more than likely *"di di'd"* out of there quickly.

On 2 May we again were mortared in the firebase with about 60 rounds. We responded with artillery from other firebases as well as our own mortars but didn't know if we hit anything.

Company C came in the next morning for its turn at the firebase. We moved out to find the position from where the mortars were fired. We found it and began tracking the enemy north. In the afternoon we came upon an NVA outpost who saw us, dropped his bowl of rice and ran. We chased, but couldn't catch him and lost him in the forest due to darkness.

We set up a night defensive position and then took up the trail the next morning. We were able to trail him into a beautiful NVA battalion base camp that was half finished. When completed, the position would have held from 300 to 400 soldiers. We estimated they had left about six hours before we got there, warned by the guy that got away. We were instructed to dismantle and destroy the camp. While we could burn logs and blow up tunnels and trenches, it was hard to destroy mere holes in the ground other than filling them with soft dirt, so we never made a real good job of it.

While we were chasing the NVA outpost, Company C put a group into the same hills where we had had our outpost action the week before and got some NVA nibbles there as well. While Company C was trolling in the general vicinity, it had taken our three attached tanks with it to provide ground support. One NVA tried to take on the tanks single-handedly. He received high marks for bravery but zero points for good judgment. Company C policed up his weapon posthumously. Eight NVA were killed while the unit was in the firebase and we were destroying the NVA camp.

A long range patrol stumbled across an NVA base camp with people in it. They were discovered and had to run for it, leaving their rucksacks and radios behind. Colonel Gannon airlifted Company A into the area immediately and notified us to return to the firebase to be inserted as well. We double-timed it back just in time to hear Company C's first lift go out. We strode into the firebase to find we were again the palace guard. I was aggravated because I thought that Company C needed the rest and we needed the fight, particularly after playing in the dirt for a day and a half. However, done was done.

Companies A and C made contact and received seven friendly WIA while killing several NVA. A media team from NBC, the news corporation, flew in to the firebase trying to get to the scene of the action. During the ensuing activity, Companies C and A had eight men wounded by friendly artillery fire, at first appearing to be an error on the part of a forward observer. Since this was only conjecture at the time, those of us not specifically involved never heard exactly what caused the problem, nor the results of any investigation. However, NBC was right there when it happened and we heard they made the most of it.

While we were in the firebase, I sent the fourth platoon back to the destroyed NVA base camp to see if anyone had returned since we had left. On a play on LT Allen's report of a few days previously, I told Bennie Bosch to annihilate them if they had, but there were no NVA. I had the impression that NVA camps were much like our fire ant beds in Texas. If you disturbed the ants, they would scurry around and fight like crazy, but throw a little ant killer on them and they would disappear and never return to that particular location again.

As if to add insult to his previous medic activities and excitement, Rountree of the fourth platoon had a sleeping bunker made of sandbags and logs collapse on him one night. He appeared to be OK, but the medic sent him back to the 18th Surgical Hospital where they gave him a short break and sent him back refreshed and feeling better. After his actions on 26 April, he deserved a little respite, even though it could have been a far more serious incident. Fortunately, our bunkers were usually built to withstand close mortar hits, so it was a good thing to find out that this particular bunker wasn't up to our normal zoning standards before a mortar blast tested it for real.

Companies A and C made another contact and found a communication complex with radios and telephones. They also took an NVA soldier prisoner. After that, Company C returned to the firebase for a rest break.

Company B had 143 fighters in the field, the most I had had in a long time. We moved out of the firebase and into our old stomping grounds, the Ia Drang Valley. I didn't have the "contact feeling," so was not worried about hitting anything too big for us to handle.

It is difficult to explain but it was almost a psychic thing. I generally had a feeling of unrest, discomfort and concern before we had a "contact". It was almost as if there were NVA vibrations in the area that I picked up prior to a combat action. It wasn't infallible, since there were several instances where I anticipated something happening in a certain region, but nothing came of it; but it was a fact that every time we had a major contact or firefight, I did have the feeling.

After a few days patrolling in the Valley with nothing to show for it, we needed resupply. Colonel Gannon came in to chat and told me to go west towards the border to check out an area, and then into the firebase for an airlift to one of the old firebases we had used previously, west of Duc Co. He told me that Division was pestering him for another captain to go to G3. I told me I would rather stay in the battalion S3 shop if I left the company. I received an enigmatic smile, but nothing else.

I heard disturbing rumors about some of the men smoking pot. I didn't know very much about drugs, except that they weren't legal and that they distorted a man's viewpoint and perception. I thought that was a pretty dangerous thing for someone in a combat unit. I didn't know how long the problem had existed, or how pervasive it was or how to stop it. I suspected that one of the supply folks in the rear was mixed up in it, and thought about bringing him to the field to live the life of Riley. I speculated that it would be difficult to control at the company level, but shakedowns at the supply depot before coming to the field, could deter it. In later years, I received a confirmation that it was indeed one of our supply clerks who was dealing pot. However, the guys in the field wouldn't have any of it and managed to get rid of most of those who tried to smoke the stuff while in the bush. Our early wave of soldiers seemed to recognize the dangers of drugs while the later ones, reflecting growing drug usage in the U.S., were less cautious.

I got a short note from Colonel Lee saying he had received a pretty good job in Nha Trang but that it was still a headquarters job, and he wished he was still with the battalion in the field.

CHAPTER THIRTY

WE MOVED WEST AND CHECKED OUT a B-52 (Arc Light) strike along the border. As usual, we found nothing. We received orders to return to the firebase for a lift out on the morning of 13 May. In order to make it by dark, we ran nearly the eighteen kilometers with Major Mercer fussing at us for moving too fast without regard for adequate security on our flanks. I told him he couldn't have it both ways; that if we were going to make it by dark, we had to move fast. In addition, the terrain was favorable for a forced march, and if we moved fast, the enemy wouldn't have time to get set up and we would just run over him. Needless to say this started another heated discussion, but since we had to keep moving quickly, I didn't take time to continue the debate. We suddenly developed severe radio difficulties, which garbled the transmissions from battalion. Not being a communications specialist, I hadn't noticed that we had difficulties talking with battalion when we took down our long antenna, and replaced it with the short-range antenna.

We arrived at the firebase just before dark, out of breath, with shaky knees but no stragglers. The eleven mile walk/run for 140 tired soldiers with full weighted rucksack and weapons was an outstanding achievement and I was very proud of my guys. The S3 and I had a discussion about my impertinence and inability to follow policies, but it was not too rancorous since we had gotten to the firebase on time, and without any thing disastrous happening. It also probably helped that I admitted my wrongdoing, and while I had not exactly promised it wouldn't happen again, the air was cleared, at least for the time being.

The morning after our forced march/run, I woke up sore in every muscle. Not only was I sore, a King cobra was stretched out on the ground next to me while I was laying on my air mattress with my poncho liner over me. I remember thinking this was not how a good day should start. I had been tired the night before and it wasn't raining, so I had blown up my air mattress and collapsed on it, thinking about the mission for the next day. I was fully clothed, except for my boots, and the snake was just lying there, probably thinking about breakfast. I didn't know what he liked for an early meal, but I didn't want to get into a discussion about it. I was afraid to get him very active and riled, so I slowly rolled out of my poncho liner and off the air mattress on the side opposite the snake. I pulled my Randall Bowie knife from its sheath on my weapons harness draped on my rucksack. All the while this guy was stretched out, not moving much, but staring at me with his little tongue flicking at me over the air mattress, testing the air. I moved very slowly and laid my rifle across his body, just in back of his head, and knelt on it to immobilize him. He quickly started squirming and thrashing his body, and because he was rather large and strong, he started moving the rifle with me on it. Before he could get

276

loose and strike either me or my air mattress, I cut his head off with my knife.

This was a technique I had perfected as a young kid in the southwest growing up with rattlesnakes. I would lay a dried sotol stalk over the snake, kill it with my knife and cut his rattles off. Then I took the body, arranged it over a red ant hill and covered it with rocks to keep predators from dragging it away. I would come back a few days later and uncover the snake. By that time the ants had cleaned the meat from the body and all that was left were the bones of the vertebrae. I then washed, cleaned with Clorox and dried the bones and strung them on cotton string as a necklace. Tourists paid a nice price for a rattle and a snake bone necklace.

At any rate, as a start for the day, it was different from dodging mortar shells or gunfire.

A little later, as I was trying to decide whether to have ham and lima beans or beef stew for breakfast, someone shared a roast leg of rabbit with me. He had killed it by throwing and hitting it with a C ration can. I thought maybe we were fighting with the wrong weapons. As the platoons came in with their morning reports, I found we had to leave five men at the firebase who couldn't travel because of suspected worms. This made me think that we might have a bigger problem.

Even though it was not in their official job description, I had each of the platoon leaders personally check the feces of those who were complaining to determine how bad the situation was. LT Allen, in particular, remembers this very clearly as one of his memories of Vietnam. As the morning wore on, we found we had about 40 more suspected cases who could travel but had to be watched. As a preventive measure, we ordered medicine for everybody. As the days went on, the medicine took care of the worm problem, but we never discovered the cause nor did we have the problem again.

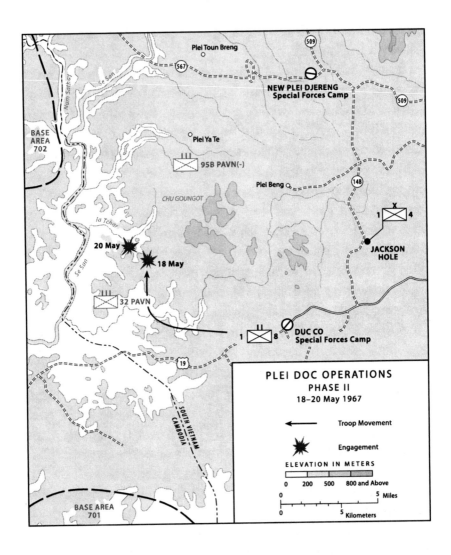

PLEI DOC OPERATIONS
PHASE II
18–20 May 1967

⟵ Troop Movement

✷ Engagement

ELEVATION IN METERS

0   200   500   800 and Above

0   5 Miles

0   5 Kilometers

About mid-day we were airlifted into a new area east of Duc Co, and moved out. I definitely had the "contact feeling" but the sun was bright, we had plenty of water, the terrain was good for moving, and it was a beautiful day. I thought hopefully it might be one of those times when I was wrong and nothing would happen.

On 14 May we were checking out a dry lakebed when I misstepped and fell down a small embankment. As I was trying to catch my balance, I put too much weight on one foot and twisted my ankle. (I have heard a story of me getting injured by a punji stake, and having a swollen leg. I have no idea from where that originated, though admittedly it sounds far more manly than just being clumsy and twisting an ankle.) One of our medics came running over and started trying to treat me for heat stroke before I was able to tell him what the problem was. I tried to go on, but only made about 200 meters before I realized I couldn't keep up with the company, so we called for a helicopter to pick me up.

Since Cary Allen was my senior lieutenant in the field, I put him in operational control of the field company until I could get back from what I thought would be a quick trip to battalion, overnight at most. A helicopter came from somewhere and took me back to the aid station at the Oasis, instead of the battalion firebase where I wanted to go. I had to almost physically fight to keep from going through all the medical evacuation stations to Dragon Mountain for just a sprained ankle. They finally wrapped it in an Ace bandage and I spent the night.

I was truly aggravated with myself for being so clumsy and was very uncomfortable about spending the night with a bunch of strangers in a place where I had no control and didn't know the professional capabilities of the guys who were protecting the place. In retrospect this was ludicrous, but at the time I was convinced that MY company, Company B, 1-8th Infantry was the most proficient company in the US Army with Companies A and C pretty close. (Being the most senior company commander in terms of time in grade and command, I had a smug elder-brother attitude I am sure the other commanders would not have appreciated had they known of it). However, even when I was in the battalion fire base or the division base camp, I never felt as safe as I did when I was with Company B in the field. They were proficient soldiers and I would have put them up against any NVA unit twice our size. Little did I know I would have that opportunity just a few days later.

I was not too kind to myself about my stupidity, clumsiness and inability to walk straight. The morning of the 15th, after one night in the Oasis, I hitched a ride back to the battalion firebase (which at that time was located approximately 3 Km west northwest of the CIDG camp at Duc Co. I volunteered to help around the S3 shop while recuperating. My former executive officer, 1LT Woodford, had been promoted to captain and reassigned to the Division operations shop (G3) in Pleiku. Our battalion was again short an assistant S3. Regardless of our continuing debates over who was running Company B, Major Mercer and I respected each other and mostly got along fine.

On the afternoon of the 16th I hitched a ride on a logistics bird to visit my company. After I had been flown out on the 14th, the company had had another dustoff. One of the platoons had stopped for a break and sent men out for security. There were already a couple of these security teams out, but they didn't know where the new one was located. As a result, when one of its members heard something and raised his hand as a warning, he got shot. He thought at first that an enemy had done it, but it was really a member of one of the other teams who had mistaken his movement for that of an enemy and had fired. Fortunately, the wounded man (SP4 Robert Miller) was evacuated and recovered.

The company looked good to me. It seemed to be doing all right without me, even though it had only been two days that I had been gone. It was good practice for 1LT Allen. Bosch from the fourth platoon had been reassigned to Division Headquarters as the Exploitation Platoon Leader in Dragon

Mountain. I would miss his passionate approach to operations, but his absence was not a major problem. Platoon Sergeant Grandstaff was quite capable of taking over without difficulty and previously had done so very effectively. As a matter of fact, I thought it was very good experience for Grandstaff since I had recommended him for a direct commission as an officer. Though the paperwork had not left Division yet, the administrative process was underway.

The next couple of days saw me hobbling around the firebase still helping the S3 shop in standing radio watches and coordinating other battalion activities.

About 12:30 on the 18th, the company reported it was surrounded and in heavy contact. There were numerous initial casualties. In the early moments of the fight, the fourth platoon had gotten separated from the company main body. It was fighting its own fight and couldn't get back to the company, nor could the company reinforce the platoon because of the viciousness of enemy fire and numbers of the NVA. Both the fourth platoon and the company main were surrounded separately.

Colonel Gannon and Captain Harton, the artillery fire support coordinator, ran for the C&C helicopter, while I hobbled to it as fast as I could and once I had loaded, we took off for the fight.

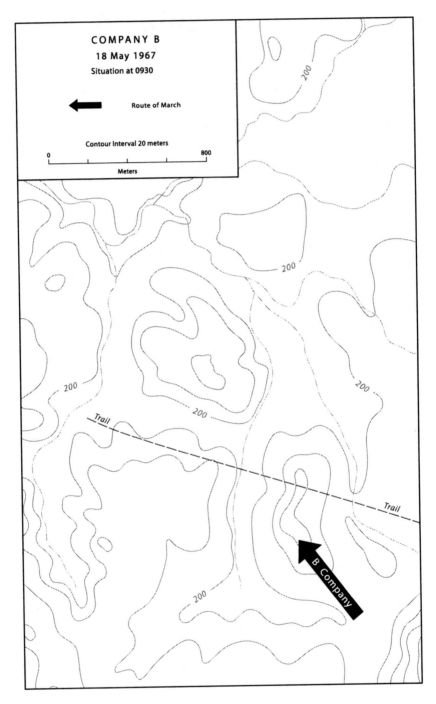

COMPANY B

18 May 1967

Situation at 0930

Route of March

Contour Interval 20 meters

0   800

Meters

Trail

Trail

B Company

CHAPTER THIRTY ONE

WHEN WE GOT TO THE LOCATION of the firefight, there was no real visible evidence of the carnage and bloodshed happening on the ground. The intertwined broccoli heads of the tall trees hid all of the action. There were slight wisps of smoke wafting through the branches but it was the only sign of activity. The artillery was firing, but their explosions were dampened by the floor of green we flew above. A few times a tree shook violently and fell crossways but there was no massive wall of explosions with trees exploding into the air or falling in large numbers. There was a wide difference of what we could see and what we could hear on the radio as we overflew the action. As LT Allen tried to give us a sitrep on the radio, we could hear the sounds of battle, the rifle fire and explosions in the background. The fourth platoon was cut off and the enemy was between the platoon and the main body. Communications with the 4th was spotty and garbled because they were in a ravine lower than the company. Allen indicated the platoon was in danger of being overrun and the company itself was still under attack by a large force. During his brief report, he mentioned the initial artillery support had been delayed.

Artillery support had not been immediate and resulted in the enemy positioning themselves where Company B was unable to come to the aid of the fourth platoon.

Timothy Gannon, Battalion Commander: *"About 48 hours before, the Division Artillery commander published instructions that were to be strictly adhered to, that artillery fire was not to be used until troops on the ground had attempted to outmaneuver the enemy — it was a memo to conserve artillery ammunition. The inference was "it better be fully justified" or commanders would be taken to task."*

1LT Larry York, the company FO who had replaced Bill Wilson, and SP4 Sam Welty, his assistant, tried to get the artillery to shoot as soon as the lead elements of the company started taking heavy casualties. It became obvious the unit was outnumbered and that maneuvering was not going to solve the problem.

Welty: *"We called for artillery and were told we could only use 10 rounds. After A Battery fired, another battery tried to fire for us and was denied permission."*

While delayed, once the artillery battalion understood the severity of the situation, CPT Harton was able to call on whatever artillery units were available and relay directly to the guns in the firing batteries. As we peered down into the forest, we could see little except the smoke of artillery rounds seeping upwards through the tops of the trees. From time to time a shell would explode in the tops of the trees and a bright flash would be visible to us in the helicopter. Men clashed and fought and died in the darkness of the jungle floor below, while we flew above in clarity and sunshine. It was surreal. I felt great remorse, guilt, and grief that I wasn't on the ground with them.

Vic Renza of the fourth platoon had started the day along with everybody else, soaked to the bone with *"not a dry spot on our bodies. Our shirts clung to us. The backpack on my back usually weighed fifty or sixty pounds. It [had] picked up ten more pounds...from the rain."*

The fourth platoon, which had point, had put Renza's 4th squad in the lead, a job Renza hated. He always felt safer walking in the middle or rear of the file.

Renza: *The terrain was hilly and thick, which made it slow moving. Every so often the word would be passed to hold up so the* CO *(Allen) could check compass readings and maps, then we would move out again. By about 9:30 or 10:00 AM the terrain started to change. The jungle became very thinned out, which made walking much easier. The terrain now was very open with no underbrush at all, just thirty to fifty foot trees, very spread out over the low rolling hills and valleys. You could now see in any direction for at least two hundred meters. Because the vegetation was so sparse, the word was passed forward to spread out even more and keep at least twenty meters between each man. We had been walking for over two hours now and I felt much better about being up front, because of the very open terrain. I felt we would never be hit by the NVA in this open jungle, because they could be seen easily from the air. I only worried about them when we were in the thick stuff. Now I could relax a little bit. By this time the sun was getting high in the sky and had burned off all the low lying fog.*

As we walked I could feel heat from the sun on my back drying out my shirt and pants. It felt good. It had been hours since any of us had been dry. I turned around and began to walk backwards, so I could feel that warm sun on my face. As I looked toward everyone behind me, there was steam coming off each man's back from the hot sun drying out their wet shirts. I knew everyone was thinking the same thing ... how great that sun felt on them. As good as it felt, I knew it wouldn't last long, because it was already getting hot. Only a little after 10:00 AM and it must have been close to 90 degrees. That was typical of the pattern in Nam. Wake up wet in the morning, dry off by 11:00 AM and be soaking wet by noon from perspiration. Then we would walk till five or six in the evening, set up in a perimeter and freeze our asses off all night, just to do the same thing all again the next day.

Because of the openness of the terrain, the company had assumed a two-column front with the fourth platoon on the left and the second on the right. The third platoon followed the fourth platoon and the first was behind the second.

Renza: *"I was now in a relaxed mood walking along holding my M16 by its handle and thinking about how f....d up the Army was, about what I was going to do when I got home and about how good the sun felt on my back. Suddenly from the rear I hear my name being called "Renza!" in a loud whisper. I turned around and it's Grandstaff coming toward me in a very brisk walk. He caught up to me, slowed and walked alongside of me at my pace. "I want you to be pace counter from here on," he said. "Every time we hit 500 meters, pass the word back to me. I don't want to end up in Cambodia by mistake." "OK, Sarge," I said. At that he headed back toward his position in the file. All I could think of was, "why me?" What a pain in the ass. Now I had to count every step. Well, it was still better than being point man. After the first 500 meters, I passed the word to the man behind me. He passed it down the line until it reached Grandstaff. Another 200 meters went by and the terrain started to get thicker again. It first began by the trees getting thicker and thicker. Then we began hitting a lot of thick underbrush and clusters of thick bamboo trees. Another 600–700 meters from my first report to Grandstaff*